STANLEY COMPLETE

PATIOS
& MASONRY

Meredith® Books
Des Moines, Iowa

Stanley Complete Patios and Masonry
Editor: Larry Johnston
Copy Chief: Terri Fredrickson
Publishing Operations Manager: Karen Schirm
Senior Editor, Asset and Information Manager: Phillip Morgan
Edit and Design Production Coordinator: Mary Lee Gavin
Editorial and Design Assistant: Renee E. McAtee
Book Production Managers: Pam Kvitne,
    Marjorie J. Schenkelberg, Rick von Holdt, Mark Weaver
Contributing Copy Editor: Kim Catanzarite
Contributing Proofreaders: Sara Henderson, Cheri Madison,
    Joel Marvin
Indexer: Donald Glassman
Contributing Editorial Assistant: Janet Anderson

**Additional Editorial Contributions from
Abramowitz Creative Studios**
Publishing Director/Designer: Tim Abramowitz
Writers: Martin Miller, Michele Pettinger
Designers: Kelly Bailey, Joel Wires
Editorial Assistant: Deb Abramowitz
Photo Research: Amber Jones
Photography: Image Studios
    Account Executive: Lisa Egan
    Photographers: Bill Rein, John von Dorn
    Assistants: Dave Classon, Bill Kapinski, Rob Resnick,
        Scott Verber
    Technical Advisor: Rick Nadke
Illustration: Art Rep Services
    Director, Chip Nadeau
    Illustrator, Dave Brandon

Meredith® Books
Executive Director, Editorial: Gregory H. Kayko
Executive Director, Design: Matt Strelecki
Managing Editor: Amy Tincher-Durik
Executive Editor/Group Manager: Benjamin W. Allen
Senior Associate Design Director: Tom Wegner
Marketing Product Manager: Brent Wiersma

Publisher and Editor in Chief: James D. Blume
Editorial Director: Linda Raglan Cunningham
Executive Director, New Business Development: Todd M. Davis
Executive Director, Sales: Ken Zagor
Director, Operations: George A. Susral
Director, Production: Douglas M. Johnston
Director, Marketing: Amy Nichols
Business Director: Jim Leonard

Vice President and General Manager: Douglas J. Guendel

Meredith Publishing Group
President: Jack Griffin
Executive Vice President: Bob Mate

Meredith Corporation
Chairman and Chief Executive Officer: William T. Kerr
President and Chief Operating Officer: Stephen M. Lacy

In Memoriam: E.T. Meredith III (1933-2003)

All of us at Meredith® Books are dedicated to providing you
with the information and ideas you need to enhance your home
and garden. We welcome your comments and suggestions
about this book. Write to us at:
    Meredith Corporation
    Meredith Books
    1716 Locust St.
    Des Moines, IA 50309–3023

If you would like more information on other Stanley products,
call 1-800-STANLEY or visit us at: www.stanleyworks.com
Stanley® and the notched rectangle around the Stanley name
are registered trademarks of The Stanley Works and
subsidiaries.

Note to the Readers: Due to differing conditions, tools, and
individual skills, Meredith Corporation assumes no
responsibility for any damages, injuries suffered, or losses
incurred as a result of following the information published in
this book. Before beginning any project, review the instructions
carefully, and if any doubts or questions remain, consult local
experts or authorities. Because codes and regulations vary
greatly, you always should check with authorities to ensure
that your project complies with all applicable local codes and
regulations. Always read and observe all of the safety
precautions provided by manufacturers of any tools, equipment,
or supplies, and follow all accepted safety procedures.

CONTENTS

CHOOSING A SITE AND STYLE

Patios, walls, walks, and other masonry features are increasingly part of home landscaping. That's no wonder. Masonry imparts a solidity and permanence unmatched by other materials. But longevity isn't all that matters in a landscape. Masonry structures improve the usability and comfort level of your yard at the same time they make it look better.

A patio, for example, can expand your home's living space, providing a place for activities you might not otherwise have room to enjoy. This makes your home more comfortable and more valuable.

A patio is more than a backyard island. While it should remain separate from external boundaries such as property lines, it must harmonize with the rest of the landscape and the architecture of your house. That's where walls come in.

Masonry walls mark boundaries, add privacy, reduce the harsh glare of sunlight, and deflect strong winds. They also organize your landscape by subtly designating where one space begins and another ends.

Consider paths and walkways too. At a minimum, they provide strictly utilitarian access to different parts of the property. They also encourage exploration of the landscape, guiding you and guests to places in the yard where flowers bloom, vegetables grow, children play, or special features open to pleasant surprises.

Patios, walls, and walks are best conceived not as individual structures, but as parts of a unified design.

Historically patios were bare, ground-level concrete slabs. What distinguishes the modern patio from its earlier form is that it's much more than a platform now. It's an expression of the homeowner's lifestyle and an important part of the landscape where it stands. Today's patio has a personality as well as a purpose.

All landscape planning starts with one question: How will you use your outdoor space? Once you have answered this question, decisions about what you should build, where the structures should go, how large they'll be, and how they should look quickly fall into place.

CHAPTER PREVIEW

Planning patios with a purpose
page 6

Planning walls
page 8

Planning paths and walkways
page 10

Assessing your site
page 12

Making patio access easy
page 16

Sizing up your patio
page 18

Siting the patio
page 20

Creating a style
page 22

A beautiful patio enhances your home and increases its value too.

Designing with color, texture, form
page 24

Putting patios into small spaces
page 26

Furnishing a patio
page 28

Adding personality with accents
page 30

Landscaping with plants
page 32

Creating privacy and enclosure
page 36

Adding amenities
page 40

Drawing plans
page 44

PLANNING PATIOS WITH A PURPOSE

Patio design begins with a look at the way you live. You'll want your patio to accommodate the kind of activities you enjoy. The best way to achieve that goal is to make several lists. Get the family together and start with a wish list: Put down everything that occurs to anyone without regard to practicality or cost. Then pare back the list to what you can afford, what you have room for, and what you have time to build.

Getting away from it all

If you need a pleasant place to sip your morning coffee or relax with a good book, design an area that affords some privacy. Simple furnishings, a hammock or outdoor recliner, and some plants to screen out the rest of the neighborhood are all you need to quickly arrange an outdoor retreat. If you'd like space for both private times and parties, you can use a narrow sideyard for your private patio, then build a large patio in the backyard (ideally off the kitchen or dining room) for entertaining. Unify the spaces with a wraparound design. If you don't have enough room or funds for both, you can make a single patio more flexible with benches or portable seating. Move them to define different areas as needed.

Entertaining

If entertaining is a priority, consider your usual number of guests. Small groups may not require more space or furnishings than your family needs. Large gatherings call for seating, dining, and perhaps even cooking areas. Decide where you would put a table for sit-down dinners or a buffet table. And if you enjoy barbecues and cookouts, consider building an outdoor kitchen with a grill, small sink, and counterspace for food preparation.

Child's play

Consider building a patio for a children's play area. You can't put the jungle gym there, but you can make sure there's plenty of open area for playing. Locate the patio so you can keep an eye on children playing there and in the yard too.

Design for flexibility so your patio can grow with the kids. A space used for a sandbox easily transforms into a small platform with the addition of a few joists and decking, for instance. Plan your patio so you can phase in improvements as time goes by.

Gardening

Plants and patios are perfect partners. Planters, window boxes, and containers beautify the space and also provide the perfect hobby garden for anyone whose green thumb appears only on weekends. Planters can be built into low walls around the patio. An avid horticultural hobbyist can incorporate cold frames—or even a greenhouse—into the design. Build your own planters from the same material as your paving or walls, or purchase commercial units that fit your patio design.

Bringing back an old patio

If your house came with a patio that makes you feel like staying inside, it doesn't mean you have to tear it down and start from scratch. Try to improve it instead. Unused patios suffer from practical or aesthetic problems. For example, if cooking space is cramped or guests have no place to sit, it's a sure sign you need more room. Often a small platform addition built from the same material as the paving will fix the problem and improve the looks of your landscape. You can finish the new material so it blends with the old (page 219).

Mix materials when practical. A ground-level redwood platform makes a great extension for an existing flagstone or brick patio. If there's no room to expand, build a detached area farther from the house and unify the two spaces with a crushed-stone path. Lay decking on sleepers to cover an old slab patio.

Always try to build on what you have. Instead of jamming a fire pit into an old cramped design, extend the patio into the yard to accommodate the new feature.

A patio doesn't have to be attached to your house—or any building. A freestanding patio separated from your home's hustle and bustle makes a great getaway spot, especially if you surround it with plants and greenery. You can build a sunny retreat or a shady haven.

If you have a spa, pool, or hot tub on a patio, allow plenty of space so it won't get in the way of other patio activities. Spas, pools, and hot tubs are major focal points as well as primary centers of activity. The raised edge on this pool creates a visual and physical border.

Entertaining sometimes requires space for large groups, but the same space can be overwhelming for smaller get-togethers. A multilevel patio solves the problem. Build an intimate patio, then add stairs down to the lawn or a larger lower-level patio.

Patios are great places for cookouts, whether you simply wheel out a portable barbecue or dedicate an area to an elaborate outdoor kitchen. Plan your outdoor cooking and dining area for convenience and privacy.

STANLEY PRO TIP

Checklist for patio planning

Good patio planning calls for taking inventory of several factors. Here are some of the things you should keep in mind.

■ **Traffic flow:** If your patio will be built between the house and other backyard destinations, such as a utility shed or play area, connect them with 3-foot-wide walkways.

■ **Views:** Orient the patio and the furnishings to make the most of a pleasing view. Don't hide a great view of the yard behind planters and other decorative elements. Do hide unsightly views (and increase privacy) with fences or plants.

■ **Sun, shade, and wind:** Nature can turn an otherwise perfect location into an uncomfortable spot. Note the patterns of sun and shade so you can provide needed shade where nature doesn't. You can move lightweight furniture as the light changes or you can make your own shade by building an arbor or overhead structure. Shelter the patio from wind by locating it carefully or by adding fences or hedges.

■ **Storage:** Make a list of equipment you need to stow, and plan storage that's easy to get to. A surprising amount fits into a small shed attached to the wall of the house.

PLANNING WALLS

Walls play many roles in a landscape. They create an identity for a space and make large areas seem less imposing by dividing them into smaller parts. Walls create a strong vertical contrast to the horizontal expanse of lawn and patio surface, helping set off the patio and calling attention to it as a prominent feature. They also serve as backgrounds for scenes and mask undesirable views.

Walls can help solve environmental problems. They can hold back a slope, for instance, thereby opening up room for a patio. When properly designed, they can keep annoying winds at bay, create shade, and afford privacy.

If you're planning to build a wall, ask yourself what you want it to do: define space, increase privacy, block unsightly views, or add architectural interest to your outdoor design? The answers to these questions may depend on whether the wall is in the front yard or backyard.

Front-yard walls

Front-yard walls should complement (or at least not conflict with) the general style of the neighborhood. The degree of design conformity required depends somewhat on whether there are other front-yard walls or fences in the neighborhood and how close they are. A low wall in a neighborhood where there are no other walls might not cause a problem, but a tall one could give the impression of a fortress. A front-yard wall usually looks best if it is short, about 3 or 4 feet.

Front-yard walls usually delineate the boundaries of a property. Unless a wall is intended to provide security, it's often used to mark those borders in a subtle and unobtrusive way. Even walls made to enclose areas for children and pets can be designed and built in an inoffensive way.

Backyard walls

Backyard walls often serve a different set of purposes; their most prominent function is to mark the property borders, like the front-yard wall. Because so many family activities take place in the backyard, the walls there must also provide privacy. Expensive barbecue grills and other equipment are often left in the yard, too, so security is another consideration. Those demands call for higher structures—6 feet is common. As an option, you can construct a brick wall with lattice or louvered panels on top (or in alternating bays) to open up the design without sacrificing privacy.

You can exercise a little more freedom when planning and designing backyard walls because it's less important to harmonize with the neighborhood. Design them to suit the style of your house and landscape.

Even short walls increase privacy. This low stone wall separates the patio from its surroundings without isolating the patio.

Combine fences or walls with plantings. Walls offer instant privacy, and plants soften their hard surfaces. Use vines for a quick cover.

A cut-stone wall forms a planter that separates formal areas of this patio from informal ones.

Filtering the wind

Building a wall to act as a windbreak requires some careful thought. That's because high, solid walls can actually make things worse. The leeward side of a wall (the side away from the wind) becomes a low-pressure area that causes wind to flow down the wall and blow more strongly into your yard. Walls with an open pattern, especially along the top edge, make more effective windbreaks. Adding lattice or a louvered panel to the top of a wall can help break up the wind and reduce it to a breeze.

Designing with materials

Walls provide opportunities to pull additional design elements into the landscape. Select objects that go with the style of your home and landscape.

Brick and stone—solid and imposing—work well with stately classic or traditional architecture. Interlocking blocks, designed for retaining walls, look at home in most landscape styles. You can combine materials to bring more variety to your design and to create unusual screens. Dress up a plain block or concrete wall with an evergreen hedge or roses, for example, for a screen that's both ornamental and impenetrable. Or further a Southwestern design by building low walls with adobe blocks and planting evergreens. No matter what your choices, aim for a unification of style throughout the landscape.

Solid-Wall screening

Solid walls provide maximum privacy and security. They function as effective boundaries that keep children and pets in the yard and unwanted visitors out. They also provide an ideal backdrop for garden beds, protecting the plants by creating a nurturing microclimate with the extra warmth and shelter plants need to survive outside their usual hardiness range.

A wall of any sort provides an instant visual backdrop for an outdoor setting, whether it defines the boundary along all sides of an area or simply encloses part of a patio. Flower borders, ponds, and sculptures stand out against walls and screens. If your yard has an old wall or fence that you'd rather hide than display, one solution is to grow climbing plants on it.

Screening for privacy

Placed strategically, walls, plants, fences, trellises, and other structures increase privacy and the comfort level of your patio. Take a privacy inventory *(pages 36–39)*

Stone walls and ledges create a dramatic scene in this yard and screen neighborhood noise and traffic.

before you start building privacy screens. Doing so will also help you discover unattractive views you may want to hide with a wall or fence.

This low brick wall creates cozy nooks as it zig-zags along the edge of the patio. The plants add softness and enhance the sense of privacy.

Location and privacy

A patio in an urban yard is exposed to more noise, traffic, and neighbors' eyes than one in the suburbs. Here it may be best to fence along all sides of the lot rather than isolating the patio. In some neighborhoods, the size of the lot creates enough separation, so you can be more selective when choosing where walls and fences will go.

 PRO TIP

How high the wall?

Before you build a wall, establish a clear idea of what you want it to do. The adage "form follows function" applies when deciding the height of a wall.

If you need a structure for security reasons, to act as a windbreak, or for total screening, you can make it 6 to 8 feet high. Conversely, structures intended solely to separate spaces can be as low as 6 inches or as high as 3 feet.

Build walls well above or well below eye level. A wall or fence that cuts your view in half is an annoyance—you'll have to stretch to see what's on the other side.

PLANNING PATHS AND WALKWAYS

Paths do much more than merely provide a route from one place to another. They unify the landscape's design elements and reduce lawn maintenance. A path or

Steps make a slope easier to climb. They also break the contours of the slope and add interest to the course of the walk.

network of paths is also a great way to add something new to an existing landscape without disrupting its character.

Before you start spreading a network of paths through your yard, consider the first rule of path design: Every path should have a purpose. To determine that purpose, answer these questions first.

■ How will the path be used? For instance, will it accommodate only foot traffic or will equipment roll over it?

■ Who will use it?

■ How frequently will it be used?

The answers will help you determine the path's route through the yard and what materials you'll need to surface it.

Function first

How do you know where you need a path? Look for signs in the landscape. A track worn in the grass, for example, shows where traffic naturally flows. You should consider building a sidewalk or path there.

Many landscapes need one or two strictly utilitarian walkways—those that simply get you from one place in the yard to another. Walks from the house to the garage or from the garage to the garden shed are typical examples. Paths like these get frequent use. They should be wide, feel comfortable and

secure underfoot, and allow you to move quickly from one point to another.

Such working paths are best laid in straight lines. For example, if getting groceries from the garage to the house is the main purpose of the walk, building a walk that winds through the garden only guarantees that people will take shortcuts through the plantings.

If you already have a sidewalk that connects the locations but isn't attractive, consider ways to improve its appearance. You can resurface or color a concrete walk or pave it with brick or stone.

Paths that are purely for appearance or enjoyment can take a circuitous route. A path joining flower beds, for example, is well-suited to a leisurely pace. Gentle curves slow the traffic yet make it easy to move materials and equipment when you have to. If you won't use the path to move materials and equipment, you can make a narrow, winding path for interest.

The function of a path also affects how you build it. You would not surface a trail for children running barefoot between the pool and the house with sharp crushed quartz, rough bark, or slick tile. Stepping-stones or pavers in a sand bed spaced for child-size steps are better choices.

How wide should a path be?

The width of a path is best determined by its principal function and the amount of traffic it will get.

The primary path that leads to your front door is usually the widest sidewalk on the property and will probably look best with formal paving. A sidewalk at least 4 feet wide allows two people to walk comfortably side by side.

Secondary paths—those leading from the primary path or to side or rear entrances—usually are narrower and may be paved with contrasting and more informal materials. Secondary paths are from 2 to 3 feet wide.

Tertiary paths, generally the least traveled, connect elements in the landscape. They are often (but not always) the narrowest; and their materials do not have to stand up to hard use. Tertiary paths and those designed for one person are 18 to 24 inches wide.

Materials must suit the purpose of the path. If you're going to push wheelbarrows along a path, continuous hard paving is best. For strolling among the flowers, soft materials or stepping-stones like these are good choices.

If you want a path that wanders through your gardens but is still suitable for the occasional wheelbarrow, closely spaced pavers or stepping-stones win over crushed bark or mulch. A path made of closely spaced stones lends itself to a leisurely pace, while stones spaced farther apart speed the journey.

Along the way

Think of a path as part of the floor of your landscape when you select materials and as a trail when you lay out the route. A trail invites you on a journey—it hints of the unknown, the unexpected, the mysterious. When you plan a new path, include elements that increase the interest and provide surprises along the way.

Curves—gentle or abrupt—and tall plants can obscure the view around the corner, creating a sense of anticipation. The surprise can be anything you choose— a shaft of sunlight piercing through the trees and falling on a gazing ball, a water feature, or some other accent. A spectacular view always provides great reward at the end of a path. Simple elements—such as randomly placed cut-stone stepping-stones—lead the eye along the path and entice people to follow it. Any kind of pattern will lure the curious, and if you include places for resting along the way—a bench, a tree stump sawn at a height for sitting, or even a wide spot in the path—you will create a rhythm within the walk that only adds to its charm.

Where does it end?

Imagine walking along a path and finding that it ends in a plain lawn or at a neighbor's chain link fence. You would probably be disappointed in a path like that.

Once you've started down a path, you expect it to take you somewhere. That destination might be a dramatic overlook above a river or lake, a simple herb garden, or the entrance to a vine-covered garden shed. (Even a utility shed can be charming.)

Paths can lead to areas for family play or pass through a wooded area to a secluded spot. They can lead to gazebos or other outdoor structures, or to entryways to public areas framed by pilasters or gates.

Some paths lead circuitously back to their starting point. This is a good way to provide a destination when your landscape lacks dramatic features, but don't forget—even flower beds can be exciting.

Paths need places to start and end. This rustic arbor marks the start of a path to a most relaxing destination—a hammock in the trees.

A path should always lead to a destination. Instead of running into a dead end at the fence, this one brings you to a pair of chairs—a nice place to sit in the garden. A small patio beside the fence could serve the same purpose.

Slip-proof your path

There are several things you can do to design your path for safety.
■ Use coarse-textured materials, especially in locations likely to get wet. Broom-finish concrete to make it safe.
■ Build steps on steep slopes instead of running the path up or down the slope.
■ Use flat stones, and slope the walk slightly to one side so water drains off instead of forming puddles. Puddles are hazards in warm weather, treacherous when frozen.
■ Remove clutter.
■ Install low-voltage lights alongside paths and steps that will be used at night.
■ Use different-size paving stones or materials of different colors to signal changes in level.

ASSESSING YOUR SITE

The terrain, vegetation, views, and climate in your yard have a major effect on your outdoor plans. Before you draw final plans for your project, study your property for factors that might require a change in the design or location of your patio, wall, or walkway.

Terrain
The contour is the most significant feature of your landscape. No site is perfectly level. Many are generally flat, however, and that will help keep construction—especially of a patio—uncomplicated. A slope might require grading the site or building a retaining wall to accommodate a patio.

Hillsides offer many design opportunities. Land sloping away from a high spot can create magnificent views, for instance. Land that slopes uphill from a patio site provides natural privacy and shelter from the wind.

If you have to level the ground to create a patio site at the bottom of a slope, you can remove soil to form a flat spot, fill in a low spot, or use a combination of both methods.

Grading and filling often creates a surface of unstable soil that settles unevenly. This can stress and crack a patio surface. Tamp and firm the loose surface thoroughly before building the patio.

If the slope's remaining soil is unstable, build a retaining wall to keep it from washing onto the patio. A retaining wall also increases the sense of enclosure produced on a patio nestled into a hillside.

Soil
Soil composition and compaction, characteristics that affect your site and how you prepare it, vary widely.

Loose, sandy loam absorbs water and drains quickly but erodes easily. In sandy loam and silted soil, local codes may require concrete footings under the perimeter of your patio.

Clay is dense and sheds water, which can create runoff problems. In this case, you may need to install swales or drainage lines that empty into a dry well or catch basin. Many local codes prohibit direct drainage of groundwater into the storm sewer system, and all codes prohibit routing drainage onto another person's property.

Sloped sites offer design opportunities as well as challenges. A series of patios, walls, and planters on this slope establishes platforms for multiple uses. Paths and stairways connecting the levels encourage exploration.

A grand stairway to a gazebo dramatizes this landscape. The wall and garden lend a sense of enclosure and privacy to the lower patio.

Sun, shade, wind, and rain
To help ensure a pleasant and inviting patio instead of one that goes unused, pay attention to weather patterns. If the sun shines on the patio location throughout the day, for instance, it might not be a comfortable place to relax in the afternoon. Harsh winds will limit the use of the patio, but a wall with an open surface could transform them into pleasant breezes. Study the way the weather affects your site, and plan accordingly.

Solar heat and light on a patio varies throughout the day—and seasonally. The earth's movement causes sunshine and shade to shift during the day. Working with nature is always more efficient than working against it, so place your patio where sun and shade patterns correspond to the times you want to use it.

What to do with the dirt?

Landscapers often level other parts of the work site with the soil removed during grading—a technique called cut-and-fill. Cut-and-fill eliminates the expense of disposing of excess soil, as well as the cost of purchasing fill dirt.

Cut-and-fill works best, of course, when the amount of soil removed roughly equals the amount needed in fill areas. If you have excess soil from grading, you can use it to construct raised planting beds or to fill planter boxes in walls.

Because you'll probably remove more than just topsoil, not all of the excavated dirt will be suitable for planting beds. Instead make berms—low mounds of earth—with it. Don't spread excess soil around trees even temporarily. Just a few extra inches of dirt over tree roots can suffocate roots and kill the tree.

Trees and shrubs offer natural shade and screening, reducing construction costs by eliminating the need to build overhead structures or fences. Container plants and a water garden help blend this patio into the verdant surroundings.

When you're planning your patio, trees, rocks, or other landscape features might seem like obstacles. Instead make them part of the plan. Building this patio around the tree close to the house makes good use of the site. Allow plenty of room for air and water to reach the tree roots.

SUNSHINE AND SHADE
Choosing your site for shade

A north-side patio, in almost constant shade, may be too cool for comfort. Locating a large section of the patio beyond the shadow of the house produces both shady and sunny areas. Consider a detached patio for comfort in a climate that's cool year-round.

A patio with a southern exposure receives sunlight most of the day, but from different angles as the seasons change. Summer sun is high; winter sunlight is low. A lattice-covered pergola could filter the summer sun but allow full sun in the winter.

Sunlight warms an east-side patio in the morning, but this side of the house becomes shaded sooner than others. That's great for morning coffee but can make evening hours unpleasantly cool in mild climates. Here, too, a detached patio provides a solution.

A west-side patio starts the day in the shade, but by early afternoon, becomes too hot to use. Here's where a wraparound patio can help, offering you a chance to follow (or avoid) the harsh sun. Use natural or man-made shade to create a comfortable site.

ASSESSING YOUR SITE *(continued)*

Observe the sun's daily movement across your property during the warm months. Drive stakes into the ground to track the changing shade patterns. Make notes and sketches to use when you put your plans on paper (see *pages 44–47*).

Notice the wind patterns in your yard. If possible put your patio in a spot that's sheltered from strong prevailing winds. Build a slatted fence or plant a windbreak to buffer strong winds. For rain protection, install a solid roof over a part of your patio.

Microclimates

If you've ever noticed a difference in temperature when you move from a patio into a yard, you've experienced the effects of a microclimate. Microclimates are small areas within a site where the weather patterns are different from the general area.

Microclimates are the result of many factors, including terrain, landscaping, and the location and design of structures.

Different materials used in structures absorb and reflect different amounts of heat and light from the sun. Plain concrete, for instance, reflects more heat and light than dark bricks. Such a surface might feel comfortably warm, but reflected light could make it seem harsh and glaring.

A dark material like brick or precast pavers won't reflect sunlight as harshly, but it will absorb heat, which can make the surface uncomfortably hot underfoot during the day. The stored heat, however, radiates during the cool evening and extends the use of your patio after sunset.

A hilltop patio feels warmer on a calm day than one at the bottom of an incline because cooler air is heavier and flows downhill. Retaining walls, fences, or house walls built around a patio that's in a low spot can trap cold air, making the patio quite cool in the evening.

Walls and fences frequently create microclimates. Where you put a wall or fence and how you build it affects the force of the wind. Solid walls usually don't reduce winds. That's because a low-pressure area forms on the side away from the wind, drawing the wind into the very area you want to protect. The wind swirls over the top and drops back down—with equal force—at a distance from the wall roughly equal to its height.

Walls with lattice panels on top or open patterns laced into the surface will reduce the force of the wind and usually provide enough screening for privacy.

If your proposed site is already shaded during the times you'll use the patio, decisions about location are easier to make. But if you don't have much flexibility in patio location, you can alter the environment.

Plant trees and other plants to shade a site that gets too much afternoon sun. A pergola over the patio can filter the sunshine, or install a roll-up awning, which you can retract when it's not needed.

Roses or vines climbing up an arbor will create a private shaded spot for outdoor reading, without blocking the breeze. Vines climbing a lattice wall cool a site that gets hot in the late afternoon. Or you could try a compromise: Build the patio in a location that has partial shade and partial sunlight during the hours of greatest use.

Picture-perfect plans

Take your camera along and snap plenty of photographs when you assess your site. Photographs call attention to details you may have missed because you see them every day.

For example, you may have forgotten that the neighbors can see right into your living room window. Photographs will remind you that you need to correct this in your patio plans. You may have gotten used to how unattractive your utility shed is. A photo will tell you that you need a lattice screen.

Photos are especially helpful when you begin putting your plans on paper. Your site analysis will be a record of the characteristics of the landscape that need attention. Use the camera to help keep track of the ideas you want to include on this drawing.

If your patio site lacks natural shade, make your own. A table umbrella is an inexpensive solution for a sunny patio. A pergola or other structure shades the patio while enhancing its style. For the future, plant a tree where it will shade the patio when grown.

*You must protect mature trees during construction—
even large trees are easily damaged. Roots extend far from
the trunk; avoid extensive excavation that might damage
them. Minimize grade changes over the roots as well;
adding even a thin layer of soil can suffocate delicate
feeder roots. Make sure paving above tree roots allows
air and water to pass through.*

*Steps down from the lawn tie this patio into the landscape. Use this type of
construction to advantage on sloping terrain or, with some earthmoving, to garner
interest for a patio in a level yard. Sunken patios require adequate drainage to avoid
collecting water and becoming a pool during rainy weather.*

*Before you build a patio, grade the site so it drains away from the house. To improve the drainage
of a damp site, dig a perimeter trench around the patio and fill it with gravel. In extreme cases,
install a perforated drainpipe in the trench and run it to a dry well or catch basin.*

Fix foundation drainage first

If water gets into your basement, don't build
a patio until you've determined the cause and
fixed the problem. The problem may simply be
that the ground slopes toward the foundation
of your home instead of away from it. If so, the
following is an easy solution.

Slope the soil next to the foundation away
from the house at least 4 feet. You may have to
bring in new soil to make a slope of this width.

Faulty or inadequate gutters and downspouts
may also be the culprits. Check the joints in the
gutters and the outlets where the downspouts
connect to them. Seal any joints that are letting
water through. Often adding an extension to
the downspout—or even just a splash block—
cures the problem.

MAKING PATIO ACCESS EASY

You will probably use and enjoy your patio more if you can see it from inside the house and get to it easily. The patio should also relate to the adjacent interior room—a patio dining area located off the kitchen or dining room, for example.

In design terms, these are *access* and *compatibility.* They can make the difference between a patio that enhances your home and one that rarely gets used.

Visual access

When you can see the patio from inside your home it has *visual access.* Seeing it is an invitation to use the patio.

To create effective visual access, locate the patio where you can easily see it through windows or doors. If existing windows or doors don't provide an inviting view, consider installing new ones. Ideally at least some of the patio should be visible from more than one room, but the best view of the patio should be from the room that adjoins it.

You don't need to see the entire patio to want to get out and enjoy it. Often a limited view is better, especially if you want a more private patio.

Landscaping your patio and its surroundings to make them more attractive entices guests outdoors. Incorporating accents that you can see from the inside, such as carefully placed container gardens, variations in the paving pattern, or a decorative insert in a wall section visible through a window, also makes your patio more attractive.

When you're considering visual access to your patio, remember to look down. Using similar (or the same) flooring materials or similar colors or textures on both the interior floor and patio surface visually links the two spaces and makes a smooth transition.

Physical access

Physical access refers to the ability to move from inside the house to the patio. The path to the patio should be obvious and easy. Doors should lead from rooms that adjoin the patio and paths should be clear.

Make a sketch of the traffic patterns in your home, then visualize how a patio will affect them. You may need to make changes to accommodate movement to the patio. For example, adding the patio on the side of your kitchen may turn the cooking area into a busy throughway. Moving or adding a door or rearranging interior furnishings can solve such problems.

Plan the entry so you can step easily from the room onto the patio. Make the patio surface as close as possible to the level of the interior floor.

If the patio surface must be significantly lower than the doorway, add a landing or an entry platform so you won't have to step down as soon as you pass through the door. A landing can prevent stumbling as you go from the house onto the patio.

If a landing is not possible, build steps. Make the steps wider than the doorway to create the illusion of spaciousness. Make each tread (the part you step on) at least 12 inches deep and keep the rise (the distance you step up) low so the stairs are easier to go up and down.

Improving access

Improving access is often all it takes to turn an underused patio into a favorite family place. If you don't use your patio as much as you thought you would, visual or physical access may be the problem.

If you feel you're on display while meditating on the patio, for instance, the site probably allows too much visual access. Add a fence, shrubs, or an overhead structure to screen the patio and enhance privacy. While areas for private use should have limited visual access, areas for public use can afford to be more open to outside views.

Inconvenient physical access from interior rooms can also reduce the use of your patio. If getting to your patio from inside is a circuitous journey with many obstacles, try rearranging the interior furniture. If the patio furnishings obstruct a natural pathway, rearrange them too. If rearrangement doesn't improve traffic flow, consider enlarging a door or adding a new one. Expanding the patio might be a solution too.

From inside to outside the best patio access is a seamless one. Nothing stops fresh air and sunshine from entering this dining room. Double doors with full-length glazing, whether open or closed, allow full visual access, making the patio part of the room.

Compatibility

When the general purposes of the indoor room and the patio are similar, the patio becomes a natural extension of the room. For this reason, the success of your patio may depend on its nearest indoor room.

A small patio where you can enjoy coffee and the morning paper is just right outside a bedroom, for example, but a large patio for parties and entertaining is not appropriate there.

For outdoor dining put the patio close to the kitchen, even if you will have a self-contained outdoor cooking space. Build-in a receptacle for trash so you don't have to carry it back into the house. Establish entertainment areas close to the living room, family room, or dining room, and maximize access with doorways from other rooms where you would entertain. Add exterior paths and walkways so guests can get to the patio without going through the house.

For a more private area, limit access. A patio that you can reach through only one room makes a private retreat. Shield your patio behind hedges or fencing.

On a nice morning, stepping right out of the bedroom onto a sunny patio gets the day off to a great start. Double doors, though not necessary for traffic flow, enhance visual access. The invitation to go outdoors is hard to resist.

Wide doors, large windows, and unobstructed views are elements that can make your patio always seem inviting. In addition to easy access, this patio's location makes it a natural extension of the dining room.

STANLEY PRO TIP

Make the right connections

To avoid traffic jams, make sure the main door to the patio is wide enough to allow easy passage and to offer an inviting view from inside the house. French doors, atrium doors, and sliding doors are especially suitable for connecting the inside and outside.

Take a compatibility inventory of your home. Sketch a floor plan and label the use of each room as active (entertaining, for example) or passive (reading). You may have rooms that warrant both labels, but one type of activity usually predominates. Match up active patio areas with active interior rooms, and passive patio spaces with passive rooms. Patio space for kids' play is better outside a family room, playroom, or den. Patio space for reading feels more comfortable adjacent to a bedroom or living room.

While you're at it, analyze the way family members and guests move through your home. Sketch in the windows and doors of the rooms and draw arrows that show the usual traffic routes. If there's furniture in the way, rearrange it to open up the view and physical paths to the outdoors.

SIZING UP YOUR PATIO

What size should your patio be? The primary design guideline is to make your patio large enough to accommodate the activities on your final planning list.

Start with a sketch. Assign each activity to a different part of the patio. Allow ample space for the activity itself, traffic flow through and around the area, and outdoor furniture, which tends to be larger than indoor furniture.

If the patio you've planned isn't large enough, expand it or look for ways its spaces can serve double duty. Perhaps one corner of the family dining space could serve as a secluded retreat. Often just moving a chair can make a small part of a larger area feel more secluded.

Give each area its own identity. Separate areas visually and physically with planters, trellises, benches, or a change in decking pattern. Structural changes make even stronger distinctions. A T-shape patio or different levels with connecting steps naturally divides spaces you can identify for various activities.

To dine outside, you need enough space for a table and chairs. Locate the patio so you have easy access to the kitchen or inside dining room. For shade, you could add a table umbrella.

STANLEY PRO TIP

Try out the site

To see if your proposed patio is large enough, rope off the area or mark it on the ground with chalk or upside-down spray paint. Then move in the furniture and equipment you'll have on the patio.

If you haven't purchased the furniture yet, use interior furnishings and add about a foot more space for each item. Figure about 2 feet square for each outdoor chair, plus about 1 or 2 feet to push back from a table.

If the patio is large enough, step back and consider its scale. It should look proportional to the house and grounds. Small patios usually do not pose a problem—they're less likely to be built next to a big house. More common is a large patio that overpowers a modest home. Start with a design that fits the uses you envision, then fit it to your budget and terrain. When you finalize the size of the patio, draw the plan on paper (see *pages 44–47*).

Large gatherings and entertaining call for open spaces and room for plenty of chairs and other seating. Arrange the furniture in groupings to establish different areas in an open space.

Multiple levels define areas for different uses on this patio. The lower features a sitting area in the garden; the higher offers seating for dining. Identifying areas in this way breaks up the expanse of a large patio.

This narrow patio easily accommodates a table and chairs for dining or casual seating. When moved into a corner, the table and chairs allow space for a couple of lounge chairs.

STANLEY PRO TIP: **Fitting function to footage**

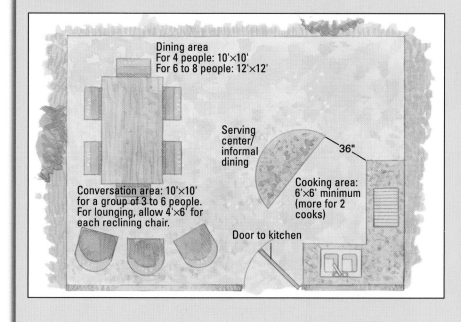

Dining area
For 4 people: 10'×10'
For 6 to 8 people: 12'×12'

Serving center/informal dining

36"

Cooking area: 6'×6' minimum (more for 2 cooks)

Conversation area: 10'×10' for a group of 3 to 6 people. For lounging, allow 4'×6' for each reclining chair.

Door to kitchen

Many patios have plenty of square footage but end up feeling cramped because they weren't planned with traffic and activity in mind. These general guidelines will help you avoid this problem.

■ For a **dining area** for four people, you'll need about 10×10 feet. For six to eight, make it 12×12 feet.

■ To accommodate a typical **round table** with six chairs, provide a circular area with a diameter of at least 9 feet.

■ A **rectangular table** requires an area 5 to 6 feet wider and longer than the table.

■ A simple **cooking area** with a grill and a small table usually needs an area about 6 feet square. Provide more room if there will be a counter, island, or large table.

■ For a single **reclining chair,** allow an area 4×7 feet. For two reclining chairs, allow 7×7 feet.

■ A **conversation area** for three to six people requires a 10×10-foot space.

■ **Pathways** from the door to the stairs and between activity areas should be 3 to 4 feet wide at all points.

SITING THE PATIO

The terrain of your property and how close you are to neighbors might limit patio shape and location. If terrain and close neighbors aren't problems, you can make a patio almost any shape and locate it almost anywhere in your yard.

Start with a look at your house and the contours of the yard. The shape of your house and the floor plan may suggest— or even dictate—a shape and location for your patio. There also may be areas of your yard that are largely unused, prime locations for detached patios.

Front-yard patios can extend the driveway or open up the area near the entrance to your home. Patios on the side of the house turn normally wasted space into prime real estate. And, of course, in any area, a patio makes an excellent companion for flower beds and plantings. Patio designs generally fall into one of the categories shown on these pages.

ATTACHED PATIO

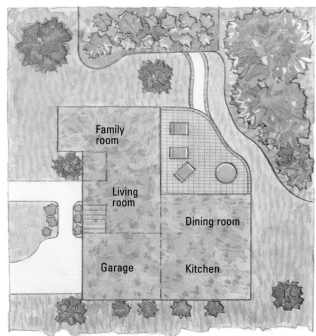

Attached patio: Locate the patio next to the house with direct access to the interior, usually the kitchen or family room. U-shape or L-shape houses offer ready-made opportunities for maintaining privacy, but that doesn't mean the contour of the patio has to be rectangular. Round off the corners, create flowing patterns with paving, and add shrubs to soften hard edges.

The contour of the attached patio follows the shape of the wooded area.

Detached patio: You can move the patio away from the house to take advantage of changing shade patterns cast by mature trees. Even though it's situated away from the house, a detached patio should in some way conform to the style of the house. Separation from the house allows you to create distinctive surface patterns that may harmonize or contrast with the house. Connect the patio to the house with a path or walkway that complements your overall landscape.

DETACHED PATIO

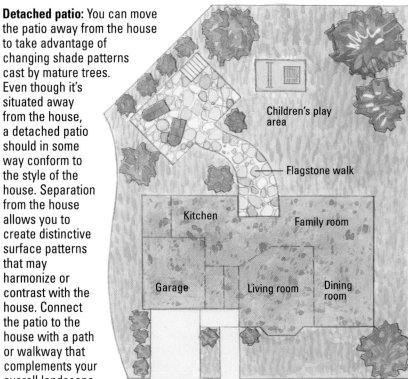

This detached patio takes advantage of open sun patterns and allows supervision of the play area.

Building codes

Building codes, zoning ordinances, deed restrictions, and easements are important considerations in determining how and where you can build your patio.

■ **Building codes:** Building codes ensure the safety of construction. Some codes treat patios as permanent structures, with regulations for footing depths and materials. Check with your building department before you build, and submit your plans for approval.

■ **Zoning ordinances:** These rules govern property use and structure placement. They may establish setbacks from property lines and the maximum size of your patio. Some cities limit patio surfaces because large areas of hardscape interfere with the natural flow of runoff.

■ **Deed restrictions:** Some communities implement deed restrictions to control architectural style. You may find restraints on the style of patio you can build and the materials you can use.

■ **Easements and rights-of-way:** There may be restrictions that limit building under or near overhead lines, and you might not be able to build a patio over underground utilities. A sand-set patio, which can be removed for access to utilities below, may be allowed.

Call your utility companies and ask them to mark the lines through your property. Most will do so for free.

COURTYARD PATIO

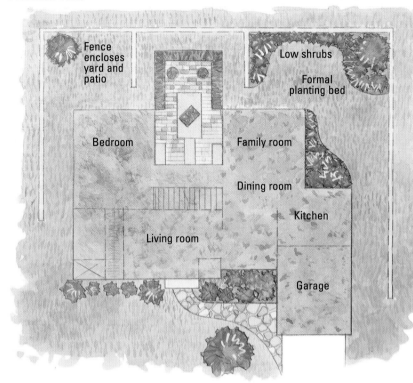

Fence encloses yard and patio

Low shrubs

Formal planting bed

Bedroom

Family room

Dining room

Kitchen

Living room

Garage

Courtyard patio: A courtyard is a great style for townhouses or any home with a small lot. If your home doesn't offer suitable walls on all sides, you can fashion them with fencing or tall hedges. Garden beds or planter boxes will turn such a spot into a private oasis. Or you can bring greenery and flowers into the space with potted plants or small trees. Install trellises and let vines climb the walls. You can even add the splash of falling water with a small recirculating fountain or an ornamental wall fountain, available in most garden centers. Avoid busy paving patterns and ornate furniture in a small courtyard—they could overwhelm the space.

Walls of the house and plantings surround this patio to create a courtyard.

Wraparound patio: A wraparound patio is ideal when you want access from several rooms. The style easily accommodates multiple uses such as (shown here) a quiet retreat outside the master bedroom, family dining off the kitchen, and space for entertaining off the family room. Curved corners, garden beds, planter boxes, and low walls separate each area and give each space a distinct character. If the size of the patio you want to build won't quite fit the open areas of your yard, this style is for you.

This design provides a large entertainment area off the family room and a sheltered patio off a bedroom.

Help with design
Ask questions. Many home centers have professional designers who can give you design advice.

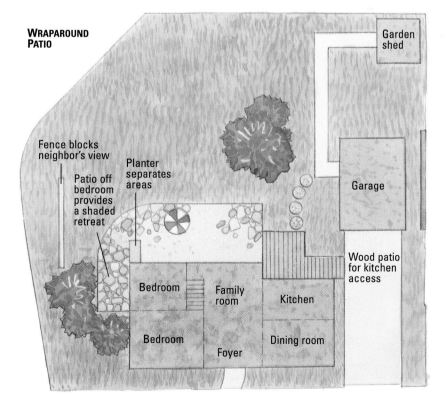

WRAPAROUND PATIO

Garden shed

Fence blocks neighbor's view

Planter separates areas

Patio off bedroom provides a shaded retreat

Garage

Wood patio for kitchen access

Bedroom

Family room

Kitchen

Bedroom

Foyer

Dining room

CREATING A STYLE

Style is a matter of details. Every part of your patio, from the type of paving you use to the patio's size and shape, contributes to its style.

Style affects more than how a patio looks; it can affect your long-term satisfaction with the patio as well. You're more likely to use the patio often if the style appeals to you and reflects the way you live.

Style by theme
A good way to approach style is to organize your landscape plan around a theme. Then make the patio an integral part of that plan.

If you decide on a classic, symmetrical look that features straight lines and right angles, a patio with rectangular planting beds on each side is perfect. Augment the effect with a border of sheared shrubbery.

For an informal style, incorporate curves into the design. A path of small stones or wood chips leading from the yard to the patio adds an informal touch. You could also curve the edges of planting beds to enhance the casual effect.

You can develop a style based on the region where you live. Use the colors and textures of nature, and take the climate and culture into account. Native plants and materials look right at home in their surroundings. Regional designs also make good budget sense—local plants and materials are less expensive and generally require less care and maintenance.

Elements from different regions often mix well with one another. A single bonsai tree won't transform your patio into a Japanese garden but could provide a harmonious Oriental contrast to a Southwestern theme.

Architectural style
You can build a style around architecture. A contemporary style, for instance, is cool, serene, and comfortable with bold shapes and colors and sleek lines. Build the patio in sections, paving each section in a different orientation. Repeat one of the patterns on the sides of your outdoor kitchen. Zigzag your patio over a series of gentle slopes, and make the pattern even more dramatic

with perimeter seating that matches the contours or angles.

Create harmony
No matter what style you choose for your landscape—even the most eclectic— it's important that its elements combine into a unified whole.

Create a sense of continuity with your house by using similar materials, colors, shapes, and patterns in your patio design.

A patio that runs parallel to a one-story ranch home creates a harmony of horizontal lines. But if you place the length of the patio perpendicular to the house, the harmony begins to be discordant.

A patio with sharp angles fits right in with a West Coast modular home and might work with an American foursquare, whose style is more neutral, but would probably look jarring on the back of a three-story Victorian, ornate with filigree and bric-a-brac.

The lines of the house aren't the only determinants. Look for design cues in the curves, angles, and free-form shapes of

A variety of colors, furniture styles, and plants combine with a concrete bench and other elements to create this casual patio.

The brick surface and balanced arrangement of furniture and container plantings follow a formal, traditional style.

property lines, swimming pools, garden beds, or slopes.

Extend your sense of harmony to accents and furnishings. Use small, carefully placed elements to provide contrast of color, shape, and texture. Gardens, edgings, walls, colored concrete, stone, tiles, bricks, logs, gates, furnishings, lights, and decorative pieces all contribute pleasing and lively accents.

Select furnishings that support the dominant design. You can find a style of patio furniture to fit almost every taste and budget, from sleek, contemporary pieces to classic Adirondack furniture, or charming, old-fashioned wicker.

If your patio is large or encompasses several smaller sections, position small groups of furnishings and decorative elements so they won't clutter the central area. Place your main patio furniture around focal points to give them greater definition.

How will you know when your design is harmonious? It will be welcoming, not jarring. It will appear to be a cohesive blend instead of a clutter of parts, and its general impression will be inviting and comfortable.

Here a formal reflecting pool connects the attached patio to the detached sitting area. Trees and plantings along the pool give the sense of being in a courtyard. Symmetry is a key element in such a formal design.

The look of the table and chairs on this patio echoes the style of the house.

A lattice screen and abundant plants make this a cozy spot for dining or cocktails.

Finding your style

Look around your neighborhood and note things you like about the houses and yards. You may find more design continuity than you noticed before. Make notes and sketches of things you like and file them in a manila folder. Clip photos from magazines for further inspiration.

When you're working on your final design, spread your notes and clippings on a table so you can see everything at once. Discard what doesn't appeal to you and keep the rest. You should notice a general theme in the images left on the table. Use the elements of that style in your patio design.

DESIGNING WITH COLOR, TEXTURE, AND FORM

Characteristics of masonry materials—their color, texture, and form—affect the project's appearance, durability, and maintenance requirements. When selecting materials for your project, make sure your choices meet your design goals and contribute to a unified landscape.

Color

Color is a prominent attribute, the one most people notice first. It's perhaps the most important design element when it comes to creating harmony between structures.

Color helps set the mood. Reds, beiges, rusts, browns, yellows, and oranges are warm tones that complement traditional settings well. Blues, grays, or black impart a cooler feel and are ideal to use with contemporary designs. Other parts, such as mortar, sand, moss, furniture, and plants, impart color. Use these elements to introduce contrasting hues to set off the color of your paving.

How much of a particular color you employ is important because the amount of a color affects how people perceive it. In small amounts, a color tends to recede or act as an accent. But a large amount of the same color becomes more prominent and could be overpowering.

Texture

The surface texture of a patio or walkway affects style, comfort, and safety. Light reflectance, surface temperature, and ease of cleaning and maintenance are all related to texture.

■ Smooth vs. rough. Smooth surfaces such as glazed tile, polished stone, and steel-troweled concrete are slick when wet and can harshly reflect sunlight. For maximum safety, avoid any material that gets slippery when wet. Small areas placed as accents do not greatly decrease the safety of the surface. Smooth surfaces are easier to sweep clean than rough ones.

Variation in the texture of natural stone provides a safe surface and gives your patio or wall an old-fashioned look. Brick and precast pavers are rough enough to provide plenty of traction even when wet and are

The coarse texture of these pavers gives the patio a rustic old-town look. The interlocking pavers' uncommon shape attracts attention. Bricks border the patio.

perfect for formal designs. Poured concrete offers the flattest, most uniform surface, and can be colored and textured—even when used in retaining walls.

■ Hard vs. soft. Brick, tile, and concrete are hard, durable surfaces good for patios and walks. Gravel, wood chips, bark mulch, and the like make resilient surfaces that are more comfortable to walk on. They can lend a rustic look that complements woodland or informal landscape designs.

If you don't want to cover the entire patio with soft materials, use them for paths and accents. Just as you wouldn't hesitate to use different flooring in different rooms inside your home, you can pave your patio with more than one kind of material.

Different kinds of paving help define different areas, separating quiet, intimate spaces from party spots.

Tile and pavers in red, gold, and earth tones are warm and inviting, and they are compatible with wood, stone, and other natural materials. They also set off plantings well.

Form

Masonry materials come in many shapes and forms. When used in a wall, walk, or patio, many of them create a visual rhythm that's pleasing as well as functional. Working with patterns, whether formal or informal, can give you unlimited creative license when designing your project. For example, varying the placement of colors in a modular material like brick breathes life into a patio surface. A contrasting shape inserted into the surface, such as a large, irregular stone set into a background of consistent-size stones, immediately draws attention to that stone and adds interest to the surface. Varying the thickness of ashlar stone in the courses of a wall produces a visual rhythm. Variations in shape and form add the element of surprise; whenever you look at the surface you'll spot another detail you hadn't noticed before.

Fixing an odd lot

If your site is an odd shape and not well-suited to the symmetry of modular materials, combine different textures and colors in a mosaic layout. Mosaics attract attention to themselves and pull it away from any irregular shapes or dimensions in the space. Don't try to hide the division between the materials; this is a situation where a sharp contrast is better.

Combinations

Mixing decking with masonry walls or paving provides additional design options. Wood-and-masonry combinations improve the appearance of your outdoor room.

Patio and deck combinations work especially well for separating areas of use. The different colors and patterns of the materials clearly indicate that the spaces they mark have different purposes.

Deck-and-paving combinations make it possible to enlarge a patio over a steep slope. Decking easily spans slopes and rough or poorly drained terrain, making it a better choice than paving when such sites are the only ones available for expansion.

When expanding either surface, select at least one material that's already in use in your yard. Then, instead of looking like an afterthought, the new material will complement your home and landscape, and the new outdoor living space will look like it belongs there.

Flagstone set in a bed of low groundcover adds a bit of patio space to the decking in this confined backyard. A stepping-stone path would fit into this landscape naturally.

The subtle colors and shapes of masonry lend themselves to creative design. Flagstone makes an appealing patchwork mosaic that dramatically transforms an old concrete slab.

PUTTING PATIOS INTO SMALL SPACES

Even if your yard is small there's probably enough room for a patio. Small spaces have some advantages: For one thing, they're easy to make secluded and cozy. A 6×6-foot section of sand-set stone provides just enough room for a barbecue grill and doesn't require a large cash outlay. Plus, you can start and finish the project in a weekend. There are many ways to make small spaces seem larger and more comfortable. The key to designing petite places is to focus on simplicity.

■ Create one large area from two smaller ones. If, for example, your patio spills into your yard without a boundary marker, it will seem larger.

■ Draw attention to the patio, not the confines of the property. Instead of letting the lawn end at the property line, sculpt its edges with flower beds. This will redirect attention to the patio.

■ Concentrate color in a patch instead of scattering flowers throughout the landscape. Groups of flowers have more impact than scattered blooms. If you use color in more than one location, repeat two or three colors to tie the areas together.

■ Whenever possible take advantage of nearby views. For example, if you live next to an attractive pond or rolling lawn, make the most of what that surrounding scenery has to offer by leaving the view open.

■ Instead of walling off the patio, place screening only as needed to enhance privacy and block unattractive views.

■ Hang wind chimes or install a fountain. The soothing sounds subdue noise from nearby neighbors or streets.

■ Install built-in seating. Built-ins take up less space than freestanding furniture.

■ Use round tables. You'll have more space around a round table on the patio than a rectangular one.

■ Scale paving patterns to the size of your patio. Small patterns and contrasting textures are confusing and busy, and will make you feel hemmed in.

Oversize pavers make this patio seem larger than it is. The visual lightness of the wrought-iron.planter and furniture add to openness.

Smart furniture arrangement makes this little patio look comfortable and inviting. Placing large items along the sides keeps the center space open and avoids crowding. The wall offers seating and a place to set things down.

Details demand attention

Details—those special decorative touches—must work extra hard in small spaces because there's no room for clutter. Finishing touches such as artwork, found objects, or architectural salvage give small spaces personality. Your small patio might be just the right size for an object that would get lost in a larger setting.

Too much of a good thing, however, can ruin an otherwise artful patio. To avoid overwhelming the space, step back and take a look at your patio in its entirety. Check for noticeable bare spots. Consider whether they function better as empty areas that draw attention to your decorating scheme or whether a potted plant, piece of artwork, or other accent could improve the setting.

Leave room around each detail or collection to set it apart. For example, if you line a wall shelf with shells, don't put another batch of small items on a table right below the shelf. If you have more things to display than you have space, store the surplus pieces, then rotate elements from your decorative stock, replacing some every two or three months.

A small satellite patio surrounded by plants is a great setting for a bistro table and chairs.

Connecting small spaces but limiting the view from one area to another makes a small courtyard seem bigger and more secluded than it is.

This small patio gives the illusion of being deeper than it is because plants and containers conceal part of the view, hinting at hidden spaces.

Make room for greenery in small spaces. Here a patch of grass and a vine-covered wall keep the scene fresh.

FURNISHING A PATIO

The right furnishings make a patio inviting and comfortable, so it's a good idea to make furniture and accessories an integral part of your planning. Furniture and accessories are part of the patio's style, adding to the patio's charm and making it more attractive. They affect how you feel about the patio, which influences how often you use it.

Furnishings and your lifestyle
The first consideration is what the furniture should look like. It's easier to answer that question by choosing furniture that reflects the purposes of the space. For example, chairs and tables for a dining area are likely to be different from chairs and tables for a lounging area. Pick colors and styles that fit into the overall design of your patio.

Be practical, too, when choosing furnishings for outdoor use. Look for durable materials that offer year-round usability. In addition to durability, your outdoor furnishings should be weatherproof and easy to move around. Select chairs and other seating with removable cushions so you can stow them during inclement weather or remove them for cleaning. If you won't use your patio in the winter, include an outside storage area in your plan so you can conveniently protect the furniture from snow and ice.

Seating—freestanding or built-in?
Seating on your patio will fall into one of two categories.
■ Freestanding seating: rockers, chairs, lounges, and dining sets with cushions. These come in more design styles than built-in units. Freestanding furnishings offer flexibility—you can move them around to change the nature of the space.

If you design your patio for entertaining, keep some folding chairs handy for overflow crowds. Make the storage area large enough to keep the chairs out of the way when you don't need them.
■ Built-in seating: planters with platform tops, attached benches, and low walls. Built-ins are less flexible because they aren't movable, but they take up less space than freestanding furniture and, cleverly designed, can also provide storage space.

Benches are the most basic form of built-in seating. Planters and walls can fill in as benches if their top surfaces are wide enough to sit on.

Stairs are an often overlooked opportunity for built-in seating. In a crowded setting, if stair treads are wide and deep enough, your guests can sit on them. Build your stairs at least 4 feet wide if you want them to serve as seating. Sturdy handrails are a must for stairway safety and can also act as grab bars to help people get up from sitting on the stairs.

An outdoor living area becomes truly inviting with the right seating. Choose furniture for comfort and style, but keep durability in mind as you shop too. Store furniture inside during the winter.

Sizing up the furniture

Buy outdoor furniture that suits your patio's size. You want it to appear comfortable, not overwhelming or lost. If you have a small patio area, use a round table—it takes up less space than a square or rectangular one. On a larger patio, you can set up conversation areas with groupings of tables and chairs or lounges and side tables. Include a serving cart, and leave plenty of room to walk around the furniture.

The bulky chairs (far left) dominate the patio and leave little room to walk. The lighter-looking chairs and table (left) are a better fit. The bench increases seating capacity without crowding the space.

Color harmony between the black furniture and the neutral stone makes this area attractive. Plants add spots of color and soften the look of iron and stone.

Flat stones around this pond offer informal, built-in seating. Stairs can double as casual seating too.

Make built-in seating comfortable

For comfortable built-in seating, follow the 18-inch rule: Place the seat 18 inches above the surface and make it at least 18 inches deep.

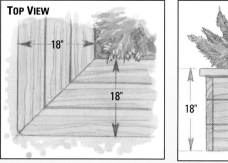

TOP VIEW

18"

18"

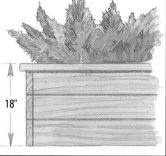

18"

ADDING PERSONALITY WITH ACCENTS

Decorations belong on your patio just as much as they belong in your home. While nature provides the ambience and some beautiful sights outdoors, you can bring your own touch to a patio. Think of your patio as a room that just happens to be outdoors, and it becomes a natural setting to decorate.

Look for nesting places

Once you've built your patio, relax on it and take it in. Notice where your gaze lingers. Those are the perfect places to put accent pieces, spots that could use decorative details. Highlight only one focal point per seating area. If you run out of patio space for decorative items, hang some on the wall.

Group similar objects to establish a theme. Folk art, antique signs, or pottery pieces invite comparison, draw attention, and take on importance when displayed together.

Grouped items act as a single focal point. If you put groups of items too close together, they'll fight each other for attention. The best spots for displaying accents have neutral backgrounds, such as a wall, fence, or green plants.

Items that don't quite count as a collection can still establish a theme. Even if the objects are different, they might have similar shapes, colors, or textures that unify them as a group.

Space the decorative items (singles or groups) far enough apart that each one gets due notice. On the patio, wooden boxes of different heights make good display stands. Coat them with linseed oil and mineral spirits (mixed half-and-half) to enrich the wood grain and color, and protect the wood from weather.

Attach shelves to the wall at different heights. Scattering the shelves on the wall rather than clustering them prevents clutter and helps create a larger display space.

If your patio is linear and formal, you can hang the shelves on the same horizontal or vertical planes. Offset the tops and edges of the shelves for variety.

Don't forget flowers and the pots they grow in. Plain, plastic warehouse pots will detract from the overall appearance of your design scheme. Discount retailers carry a wide variety of stylish, inexpensive containers made to match almost any theme.

The style of your seating influences your patio's personality. A simple board bench would work here, but this new Spanish revival from an import shop adds a touch of old-world charm.

A dull corner becomes a lively place when dressed up with rustic country crafts, a few vintage tools, and a potting bench.

Stone pillars with lamps highlight the steps that lead to this flagstone patio. The low wall creates a rugged texture behind the plants around the patio.

Look for statuary in styles and sizes harmonious to your patio. Standing guard at the steps from path to patio, this statue lends a classic aura.

Look for unusual items, such as this moss-filled basket in the shape of a shoe. Then find the right spots on ledges, shelves, walls, and tabletops to display your found treasures.

Fancy this...

Worried about the right or wrong way to display personal details on your patio? Don't be. There aren't any rules—only suggestions.

■ Mobiles and wind chimes catch the breeze and add a vertical element to the predominantly horizontal lines of the patio. Wind chimes add lively sound.

■ Seashells and other small objects have more appeal when they appear half hidden behind the sides of shadow boxes.

■ If there's an object you can't live without, but there's no obvious way to display or support it, lean it against a flowerpot on the patio.

■ Mount driftwood on a blank wall and train vines to drape its contours.

■ Paint a piece of battered barn wood to look like a circus clown, a butler, or another character. The contrast between the color of the weathered wood, its rough texture, and the paint is reminiscent of folk art. On a smaller scale, hang a similar small figure from the rafters of an overhead structure.

■ Stand a weather vane in a flowerpot that's thick with blooms to draw attention to the seasonal color of the blooms. Create a sculpted array with metal flowers arranged in rows. They make an interesting foil rising behind containers planted with the real thing.

■ Old sporting goods and backyard game equipment are appropriate dressings for a patio. Display croquet mallets and balls in a croquet rack, as if ready to use, for instance. If you're a golfer or tennis player, decorate with retired clubs or racquets. Stand clubs in a used golf bag or hang racquets on a wall.

■ Consider replacing your metal or vinyl-clad storm door with a well-made wooden screen door. Home centers carry them in a variety of styles with both plain and decorative panels.

■ Hanging old silverware or other unexpected (small) objects from an arbor makes a delightful display. Sparkly or silver objects reflect random light patterns onto the patio.

■ Add color with home-sewn pillows covered with colorful patterns in acrylic awning fabrics. Acrylics won't fade like cotton canvas fabric, and hold up a long time even when exposed to weather. Use synthetic fillers to stuff the pillows.

LANDSCAPING WITH PLANTS

Use plants to integrate a patio or wall with other elements in your landscape. You can grow plants in garden beds beside or near the structure or in containers placed on the patio or any wall that surrounds it.

If you haven't yet built your patio but you do have garden beds in place, situate the patio where it offers the best views of the plantings. If you don't have garden beds, plan their location, contours, and plantings when you plan your patio so the flower beds and patio enhance each other. To extend the garden, you can grow plants in containers on the patio itself—right to the doorway of your home if you want.

Container gardens are ideal for placing plants on or around patios or walls. They help make outdoor structures seem a natural part of the landscape instead of an architectural add-on. Container gardens are especially practical when the site (or project budget) prohibits complex landscape installations. Imaginatively placed containers turn even the most basic patio

into a garden paradise.

You can use plants to solve many design problems. Flower beds with a rear border of shrubs and tall plants beautify (and hide) the unattractive space where the patio approaches the edge of the property. A hedge naturally screens out an unattractive view. Potted trees offer shade and privacy, as well as fruit. Large planters help establish and enforce traffic patterns.

When you're ready to integrate plants into your landscape design, first decide where they should go. Your design sketches show where you need shade, privacy, and shelter. Simply pick plants that do the job.

Making the beds

Before you decide what to plant, you must first determine the shape of the bed. Experiment by laying out a garden hose to create a pleasing outline. Curved lines generally look more interesting than straight lines, even bordering a square site. Mark the contour on the lawn with upside-down

spray paint or powdered chalk, roll up the hose, and dig the bed into the soil.

Plant in tiers, with the shortest species in front, and gradually increase the height of the plantings toward the rear of the bed. Tops of plants adjacent to the patio should be lower than eye level for seated people, unless the plants are intended to screen out a view or enhance privacy.

Making use of trees and shrubs

Trees are the environmental workhorses of the natural world. They cast shade, reduce erosion, and clean the air. Shrubs are excellent transitions between larger elements—other trees, sheds, or patios, for example. They're a great substitute for trees where trees won't fit.

Trees and shrubs are either deciduous (they lose their leaves in the winter) or evergreen (they keep their leaves), but these are not the only criteria for selection.

Research species and select those that will adapt to your climate and the soil

Plenty of planters and pots provide lush seasonal landscaping that softens the edges and corners of this patio. Select blooming plants carefully so you have a variety of color throughout the year.

Plantings along the borders integrate this patio with the surrounding yard. The garden beds provide color and texture that contrast with the stone. Taller trees and shrubs behind the beds make a privacy screen.

conditions in your yard. Consider the mature size and growth characteristics. The sapling you buy today may root under your patio or into your foundation in 10 years. And many trees drop seeds, twigs, and blossoms that call for constant cleanup. Others are susceptible to diseases and insects. Some trees, especially fast-growing ones, are prone to storm damage; dead or broken branches above a patio are hazardous.

Groundcovers

Low plants that hug the ground reduce erosion and serve as a living palette for other plantings. Wide, sweeping beds curving around a patio define areas without dividing the space into smaller parts. Where grass won't grow, a groundcover usually will. And it won't need mowing.

Container gardens

You can grow just about any kind of plant in a container, even when you're faced with hot, dry weather or little space. Containers also allow you to quickly change the arrangement of your plants.

Before you plan your planting scheme, spend some time sampling your patio's views. Check the view from the adjoining interior room as well. Wherever you see distractions, such as power lines or the neighbor's storage shed, block them out with a plant in a container. Wherever you need more privacy, plant a shrub. Tall species furnish screening without making the patio seem isolated.

Look for empty corners, blank walls, unattractive structures, and unruly plants on the property line. Dress these areas with container-grown plants. For a unified look on a large patio, plant the same kind of plant in more than one place. The repetition of color and texture will link the spaces.

Boxes and baskets

Window boxes and hanging baskets are the perfect containers for a composition on a small scale.

To keep maintenance and care to a minimum, all the plants in a window box or basket should have the same nutritional requirements and the same needs for sunlight or shade. That doesn't mean you have to plant just one variety. Combine several plants that have blooms of similar colors with plants that have different, contrasting textures. A fine-textured species, such as baby's breath, contrasts nicely with a species that has spiky foliage, such as rosemary. Tall, upright forms, such as coneflowers, make a good backdrop behind low-growing or trailing flowers.

Window boxes and baskets are perfect for growing edible plants too. Lettuces, herbs, and edible flowers create an outdoor salad in a basket, ready for the picking.

Build your window boxes as deep as possible—10 to 12 inches of soil allows room for adequate root growth. Be sure, however, the window boxes don't interfere with the natural traffic patterns that cross your patio. While deep window boxes are

Tall urns overflow with flowers that complement the plantings in the surrounding ground.

A short course in plant buying

Plants for your patio will be close to you, not in a garden far across the yard. So follow a different strategy when you buy plants for patio containers.

■ Buy plants that are at their best in the season when you'll use your patio. Flower beds are big enough to accommodate a variety that will last throughout the seasons. Containers aren't.

■ Choose low-maintenance varieties, those that don't demand deadheading and other botanical chores.

■ Select species whose mature sizes will not overwhelm their surroundings and won't need a lot of pruning to keep them that way.

■ Include fragrance on your list of criteria. Some flowers may be too fragrant to be near.

■ Give your plants an environment in which they'll thrive. Buy plants suited to your zone (see the USDA plant hardiness zone map, www.usna.usda.gov/Hardzone/ushzmap.html).

■ Balance flowers and foliage. An overwhelming display of blossoms can be just that. You'll show off your choices more dramatically against a backdrop of foliage. Vary the texture of the plants—the shape and size of their leaves—and their colors too.

■ Find your favorites first. Then build the rest of your choices with plants that provide attractive complements or contrasts.

■ Set plants on homemade display benches. Woods commonly used to build outdoor structures—pressure-treated lumber, cedar, cypress, and redwood—turn various shades of gray if left untreated, providing an excellent neutral backdrop for plants. The brown tones of stained wood also contrast with the greens and other colors of container gardens.

LANDSCAPING WITH PLANTS *(continued)*

better for your plants, they're not worth it if you have to avoid their sharp corners every time you pass.

If you build your own boxes, drill at least two holes in the bottom for drainage and insert a sheet of rigid foam insulation inside the front before filling the box with soil. The foam will keep roots cool and reduce soil-moisture evaporation. Then, before planting, mix water-retaining polymers into the soil. The pellets swell when wet, retaining moisture. See the polymer instructions for the proper proportion of pellets to soil.

Water window boxes daily or, if needed, twice a day during hot weather. To determine when the plants need watering, poke your finger into the soil about ½ inch deep. If soil feels dry to the touch, it's time to water.

Groundcover plants between the pavers soften the paths leading to this patio.

Trees and shrubs provide a soothing background view for this patio.

A plant stand adds a focal point in front of this garden wall.

Plants almost seem to spill out of the abundant flowerbeds and into the containers on this patio.

A rosebush against the wall and rustic furniture add cottage charm to this patio.

Groundcovers make this patio a grid of greenery .

CREATING PRIVACY AND ENCLOSURE

Without a fence, wall, hedge, or some other way to establish borders, a patio is an exposed and uncomfortable place. You'll feel more at home sitting on a patio that offers at least a small amount of privacy and enclosure—enough to make the space around you seem secure.

Planning for privacy

Consider privacy throughout the planning stage of your patio. Will neighbors have a clear view of the site? Will your patio (and people on it) be visible from a public street or sidewalk? If so, you need to create privacy.

The solution may be as simple as building your patio on a less-exposed side of the house or tucking it into a corner. Stand in different places on your proposed patio site several times during the day and evening. If you don't feel a sense of security and privacy, look for places where you could add a privacy fence, wall, or trees and shrubs. Consider alternate locations for the patio if necessary. While you're checking the site, make a list of unsightly views you want to hide.

Screening

The screening used to enhance privacy or block out unwanted views can take many forms. Which one you use depends on how you plan to use each area of your patio.

Cozy spots for reading, conversation, sunbathing, or meditation call for plenty of shelter. Pools and spas need privacy and a windbreak. Walls, high fences, or dense evergreen plantings are good choices for screening these places.

Areas for parties, large family gatherings, or children's play by nature are more open. Partial screens of latticework, low fence panels with open infill, airy trees, or seat walls are adequate for these places. They can also hide unsightly views, such as garbage cans, air-conditioning equipment, utility hookups, or the back of a neighbor's shed or garage. Train a vine to grow into the screen; the foliage ultimately will hide the screen, drawing it into the landscape.

No matter what kind of screening you pick, make sure you locate it strategically. Study the location and the angle from which you see an unattractive object, then place

screens between it and your vantage spot. The closer you can put the screen to the object, the better you will hide it.

The same goes for a privacy screen— the closer it is to the patio, the more privacy it offers. Before you encircle your patio with a privacy hedge or fence, find the places where outsiders can see in. Few patios need complete coverage. Block the most open views. More open, friendly screening, such as lattice, picket fencing, or ornamental iron fencing, is often all you need.

Defining space

The acknowledgment of space usually doesn't occur until something encloses or defines it. Defining space—visually separating one area from another— is an important aspect of patio planning.

For example, you'll need some physical structure to separate an intimate dining area from larger entertainment areas. Otherwise you might feel like you're in a public place, even if you are screened from public view.

Inside the yard or on the patio, a brick or stone wall or fence 18 to 30 inches tall is

STANLEY PRO TIP

The right height

Put your outdoor ceiling at a comfortable height by following these design tips.

Tree branches 15 to 20 feet off the ground may not seem high, but they could be high enough to make people at a dining table feel uncomfortable. Fix the problem by setting up a table with an umbrella.

Patio space that's intended for intimate activities such as family dining, reflection, or solitary reading benefit from cover that's 10 to 12 feet above the patio surface. Party space feels comfortable with ceilings up to 20 feet high.

How much of the patio should you cover? It's usually best to shelter at least one-third of the patio's surface area.

A screen house shelters this patio's outdoor sitting room. The screened walls render a sense of privacy and enclosure and allow breezes to enter without bothersome insects. A structure like this often becomes the difference between a patio that gets used and one that sits idle.

adequate to separate spaces. A wall that defines the lot line should be 3 to 6 feet tall.

Implied definitions

The need to separate one space from another doesn't mean you have to build actual walls. Perceived walls often do a better job of defining space than solid walls, and they don't seem quite as intrusive.

Perceived walls—ankle-high plantings, built-in seating, even shrubs and trees—imply separation without actually isolating areas from one another. They interrupt both visual and physical movement but don't block views. In this way, they direct traffic and define space without making you feel isolated or claustrophobic.

Plants and flower beds can suggest walls or borders. They're especially useful in helping establish outdoor room spaces.

Low hedges and small trees serve the same purpose in the larger landscape, to visually separate the patio from the yard for instance. Shrubbery effectively blocks physical movement but not the view.

Built-in or freestanding benches, raised planters, or even a change in the paving

pattern adequately distinguish one space from another. Freestanding furniture also differentiates areas without completely enclosing spaces, and you can rearrange the division of space to meet different needs. This can be especially useful when you need to separate two spaces that have closely related purposes, such as a family dining area from a party space.

Overheads

Overhead space, or the lack of it, has a great impact on comfort—both indoors and out. Think of a high, vaulted ceiling. It's awe-inspiring but leaves you feeling a bit overwhelmed. Low ceilings, on the other hand, create an oppressive atmosphere. The same holds true outdoors. Many outdoor areas need some kind of physical limit overhead—but just in the right amount—in order to be comfortable. How much of an overhead ceiling you'll need in your outdoor room depends on how you plan to use the space.

An area designated for entertaining large groups will feel more comfortable left open to the sky or provided with a high overhead

structure. Private spaces, such as those you'll use for dining, talking, or relaxing, will feel more cozy with less height overhead. Just as you can imply the presence of a wall with plants and low structures, you can suggest a ceiling too. Train a vine across the back of the house about 8 feet above the patio for a simple way to bring a sense of security to the corner where you will sit to read your Sunday newspaper, for instance.

You can, of course, come up with more elaborate solutions. You can build an overhead structure—a two- or four-post arbor, a pergola, or a canopy. You can even install a fixed or retractable awning.

Such additions increase your sense of enclosure, provide protection from the weather, and turn an average-looking patio into a unique part of your backyard.

Overheads with slatted roofs make mottled shade. With some careful planning and a thorough site analysis *(pages 12–15)*, you can control the amount of shade provided throughout the day.

A solid roof makes shade all the time and offers some protection from showers. The roof over an attached patio usually looks

A curved wall with a water bowl sets off this patio's sitting area, making an outdoor room.

Placing this small patio close to the fence screens it from the neighbors and still affords a generous view of the garden.

Open rafters overhead shade and enclose a patio without completely covering it.

Limit heavy screening

Without forethought, screening can quickly turn into a stockade. Build walls, high fences, and dense hedges only where you need maximum screening.

CREATING PRIVACY AND ENCLOSURE *(continued)*

best if it matches the style and color of the house roof. When possible, extend the line of the house roof into the patio cover. A solid roof over a freestanding patio can be design feature—a cupola roof or a pyramidal shape, for example. A patio is a great place for a gazebo.

No matter what kind of overhead you build, make it look like an integral part of the design, not an afterthought. Repeat a detail of your house—a molding or post style, a color, or a material—so the structure looks like it belongs with your house and yard.

A fence or wall contributes to the style of your patio. This brick-and-wood fence and arched gateway set a tone of traditional elegance.

A curve in the wall carves a niche for a table and chairs. The low wall allows a view of the garden, then steps to a higher level for more privacy.

A rustic stone wall perfectly pairs with this patio of moss-surrounded stepping-stones.

A vine-covered pergola over a detached patio provides an inviting outdoor sitting room, complete with lighting and a fountain.

Don't wall yourself in

Avoid turning your yard into a fortress. Place barrier-style screens, such as solid walls, high fences, and dense, straight hedges, only in areas that require maximum screening. Everywhere else, use the least amount of screening possible.

A gazebo offers shelter from the elements and a focal point for this natural setting. Low walls define the open patio.

A slat roof casts dappled shade over the patio's sitting area. Vines trained on the uprights and roof camouflage the hard edges of the structure.

ADDING AMENITIES

Amenities such as lighting, a cooking area, or storage space increase the comfort and convenience of your patio and make it more inviting. The benefits of including any amenity depend on how you plan to use the patio.

Consider outdoor lighting for any patio. It costs little, but extends the use of your patio, increases its safety, and makes your house more secure, even when you're not using the patio.

Lighting
Patio lighting requires some planning, but installation is straightforward (see *page 41*). A low-voltage lighting system is easy to install. Line-voltage lighting is more complex, but installation is still well within the skills of the average do-it-yourselfer.

Before you install any system, it is useful to understand some lighting principles. Outdoor lighting fixtures come in a multitude of styles for different uses. Your outdoor lighting will best serve and enhance the beauty of your landscape if you rely on the following variety of lighting strategies.

Uplighting highlights an object by casting light up from a low position. The fixture is usually in front of the object so the beam shines away from viewing areas and grazes objects, highlighting their shapes.

Downlighting lights large areas from above—it's good for steps, paths, floors, and tabletops. Mount the fixtures on trees with conduit and hardware that won't harm them, or fasten fixtures to overhead rafters. Keep the fixtures out of sight and aim them to minimize stray light. Thread wires through the centers of hollow columns or press them into the grooves routed into overhead posts.

Conceal the fixtures to focus attention on the lighted object or area. Fixtures may cast their bright light a long distance, so aim them carefully. Place them so the bulbs aren't visible from any angle.

Decorative fixtures add style. Some mount on posts, others attach to walls. Choose fixtures that fit your patio's design theme.

Path lights illuminate a walkway, linking your patio to other parts of the yard. They're made to order for lighting short flights of steps or to mark points of entry.

Outdoor kitchen
Almost everyone believes food tastes better when it's cooked outdoors. An outdoor kitchen on your patio—even a basic one with just a propane grill and a work surface—inspires cookouts.

An outdoor kitchen complicates the construction of the patio, so be sure the benefits of adding one are worth the extra cost. Adding a basic kitchen is inexpensive. If you spend more, you can have an outdoor kitchen with a deluxe gas range, a rotisserie, built-in cabinets, built-in refrigerator, and even a kitchen sink.

No matter what kind of kitchen you desire, where you put it is important. The best location offers both convenience (close to the indoor kitchen) and safety (distant or insulated from combustible material and away from traffic patterns).

For a simple cooking spot, place a portable grill at the edge of the patio, close to the indoor kitchen. Keep it out from under eaves and overheads. When it isn't in use, hide it behind large potted plants on platforms with casters or other movable screening.

Construct a built-in grill with fireproof materials that conform to local building codes. Whether portable or built-in, keep your kitchen out of the main traffic route and make sure it doesn't block attractive views. Provide enough room for preparing and serving food and for storing utensils. If you're short on space, tuck cooking items into a bench or screened cabinet.

Equip your patio kitchen with outdoor-grade appliances that meet building codes and will withstand weather conditions. Waterproof countertops made of marble, metal, or tile withstand the elements. If you build the countertop with an 18-inch overhang on one edge, you can use it as a bar or dining counter.

Storage
Planning adequate storage is part art, part science. Like all patio design, storage starts with a list of everything you might want to keep on the patio, such as firewood, furniture covers, pet supplies, hoses, chair cushions, garden tools, and barbecue utensils. Without a home, all that stuff can turn your patio into a large storage area, and you won't enjoy it—or use it—as much as you planned.

Opportunities to create storage space exist both on and around the patio. On the patio surface, vertical cabinets made from cedar, redwood, or painted pressure-treated lumber serve as attractive and functional accents. Sketch out the size of the cabinet before you build it, allowing enough room for the items it will house. Then adjust the proportions so they are pleasing to the eye. When you have the size right, design a framed door with an infill pattern that complements the overall style of your landscape theme.

Patio boxes, handmade or commercial, are popular storage places that double as seating. Buy freestanding benches with lids—or build them into the perimeter of your patio. Paint a child's toy box with exterior paint and use it as an outdoor coffee table and a place to store chair cushions. Keep pet supplies and birdseed in watertight tins decorated with painted designs of your choice. A decorated mailbox provides a dry place to store hand tools and garden gloves in an unusual accent. Stand a baker's rack in front of a blank wall and line up your empty flowerpots, baskets, and watering cans.

An outdoor cooking area takes your patio to another dimension. For a simple approach, park a portable grill on the patio. Or you can build a more elaborate outdoor kitchen with a built-in barbecue grill like this one.

Water features

Water gardens bring the sparkle and soothing sound of water to your patio. A simple birdbath or a small container water garden might be all you need, but first explore the many sources for freestanding fountains or wall-mounted units available. Many are easy to install and affordable.

Even an elaborate patio pond is relatively inexpensive. For example, if you can incorporate an open area into your plans, you can excavate a hole for the pond before you lay the patio paving. Then line it with whatever liner you've chosen before building the base. When you lay the paving material, cut the individual pieces around the pond's opening so they look more natural. In a contemporary setting, make straight cuts to match the style. Add a

submersible pump and pots with water plants to complete the oasis.

A preformed, rigid pond liner creates an even larger pool on the surface of the patio. Follow the manufacturer's directions when building the framing, and pay special attention to the need for a footing to support the structure below ground. Camouflage the edges of the liner with landscape timbers, rocks, or paving material.

Stagnant water breeds mosquitoes, bacteria, and algae and also collects silt and debris, so install a submersible pump to recirculate water over a waterfall or through a fountainhead for aeration. Set the pump on a stone or brick on the bottom of the pond to minimize clogging, and skim the surface periodically to remove debris.

Lights let you enjoy the patio after dark and add a touch of style during the day. You'll find light fixtures to match any patio design.

Lights set an almost magical scene after dark. You can install lighting fixtures to provide uniform lighting or to create dramatic areas of light and shadow.

Voltage: line or low?

Outdoor lighting runs on either line voltage (the 120-volt AC power in your house) or low voltage (12-volt DC power provided by a transformer). Installing a line-voltage system is a job much like house wiring—a homeowner with experience in electrical work or a licensed electrician can do it.

You'll need line voltage for outdoor appliances. Installation requires conduit, fittings, junction boxes, receptacles, fixtures, and wire. Most outdoor line-voltage systems require a permit and approval from a building inspector.

Most low-voltage systems don't require a permit and are designed for do-it-yourself installation. They do require a line-voltage outlet for the transformer to plug into.

Several kinds of fixtures are made for both systems, but line-voltage systems offer more options.

ADDING AMENITIES (continued)

Spas, hot tubs, and pools

A spa, hot tub, or soaking pool is a popular patio addition, but installing one requires careful planning. It's better to select the pool first so you can incorporate electrical, water, and drain connections into the patio design. For aesthetic reasons, and to prevent damage, you'll want to conceal wires and plumbing but make sure they're accessible for maintenance. An outdoor pool must meet local code requirements, so have your plan checked and approved before you spend any money.

Fireplaces, fire pits, and chimineas

Fire—whether in a fireplace, fire pit, or chiminea—is the ultimate focal point in both indoor and outdoor settings. Nothing matches the comforting glow of an outdoor fire, an amenity that's easy to include in your patio plans.

A fireplace is the most labor-intensive and expensive option. Building one requires a concrete base and a permanent, safe location. You can include a rotisserie and a brick-lined warming oven in the plan, and use your fireplace for cooking and keeping food hot.

Freestanding gas and wood-fired pits have become widely available for installation on patios. Lined with firebricks and surrounded by a wide, fire-resistant coping such as stone, their open flames resemble campfires. Provide plenty of floor space on all sides of the pit to keep people a safe distance from the flames and to prevent sparks from jumping out onto flammable material. Keep an extinguisher handy, as well as a cover to smother flames that grow too large. The cover also helps contain sparks, which otherwise might blow out of the pit when the party is over.

Chimineas are portable fireplaces that look like ceramic potbellied stoves. They originated in Mexico and have become popular in the United States. Place a chiminea on a metal stand or firebrick platform to keep the patio from overheating. Chimineas are not designed for cooking or winter weather. Store them indoors when temperatures fall below freezing.

A spa or hot tub is a natural enhancement for a patio, one that calls for careful planning. Pools, spas, and hot tubs usually fall under local building code requirements, so check with your building department before finalizing your plans.

Gathering around a fire is a time-honored outdoor ritual. A fire pit on the patio is a great place to spend a chilly evening or to have a wiener roast. You can design and build your own fire pit (check your building codes first) or purchase a commercial unit.

A tiled pool partners well with the traditional style of this patio. The poolside kitchen and dining area invite swimmers to spend an entire day.

Stone walls, a waterfall, and plantings welcome this informal pool into the landscape. The stone patio and pool deck carries on the natural look.

STANLEY PRO TIP: **Lining up the utilities**

Before you build your patio, plan the utility requirements. Once you've built the patio, it will be difficult to add water and gas lines and underground wiring. Run utilities underground to maximize safety and minimize clutter. Plot the runs on paper and rough them in before you dig footings.

A water feature will require installation of a pair of 2-inch schedule-40 PVC pipes under the patio site. Draw them in your plans so they run like tunnels under the patio, from one end to the other. Run the electrical cables and smaller pipes for water through the sleeves. The sleeves protect wires and pipes and allow you to remove them for repair or replacement without digging up the patio. Any water leaking from a line break flows through the sleeve and out of the site instead of seeping into the soil under it. Run power and water lines through separate sleeves.

Spa installations are more complex because they require both running water and a drainpipe. Spas, ponds, fountains, and waterfall pumps also require electrical outlets with ground-fault circuit interrupters (GFCIs). Lighting systems require electric lines. For an outdoor kitchen, consider installing a permanent natural gas line for a gas grill so you won't have to deal with propane tanks. The orifices for gas and propane appliances are different—make sure your grill is fitted with the right ones.

Install an exterior phone jack, even if you use cordless phones indoors. You'll eventually want to carry on conversations off the patio, and the indoor cordless phone signal might not reach that far.

To bring television to the patio, you'll need an electric outlet and cable or satellite connection. To provide music, it's easy to run speaker wires from your stereo system to weatherproof speakers on the patio.

DRAWING PLANS

You can draw plans for your patio, wall, or walk yourself even if you're not a draftsman. Some graph paper (use paper with a ¼-inch grid), a sharp pencil or two, a good eraser, a ruler, and perhaps an architect's scale are the tools you'll need.

Before you sit down to produce your plans, check with your local building department to see if it has specific requirements for the way plans are presented.

Follow this sequence to develop your plans: Start with rough sketches that show the basic contours of the structure; move on to scaled drawings; then create final drawings that illustrate the details of any specialized construction procedures.

Satisfying the inspector

Most building departments do not require architect-quality plans, but do want to see how all the pieces of a structure fit together. Inspectors don't like to squint over unclear drawings, and they may want to see a complete list of materials you plan to use.

Produce at least one plan view of a patio or walkway (how the structure looks from overhead) and one cross section that will show footings, excavation depths, how you intend to build the base, and any reinforcing elements like rebar or wire mesh. For a wall, you'll need "elevations" (drawings that show how it looks from the front and side).

Plans save time and money

With a complete set of drawings in hand, you can more easily estimate materials. Detailed drawings can also help you spot ways to save money on materials. For example, if the patio requires forms that are 12 feet 2 inches long, you will need to buy 14-foot boards—that means wasting nearly 2 feet of each piece. By shortening the deck a few inches, you can buy less expensive 12-foot boards.

Drawing plans enables you to solve problems before you start building— wasted pencil lead is less costly than wasted materials and time. The more detailed your drawings, the more likely you are to catch design flaws that would otherwise slow construction of the project. And if you have some or all of the work completed by a contractor, plans are invaluable.

All plans start with sketches—usually many of them. Narrow your preliminary ideas to the best ones for your final design. Following the planning sequence in this chapter will help you design a patio that meets all your needs.

Computerized landscaping

Some home centers and lumberyards will help you lay out your patio, wall, or overhead structures and draw plans using computer software. Bring in a rough drawing with dimensions (height, width, and length) and ask for help. If you're computer savvy yourself, browse the Internet for similar planning software you can use.

Most programs produce several drawings—a plan view, an elevation, and a perspective view. Many also will produce a bill of materials you can take shopping.

Some programs have limitations, displaying only a few material styles and lacking the capacity to plan unusual or odd-shape designs. Structural requirements that differ from typical building codes may not be covered. Most professional contractors draw their plans by hand. It's quicker and more flexible.

Revive an old patio

If you have a patio that needs renovation, use the planning steps to turn it into an enjoyable, usable space. Start by noting faults and assets, just as if you were planning a new patio.

If the area is too large, subdivide it into smaller, more intimate spaces with planters, container gardens, or movable seating. Perhaps you could add an outdoor kitchen, fire pit, or water feature, as described on *pages 40–43*. Maybe all your patio really needs is a new dining space and a spot to set up a portable or built-in grill.

If the patio is too small to entertain guests, build an extension *(page 6)*. If you don't have space close to the existing structure, build a detached patio farther out in the yard and connect the two with a boardwalk or path.

To make an old concrete patio more attractive, consider mortaring brick or stone paving to its surface *(pages 54–57)*.

Making a landscape plan

Putting plans on paper requires discipline. The task will proceed smoothly if you approach it one step at a time.

A patio, wall, or path plan starts with a base map, which is simply a scaled drawing of your property. You can zip through this step by locating your plat map—it's probably among the papers you received when you bought your house. You may also find a plat map at your county clerk's office. Once you have the map, have a copy shop enlarge it to 24×36 inches.

If you can't find a plat map, make one yourself. With a 100-foot steel tape measure, a sketch pad, and someone to help you, measure your property and make a scale drawing of its important features. Here's what a base map should include.

■ Dimensions of your property and location of property lines.

■ Outline and dimensions of the house and its position relative to property lines.

■ Exact locations of exterior electrical outlets, dryer vents, and water supply—anything that protrudes from the side of the house where you plan to locate the patio.

■ Locations and dimensions of all exterior windows and doors, including the distance from the ground and which rooms they represent. Show them all, not just those on the deck side; you may change your mind about the patio location.

■ Positions and dimensions of any outbuildings, such as garages and storage sheds, and other major landscape features, including large trees, playground equipment, and planting beds.

■ Dimensions of roof overhangs and locations of downspouts.

■ Locations and dimensions of existing walls, fences, stairs, walks, and driveways.

This map will show everything you need to know when you plan your patio.

Making a site analysis

Once you have a record of your property's existing elements, note what's right and what's wrong with it. Tape a piece of tracing paper over your site plan and trace the major elements. Gather up the notes and the sketches you made when you conducted an inventory of your site *(pages 12–15)* and transfer the findings to the tracing paper.

(Leave your site plan unmarked—you might need it later.)

A site analysis is a bird's-eye view of conditions in your yard, both the things you like and those you would like to change.

Note the prevailing winds; you don't want your patio situated in a wind tunnel, so you may need to move it or build windbreaks.

Draw arrows to indicate predominant drainage patterns so you can avoid putting your patio or wall on swampy soil. If the best location is in a runoff area, you may have to build a drainage system to divert the water.

Indicate where the shade falls and where the sun is strongest during the part of the day you plan to use your patio most.

Make note of neighbors' views and plan for privacy. Also note the things you want to shield from your view.

You don't need to indicate solutions for each of these situations yet; that's a step you will take later.

Remember to include the elements you consider assets—pleasant views, the direction of cooling breezes, or natural areas that you could link to your patio via pathways.

TYPICAL BASE MAP

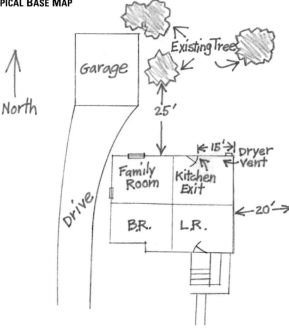

TYPICAL SITE ANALYSIS

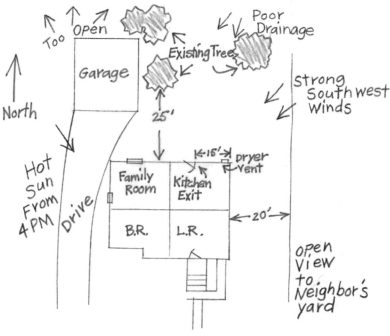

DRAWING PLANS *(continued)*

Making a bubble plan

A bubble plan is simply a base map with circles containing notes on it. The bubble plan will probably be the most useful planning tool you'll use.

Bubble diagrams encourage you to try different ideas. They are designed to let your imagination run free so you can look at different situations to come up with the best landscape plan. The site analysis you prepared *(page 45)* is a snapshot of your landscape as it exists; the bubble plan helps you imagine how things could be.

To draw a bubble plan, tape a sheet of tracing paper over your site analysis and retrace the house and major features of the landscape. You should be able to read your site analysis notes through the top sheet, but if you can't, lay the site analysis to the side and use it as a guide.

Now look at the various areas in the yard and brainstorm how you could use them. Draw circles on the paper, identifying the purpose of each area—disregard budget limitations or time constraints for now.

When you make a bubble diagram, think about the purpose or function of an area first. Consider the kind of structure you need later. If you decide you're ready to finalize your design after you've drawn your first bubble plan, take a second look. There's a good chance you've forgotten something.

Use abstract terms at this stage. For example, label an area close to the house as "entertainment," if you wish, but don't identify it specifically as "patio." You may discover other areas with the same purpose and find in later planning stages that a patio doesn't belong there at all. Similarly, "privacy" or "increase privacy" would be better labels than "fence," "wall," or "trees." Indicate various needs in a general way and move them around to make the best use of your landscape.

If you want a place for entertaining large groups and a smaller space for family dining, move the bubbles around to see where they might fit. One solution might be to place them on different sides of the house. They might work with one area attached to the other. Or you might see a way to have one area completely removed from the house and the two connected by a path. Maybe you wouldn't connect them at all. With the bubble plan, you can test all the options.

The final touches

Once you have found the best solution for your property, sketch in the structures that meet the purposes you have defined. Get as close to scale in this version as you can. It will be the launching pad for the plan views and elevations you'll take to your building department for approval.

Put in the main structures first—the patio, steps, walls, and paths—and modify them if necessary. For example, if a rectangular patio doesn't look quite right or if a large oak interferes with one of its corners, don't reduce the size of the patio. Round the corner or cut it at 45 degrees. If the walk from the patio to the garden bed strikes you as straight and boring, put curves in the path.

Trees and plants come next. Add planting areas with contoured bed lines, and use circles to designate new trees and shrubs. Then label the rooms in your house and make one last check to see that the uses of exterior space are compatible with the space inside. Finally make notes of the tasks you need to accomplish: "remove this tree," "build fence here," "replant this garden," and so forth.

TYPICAL BUBBLE PLAN

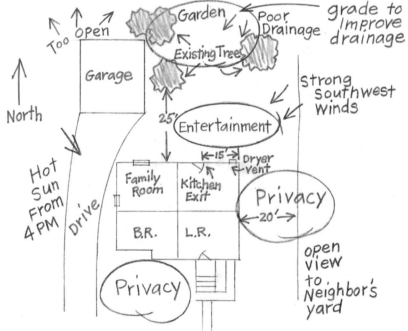

Dealing with inspectors

Building inspectors have an important job: They assure that structures built in their jurisdictions are strong and safe. To accomplish this goal, they have the authority to stop construction on any job they believe is being built incorrectly.

Work with an inspector in a respectful, businesslike manner. Present clean and complete drawings and materials lists. Find out how many inspections you will need to check your project and be ready for each. Do not cover up anything an inspector wants to look at, or you may have to dismantle your work. It's seldom a good idea to argue with an inspector. He or she knows more than you do, and getting on the bad side of an inspector can make a job miserable. Comply exactly with all of the inspector's directions.

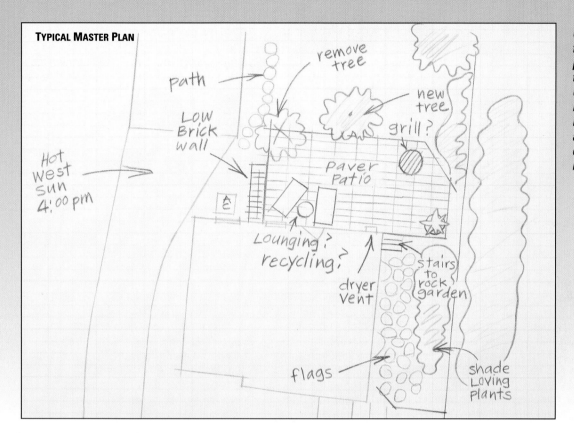

TYPICAL MASTER PLAN

path
remove tree
LOW Brick wall
new tree
grill?
Hot west sun 4:00 pm
Paver Patio
E
Lounging? recycling?
dryer Vent
stairs to rock garden
flags
shade Loving Plants

Creation of the master plan is the final stage of planning. The master plan shows the steps you will take to make your ideal landscape. On the master plan, you should identify structures you will build, locations of gardens and plantings, and major alterations to the existing landscape, such as tree removal or grading.

REFRESHER COURSE
A quick look at patio planning

Putting your plans on paper is the final step of the planning sequence. This allows you to sort out the considerations involved in locating and designing a patio that fits your site, reflects your personality, and will provide you with enjoyable space for years to come. Here's a quick glance at the things you should keep in mind when committing your design to paper.

Planning for purpose
List all the activities you foresee for your patio: lounging, barbecuing, entertaining, soaking in a spa, container gardening, and more. In your design try to accommodate as many of these activities as possible.

Size and shape
Unless you expect to entertain large groups, there's little need for a huge patio. Just make sure you have ample space for all the activity areas you need.

A rectangular patio provides the most available space, and a simple shape is often the most attractive design. But don't be afraid to add angles. An octagonal patio holds a round table nicely. Simple 45-degree angles add visual interest, often without sacrificing much space.

Consider dividing the patio into two or more sections: one area for lounging and another for dining and cooking. Orient one section at a different angle, or use planters or steps to create a transition between the two areas.

A patio doesn't have to be right next to the house. A peninsula or an island patio offers a pleasant retreat from daily life.

Situations for comfort
As you plan your patio, note the sun and wind patterns in your yard. Situate the dining area in evening shade. Provide a lounging area with part shade and part sun. Put in plantings or a fence to minimize wind gusts.

Include amenities
Don't neglect the add-ons that make a patio more than just an outdoor floor. Consider an overhead structure or trellis to provide shade as well as a trellis for climbing plants. And you can add a high railing with lattice panels to increase privacy and screen undesirable views.

Built-in planters and benches are great for unifying different areas of a patio. You can use large flowerpots and attractive furniture, which can be moved to suit the occasion, the same way. If so, allow space for them in your plan.

Plan for lighting as well. Low-voltage lights are inexpensive, easy to install, and can be mounted around the patio. You may also need additional line-voltage lighting and an electrical receptacle or two. For comfortable breezes on a still evening, think about installing a ceiling fan for a covered patio. Consult an electrician about extending wiring from the house or adding a new circuit for electrical features.

TOOLS & MATERIALS

Masonry projects usually require more tools than other do-it-yourself home improvements. Most homeowners, however, already have many of the basic tools: a level, tape measure, framing square, pry bar, framing hammer, and perhaps a small sledgehammer and cold chisel.

In addition to basic tools, you will need shovels, rakes, an electric drill, and other tools that you may already have. Specialty tools, ranging from a cement mixer to cement-finishing floats and trowels, are readily available at rental shops. You may also have friends or neighbors who have done masonry projects and can lend you what you need, along with some firsthand advice and experienced hands-on help. If you plan to do several masonry projects, it's probably worthwhile to buy some of the equipment.

Choosing tools
Buy any basic tools you're missing—consider them an investment in future projects. You will use them long after your patio or wall is finished, so invest in high-quality tools. Cheap tools often break or bend easily, don't work well, and may be less comfortable to use. When you buy cheap tools, you risk having to take a trip to the hardware store to replace a broken tool right in the middle of your project.

You can rent many of the other tools you'll need, especially those which are large and expensive or the ones you'll use just once or infrequently. Make a list of those tools and estimate when you'll need them. Then rent the tool just when you need it, rather than spending money to have it sit idle while you work on other parts of the project.

Choosing materials
A multitude of bricks, pavers, stone, concrete, and other masonry materials add up to a wide range of possibilities for your project. Deciding which materials to use and how to use them are important design decisions. Begin with a general idea of the look you want, then visit your local brickyard, quarry, landscaping center, or tile retailer to see which materials will bring your vision to life. Get samples so you can visualize what textures and colors will harmonize with your house and yard. In the early stages, stay flexible about your design. Then, as you narrow your choices, consider the skills, time, and cost for the job. You may want a rubblestone wall at first, for instance, but later decide the heavy work required is not for you. Instead you opt for ashlar stone, which is more costly but easier to lift, set, and cut.

CHAPTER PREVIEW

Layout tools
page 49

Excavating tools
page 50

Mixing tools
page 51

Cutting tools
page 51

Finishing tools
page 52

Tiling tools
page 53

Safety gear
page 53

Brick
page 54

LAYOUT TOOLS

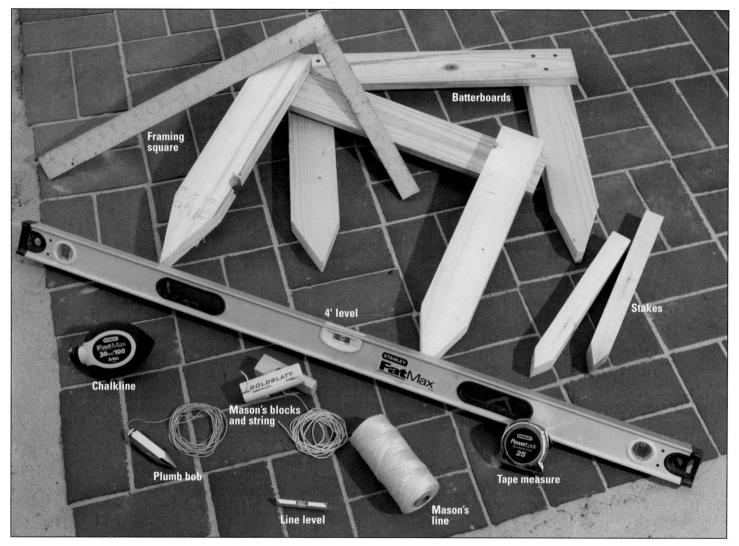

Framing square

Batterboards

4' level

Stakes

Chalkline

Mason's blocks and string

Plumb bob

Line level

Mason's line

Tape measure

Stone
page 56

Precast concrete pavers
page 58

Tile
page 60

Concrete block
page 62

Poured concrete
page 64

Stucco
page 66

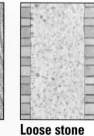

Loose stone
page 68

Mortar
page 70

EXCAVATING TOOLS

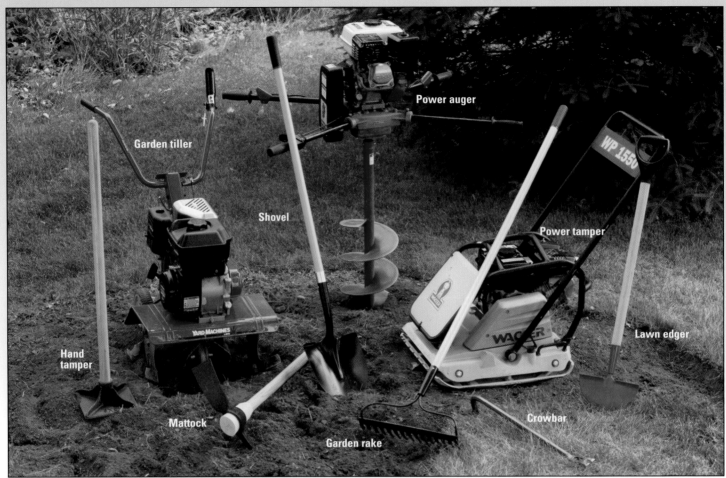

Garden tiller

Power auger

Shovel

Power tamper

Hand tamper

Lawn edger

Mattock

Crowbar

Garden rake

Most masonry projects require digging and earthwork. Whether you are setting stepping-stones or digging footings for a wall, you will probably have to cut through sod with a spade or **lawn edger** *(above)* to remove soil. If you have to remove a large amount of sod—to construct a patio, for instance—rent a **power sod cutter**. This machine cuts sod into strips and slices under the sod to separate it from the soil so you can roll it up and reuse it elsewhere in the landscape. When you have to excavate a large area, loosen the soil with a **garden tiller** first to make digging easier. If you have to dig a number of postholes for footings or to build an overhead structure or fence for your patio, rent a **power auger.** The two-person version in the photo *above* will bore through soil and small roots easily.

You can use a **hand auger** or **posthole digger** if you have just a few holes to dig.

You'll need a **tamper** whenever you excavate or fill an area. Sand and gravel base material for concrete and stone surfaces should be tamped too. A hand tamper works well for small areas, but consider renting a **power tamper** for large patios and long paths or walks. In footings and holes, you can tamp with the end of a 2×4.

Mix mortar in a **mixing tub** *(opposite page, top)* rather than a wheelbarrow. The shape of the tub makes thorough mixing easier. A **mason's hoe** with holes in the blade also makes it easier to mix mortar properly. You can mix concrete in either a tub or **wheelbarrow;** mixing it in a wheelbarrow makes transporting the concrete to the site and pouring it into place easier. A tub would be handy if you are mixing concrete for

postholes; you could place the tub near the postholes, mix the concrete, and shovel it into the holes.

If your project requires mixing more than a dozen or so bags of premix *(see page 63),* rent a **power concrete mixer.** Consider ordering ready-mix concrete for any job that requires more than one cubic yard.

Cutting masonry materials is easiest with special tools such as the **drysaw, brick splitter,** and **tile cutter** shown on the *opposite page, bottom.* You can rent these tools. You'll need standard carpentry tools for building forms. Special tools for finishing concrete and laying tile are shown on *pages 52 and 53,* along with safety equipment. Always wear safety glasses and gloves when working with masonry materials. A dust mask or respirator will protect you from dust when cutting materials.

MIXING TOOLS

Cement mixer

Wheelbarrow

Mixing tub

Mason's hoe

CUTTING TOOLS

Reciprocating saw

Bricklayer's hammer

Cordless drill

Mini sledge

Circular saw

Brick chisel

Cold chisel

Angle grinder

Drysaw

Brick splitter

Jigsaw

Tile cutter

FINISHING TOOLS

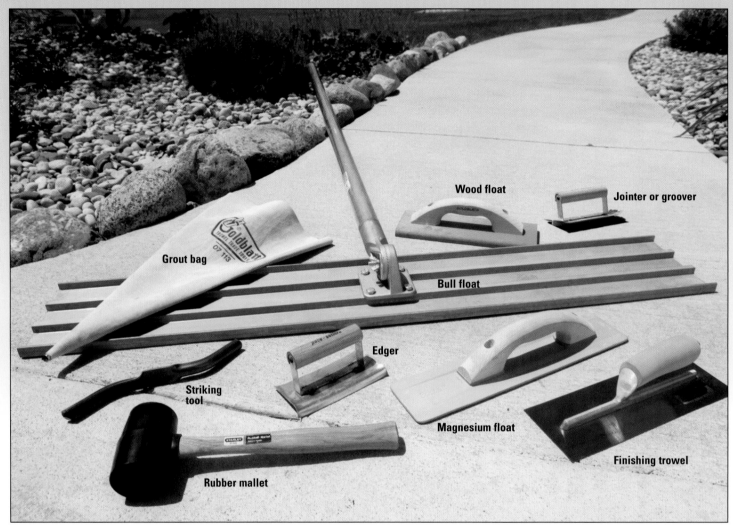

Grout bag

Wood float

Jointer or groover

Bull float

Striking tool

Edger

Magnesium float

Finishing trowel

Rubber mallet

Renting tools

For some homeowners, buying new tools is part of the enjoyment of a home improvement project. But when it comes to masonry projects, there are some tools you won't ever need again once the job is done. If you need a tool only once, renting it makes more sense than buying it. Don't pay for idle time: Rent a tool only when you're ready for it.

Here are some of the tools you may need to rent for the construction of your patio.
■ Excavating equipment to clear the site.
■ Hammer drill to install masonry anchors in a brick or stucco wall.
■ Power auger to dig holes for footings.
■ Power mixer to prepare concrete.
■ Reciprocating saw to make cuts where

a circular saw can't reach.
■ Bull float for large concrete slabs.
■ Sod cutter to make sod removal easier.
■ Rototiller to break up soil for excavation.
■ Wet saw or snap cutter to cut large amounts of tile or other masonry materials.

TILING TOOLS

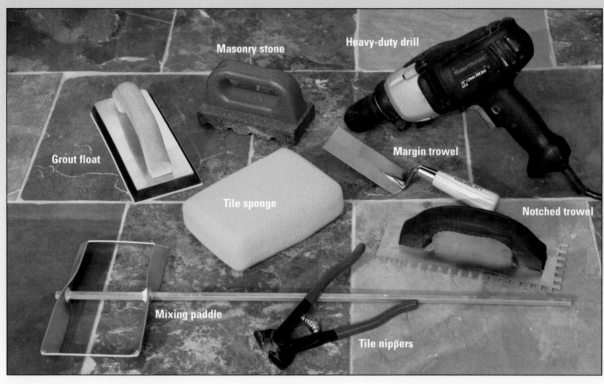

Masonry stone

Heavy-duty drill

Grout float

Margin trowel

Tile sponge

Notched trowel

Mixing paddle

Tile nippers

SAFETY GEAR

Respirator

Knee pads

Rubber gloves

Particle mask

Work gloves

Safety goggles

Safety glasses

Ear protectors

BRICK

Brick is one of the oldest building materials. Museum samples date back 10,000 years. There's a brick for every use you can think of. The most common are face brick, pavers, firebrick, and building brick.

Picking a brick

You'll probably choose brick for your project based on its color and texture. Colors range from reds and burgundies to whites and buffs. There are a variety of face textures. Other factors that play into your final choice are durability, maintenance requirements, the grade of the brick, and how you intend to use it. No matter what you choose, the brick grade must match your area's climate.

Pavers, face bricks, and building bricks come in three grades based on the severity of the weather they can endure. NW (no weather) brick is for interior use only. An MW rating means the brick will stand up to moderate weather conditions, including frost and some freezing. SW brick withstands severe weather, including freeze-thaw cycles. Use SW brick for patios.

MW is good for exterior walls in mild climates, but SW is a more durable choice.

■ **Brick for patios.** When choosing brick for patios, avoid common brick, face brick, and firebrick, varieties not designed for paving. Some good choices are:

Pavers are hard and resist moisture and wear. Some types have rounded or chamfered edges, a feature which makes sand-set installations easier and more attractive.

Salvaged brick from old buildings and streets frequently comes with chunks of mortar left on, which many designers feel adds to its charm. You may have to chisel the mortar off for some uses. Salvaged brick varies widely in durability, however. If you like the look but not the risk, you can approximate a used-brick appearance with manufactured salvage brick.

Adobe pavers, impregnated with asphalt, resist water almost as well as clay brick. They are not fired at high temperatures, however, so they won't stand up to hard use. Install them in sand in dry climates where the ground doesn't freeze.

■ **Brick for walls.** Common brick and face brick are good wall bricks. Common brick is less expensive and most are manufactured with three or more vertical holes that make them lighter and easier to work with. The bricks build a stronger wall, too, because the mortar keys onto the edges of the holes. Standard modular bricks are $2\frac{2}{3}$ inches thick, engineer bricks are $3\frac{1}{5}$ inches thick.

Designing with brick

Brick enhances any landscape. It conforms to gentle terrain changes, mixes easily with other paving materials, makes an excellent border for other path and patio materials, and if properly installed requires little maintenance. Pavers are set in a sand base (the easiest installation method) or mortared to a slab (a more time-consuming, costly, and permanent installation).

In damp climates and shaded areas, moss grows readily on brick and may make the surface slippery. Brick with smooth or glazed surfaces can become slick when wet.

There's almost no end to the variety of brick available. It comes in countless sizes, shapes, and colors. Availability varies according to region and manufacturer, so consult with your brick dealer when you are planning your project.

BRICK PATTERNS

Basket weave

45° herringbone

90° herringbone

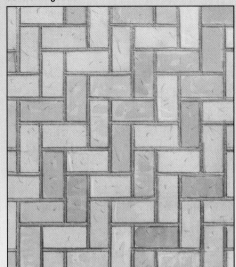

Running bond

Offset bond, bricks on edge

Diagonal bond

Brick patterns

Before you decide which brick you want to use, consider the pattern you want to lay down. Pattern affects the look of your project as well as the amount of time and money you'll devote to it. The simplest pattern is the running bond, in which each succeeding course is offset by one-half brick. It can be used to build walls and patios. A variation that's only slightly more complicated is the common bond, which is a running bond pattern that employs header bricks (bricks placed perpendicular to the rest) on a wall and half brick on a patio. The headers and half bricks are set every sixth row. Other variations are more complicated combinations of headers (or half brick) and stretchers; they require more brick, produce more waste from cutting, and take more time. Patterns such as the herringbone and basket weave are used only on horizontal surfaces, such as patios and walks.

Design tip

Vary brick colors to add interest to a brick wall, walk, or patio. Keep the contrasts subtle—red-brown bricks interspersed with dark red bricks, for example, will look more pleasing than sharply contrasting colors. Bricks set on edge expand your design possibilities, but the smaller surface of the edges will require more bricks— and a larger budget.

STONE

Whether you build a stone patio, walk, wall, or stairway, it's hard work. But it's also immensely rewarding. The result of your effort is always a one-of-a-kind structure that expresses personal artistry and demonstrates craftsmanship. Stone projects take longer than most projects made from other materials, but many homeowners believe the final result is worth the time and effort.

Although some stone is suitable for use in walls as well as patios and walks, that suitability is determined generally by the size and shape of the stone. It's also worth noting that the names of stones are not necessarily consistent from one distributor to another. The term "rubble," for example, may include river rock and fieldstone at one retailer but not another. Be sure you understand how a dealer is using a term when you inquire about their stone.

Stone for patios and walks
Flagstone is quarried stone fractured— or cleft—into flat slabs 1½ inches thick or thicker. It is often used for paving and works well set in sand or mortar. Flagstone comes in many varieties; slate, bluestone, limestone, redstone, sandstone, and granite are the most common. Irregular shapes make it ideal for either free-form or geometric patios or walks. It is often used for stepping-stones.

Cobblestone is small stones of a relatively consistent size cut for use in walks or paths. Cobblestones are square or round, flat or slightly domed. Their surfaces have subtle variations in the visual rhythm. The stones' small size makes installation easy but time-consuming.

Cut stone is flagstone with straight-cut edges and square corners. Pieces range from about 1 foot to 4 feet wide. Thickness varies; cut stone for paving should be at least 2 inches thick to avoid breakage. You can install cut stone in the same manner as flagstone, but its overall appearance will be more formal.

Stone for walls
Fieldstone is literally stone that's gathered from fields. It comes in various sizes and is almost always round. It's suitable for both dry-stacked and mortared walls. Some quarries offer split fieldstone with at least one cleft edge that makes wall-building easier. Some dealers include river rock, a smaller variety, in the fieldstone category.

Rubble is quarried small stone of irregular sizes, usually with one cleft face that makes mortaring easier.

Ashlar is cleft stone cut into fairly regular shapes with relatively flat sides. Ashlar stone comes in different thicknesses, a characteristic that makes an interesting look when stones are placed in alternate courses on either a dry-stacked or mortared wall.

Stone veneer is natural stone or a stone look-alike cast from concrete or synthetic material. It's cut or molded in thin sections for application as a cosmetic facing material on walls.

Designing with stone
Stone's random shapes and varied surface textures bring a rough-hewn character to the landscape. Even in mortared installations, stone imparts a casual, rustic quality, effortlessly complimenting woodland, cottage garden, and natural design themes.

Flagstone

Rubble

Fieldstone

Stone veneer

Ashlar

Cobblestone

STONE PATTERNS

Flagstone patterns

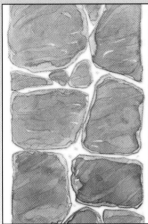

Equal sizes

Mixed sizes

Cut-stone pattern

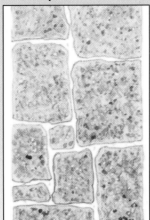

Equal sizes set in offset bond

Fieldstone wall

The overall tone of a patio design is set by its contours more than the type of stone. Stepping-stone patios usually look casual. Sand-set and mortared patios can be formal or informal, depending on their contours.

Dry-laid or sand-set stone doesn't require specialized skills or equipment and resists frost heave. Porous stone, however, may absorb water and crack in freezing temperatures. Natural depressions in flagstone can collect water and become slick when frozen. Slate is slick when wet.

Stone patios and walls can last forever with little or no maintenance. Stepping-stone projects require periodic weeding and occasional resetting and leveling. Mortared installations require a concrete slab and mortar bed.

Large stone will cover an area more quickly than smaller stone but may prove harder to move, cut, and design.

Ashlar wall

STANLEY PRO TIP

Buying stone

Stone is generally sold by the ton or square yard. For a patio or walk, one ton of larger stone covers about 13 square yards. Before placing your order, determine your patio or walk's area or the volume of your proposed wall. Your supplier will convert this measurement to tonnage, if necessary.

For small projects, visit your garden center or building-supply retailer; some sell individual stones for small projects.

For a large project, purchase stone in bulk from a local quarry or stone yard. Order cut stone and ashlar on pallets to reduce breakage. Hand-picking your stone increases costs considerably. Stone native to your area is most economical.

Design tips

To increase the formality of a patio design, keep straight edges on the perimeter or use modular edging, such as brick. Use large stones to pave large expanses of landscape, smaller units in smaller yards.

Unlike other materials, stone structures are best designed on-site. Lay flagstone into the side of the patio site and experiment with patterns and pleasing arrangements. Separate wall stone into groups of similar size and shape and intermix stones from these groupings as you create a design.

Rubble wall

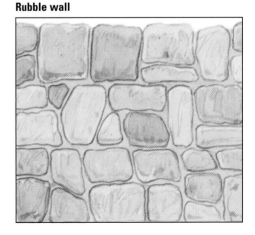

PRECAST CONCRETE PAVERS

Precast concrete pavers are the most recent addition to the catalog of masonry paving materials. They were developed in the Netherlands in the 1950s. Initially sold only as gray concrete squares, they are now widely available in an array of sizes, shapes, and colors.

Cast in molds, these concrete pavers often resemble brick, stone, and tile. The brick pavers, perhaps the most popular pattern, are now getting competition from other shapes: circles, chamfered squares, diamonds, hexagons, octagons, crescents, and fans. Interlocking styles and textures with embedded terrazzo and aggregate are newer options.

Unlike brick, which is made of fired clay, concrete pavers are cast from dense, pressure-formed concrete. That makes them more durable than poured concrete. Some paver manufacturers claim their products are virtually impervious to oils and other stains, making them ideal for driveways.

Sizes, shapes, and types

A few years ago concrete pavers were easy to classify, and the natural tendency was to compare them with brick. With more designs available, however, pavers don't fall so easily into categories. Some pavers are thinner and lighter than brick; others are heavier. Most pavers range in thickness from 1½ to 2½ inches (that of common brick). Some are thicker. You'll find pavers in the shape of rectangles that measure from about 4×6 inches up to 24 inches square. There are also geometric shapes about 2×4 inches, and keyed and triangular shapes that make circles and fans. Most precast pavers are set in a sand bed, but you can mortar some of the thinner styles to a slab.

The method of installation varies for different types of pavers. There are interlocking pavers, standard pavers, and turf blocks.

Interlocking pavers resist lateral movement because their shaped edges fit together, linking the units. They stay in place even under heavy loads and weather changes. Some styles require cutting to fit a patio or walk. Others come with premade corners, edges, and end pieces.

Standard pavers are rectangular or square. They are less stable than the interlocking variety. Like brick, they may shift over time, especially if set over poorly drained soil.

Turf blocks have an open design with holes for planting grass. They are strong enough to use in driveways (see *page 63*).

Designing with precast pavers

With so many styles, colors, and textures available, you can easily find a precast paver that will match your outdoor landscape theme. Warm colors predominate—reds, browns, and earth tones—but pavers also come in black, grays, and off-whites. Textures are also plentiful, from smooth to stamped designs.

Although precast pavers look at home in both formal and informal landscapes, their modular uniformity suits formal designs the best. Geometric patterns such as circles,

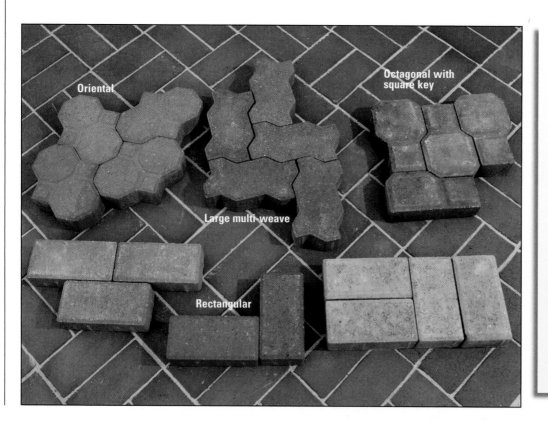

Oriental

Octagonal with square key

Large multi-weave

Rectangular

Design tips

The relationship of the size of each paving unit to the overall size of the patio or walk is an important design consideration that's easy to overlook. A paver that's too small in relation to the space you're covering can result in a busy look. On the other hand, large pavers take less time to set because each unit covers more area, but their size may overwhelm your installation.

In the planning stages, if you sense that your design will end up looking too busy, consider a larger paver. Or if it's a rectangular unit, consider setting it with wider spacing. Planting groundcovers between gaps can minimize the busy look, and the green plants help frame the pavers, adding another design element.

fans, and crescents that are difficult or impossible to achieve with other materials, can be done with pavers.

Standard rectangular pavers must be cut to create geometric designs, but so many geometric varieties are now available that you should be able to find a style that

minimizes or eliminates cutting. Some pavers have tabs cast in their sides, which automatically space the pavers for sand-set patios and walks.

Tightly set sanded pavers usually will not require weeding, but they may require resetting from time to time.

Like brick and stone, the smaller sizes of precast pavers conform easily to minor variations in terrain. Pavers mix well visually with other paving materials.

Make your own precast stepping-stones

You can cast your own stepping-stones with premixed concrete and homemade or commercial forms. Rectangles and squares are the easiest to make yourself. Commercial forms, available at garden and home centers, come in a wide variety of shapes. You can also use commercial precast stepping-stones as a base for mosaic pavers.

Skin deep

Be wary of inexpensive pavers. Most likely the cost savings comes from the way the pavers were colored. Look carefully at the depth of the color, and avoid pavers with shallow color. Colors applied only to the surface wear off quickly, exposing bare concrete. Buy pavers that have pigment impregnated throughout their thickness.

STANLEY PRO TIP

Buying precast pavers

Building-supply dealers, concrete suppliers, landscape stores, and home and garden centers sell concrete pavers individually, by the square foot, or in banded cubes with enough pavers for about 16 linear feet.

Compute the area of your patio or walkway and divide it by the area covered by the particular paver style as recommended by the manufacturer or distributor. Order 5 to 10 percent more if your project will require a lot of cutting.

MOSAIC PAVERS
Add style to plain pavers

1 Remove the cured stepping-stone from its form and apply ¼ to ½ inch of latex-modified thinset with a notched plastic trowel. Press broken pieces of ceramic tile mosaic in the mortar, leaving a ⅛- to ¼-inch gap for grout. Scrape off excess mortar with a spatula and tile the remaining stones.

2 Mix up enough latex-modified grout to cover the stones. Force it into the gaps with a spatula or a grout float. Remove the excess grout with the edge of the spatula and smooth the grout along the edges of the paver.

3 Let the grout set for 10 to 15 minutes, then clean off the stones with a wet sponge. Rinse the sponge often, but don't pull the grout from the gaps. Let the stones dry 24 to 48 hours, then buff with a soft cloth and set them in a sand base in recesses on your path.

TILE

Tile offers more sizes, shapes, colors, and textures than any other paving material. Selecting tile for a patio or pathway is much like selecting tile for a kitchen or bathroom, with a few additional factors to consider.

The first thing to look for when selecting outdoor tile, for safety, is a slip-proof surface. The second thing is freeze-resistance. Will the tile withstand the winters where you live? The third standard the tile must meet is durability. Can it weather the hard use of an outdoor patio or walkway?

A complication you'll encounter is that not all tiles within a category have the same characteristics. For example, some terra-cotta tile is machine made and serves well outdoors (in some climates). Other terra-cotta tiles simply are not strong enough for outdoor use. Ceramic tiles are not equivalently dense and waterproof, either.

All of the tiles described on these pages can be used for outdoor applications—in certain climates. Before making a selection, be sure the tile you choose is suitable for outdoor use in your area. Your tile dealer can tell you which tiles are suitable.

All tile must be set in mortar on a smooth concrete slab over a gravel base. Set properly, tile needs little or no maintenance.

Here are some tiles to consider:

Terra-Cotta tile is a low-density, nonvitreous (absorbs moisture) tile suitable for dry areas in some moderate climates. It is not a true ceramic tile because it is fired at low temperatures. Surface defects are common and admired as part of its look. It is sold in pieces from 3 to 12 inches square and in other geometric shapes.

Porcelain tile, made of highly refined clay and fired at extremely high temperatures, is vitreous (it absorbs little or no moisture). Sizes range from 1×1-inch mosaics to big 24-inch squares. Some have stonelike textures. Tile with an absorbancy of 5 percent or less is suitable for use in freezing climates.

Quarry tile, extruded and fired at high temperatures, comes as a semivitreous (somewhat absorbent) or vitreous product. Made in ½- to ¾-inch thicknesses, it is fired

CERAMIC AND CEMENT-BODIED TILE

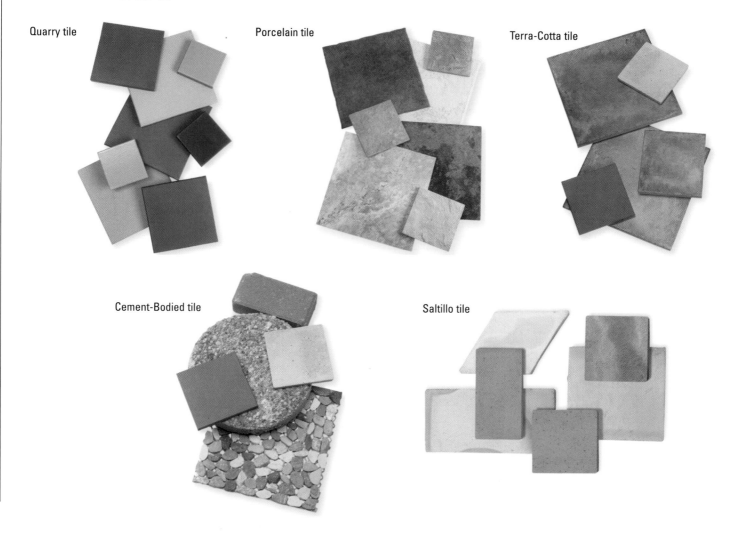

Quarry tile

Porcelain tile

Terra-Cotta tile

Cement-Bodied tile

Saltillo tile

unglazed in many colors, sizes, and shapes such as 4- to 12-inch squares and hexagons and 3×6-inch or 4×8-inch rectangles.

Cement-Bodied tile, made of a cured mixture of sand and mortar, is a nonvitreous tile with excellent durability. Cement tiles are available in squares or rectangles ranging from 6 to 9 inches and in mesh-backed paver sheets (up to 36 inches square) that give the look of cleft stone.

Saltillo tile is not a true ceramic tile because it is dried, not fired. It enjoys wide use in rustic and Southwestern designs. Available in squares, rectangles, octagons, and hexagons in sizes that range from 4 to 12 inches, it is a low-density, nonvitreous product suited only to warm climates.

Stone tile is increasingly popular. Natural stone materials cut into uniform tiles include marble, granite, limestone, sandstone, slate, quartzite, and shellstone (granite with embedded fossilized shells). Ask your tile dealer to recommend a stone tile that's suitable for outdoor use. Most are best used only in moderate or warm climates. For tile with a rough, rustic character, seek out tumbled tile which has been acid-treated and tumbled in sand.

Designing with tile

Tile is an excellent choice for formal landscapes, but it's not limited to them. Tile's modular dimensions fit almost any design scheme. Many varieties for outdoor use are available in earth tones (subtle tans, reds, and browns). Make sure all the tiles you buy come from the same lot. Check their lot number to ensure consistent coloration. Tile suited to the outdoors usually has a slightly roughened surface and its high density will support heavy loads and hard use.

Quality tile is more expensive than other surface materials, and it's susceptible to cracking on uneven surfaces.

STONE TILE

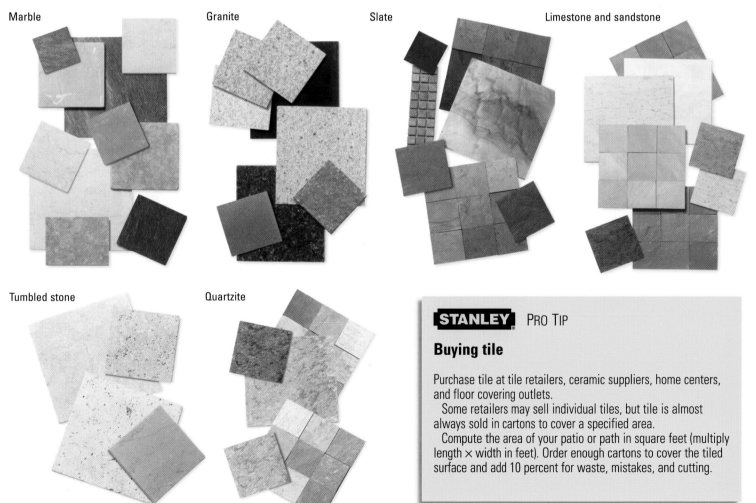

Marble

Granite

Slate

Limestone and sandstone

Tumbled stone

Quartzite

STANLEY PRO TIP

Buying tile

Purchase tile at tile retailers, ceramic suppliers, home centers, and floor covering outlets.

Some retailers may sell individual tiles, but tile is almost always sold in cartons to cover a specified area.

Compute the area of your patio or path in square feet (multiply length × width in feet). Order enough cartons to cover the tiled surface and add 10 percent for waste, mistakes, and cutting.

CONCRETE BLOCK

Low material and installation cost, along with outstanding durability, make concrete block a practical choice for walls. Concrete block (often called cement masonry units or CMUs) are less expensive than other wall-building materials, are relatively easy to install, and won't rust, rot, or decay. Many blocks now have decorative face patterns, offering options to plain structural blocks.

Concrete block is cast in forms using a high-density mixture of sand, cement, and aggregate. Although building blocks are often generically called cinder blocks, a true concrete block differs from a cinder block. Cinder blocks are made with aggregates of clay or pumice. They weigh less but fracture easily. If you're looking for a worry-free, long-lasting wall, use concrete blocks.

Most blocks have webs that separate two or three cavities called cores. This type of construction reduces the weight of the unit without compromising its strength. Rebar is often placed in the cores, which are then filled with concrete to strengthen the wall.

The basic building unit is the stretcher block, which has flanges on both ends. The blocks are butted together with mortar applied to the flanges. End blocks and corner blocks have one or more flange faces so they present a smooth, outside finished face. You will also find cap blocks, thinner, solid, flangeless blocks used to cap the top of a wall.

Most walls are built from a block measuring $7\frac{5}{8} \times 7\frac{5}{8} \times 15\frac{5}{8}$ inches. When laid with a standard $\frac{3}{8}$-inch mortar joint between them, the block dimensions become $8 \times 8 \times 16$ inches. These dimensions are the most common, but concrete block comes in a wide variety of sizes and shapes. Before you make plans for a wall, visit local building-supply dealers and research the available blocks. The sizes and shapes you find might make you decide to reconsider the wall design or dimensions.

Designing with concrete block

Normally structures built of standard concrete blocks are finished with a facing material such as stucco, brick, stone, or veneer facing. For some uses, the facing is left unfinished; other times, it's painted.

Block is available in a variety of shapes, colors, and textures. Such architectural blocks need no additional facing material or finishing. Many are cast to look like cleft stone. Others are manufactured with fluted or scored surfaces, ribs, and faces recessed with geometric patterns. Homeowners use blocks with open designs to make screens. You'll even find some that look like wood—use them to build a structure that looks more like a fence than a wall. If your budget allows, you may opt for prefaced blocks in a rainbow of colors and colored glazes.

A mortared concrete block wall must be built on a solid concrete footing with dimensions and reinforcement that conform to local building codes.

Architectural block comes in a huge variety of shapes and sizes, allowing the homeowner to use concrete block as a truly creative design element in the landscape.

The group above is a sample of the many sizes and shapes that standard concrete building units come in.

Interlocking concrete block

You can also buy concrete blocks that don't require mortar. Interlocking concrete blocks rely on different methods to hold them together. Some are cast with flanges on one side that hook one course to the preceding one. Others use pins engaged in holes. Still others use a system of the blocks' own concave/convex ridges or depressions. Another style provides a low-labor way to build a curved wall without cutting a large number of blocks. Most interlocking blocks are available in various surface textures and colors. Such blocks can save much time and effort in do-it-yourself projects.

Interlocking blocks rely on pins, flanges, clips, or ridges to hold them together. Mortar is not needed, saving construction time. They are an excellent choice for curved or retaining walls.

The only block you need to mow

Turf block isn't technically a concrete block in the same sense as the block used in building walls. It's a precast concrete paver formed from pressurized concrete. Its compressive strength is such that it can withstand the weight of automobiles and trucks. Thus, it makes an unusual driveway surface that lets grass grow up through the recesses. It's also suitable for paths and walks, although the recesses make a rough ride for wheeled garden equipment.

STANLEY PRO TIP

Buying concrete block

You'll find concrete block at all major home improvement centers and some lumberyards.

To estimate how many standard 8×16-inch blocks you'll need, figure that 100 square feet of wall will require roughly 113 blocks.

You can get a more precise estimate with the following calculations:

■ Multiply the length of the wall in feet by .75 to get the number of blocks in each course.

■ Multiply the height of the wall in feet by 1.5 to get the number of courses.

■ Multiply the two results together to get the total number of blocks.

■ Subtract the number of corner or end blocks you'll need and order 10 percent more to allow for cutting, mistakes, and breakage.

POURED CONCRETE

Poured concrete, which is a mixture of cement, sand, aggregate, and water, is a much more versatile building material than people give it credit for. It is placed as a liquid, so it can flow in and fill forms of any shape you can think of. When it's cured, it can stand up to heavy loads, inclement weather, and hard use.

One drawback is that in its natural state, it's gray and textureless, and, to many, presents an uninspiring face. By applying coloring and stamping techniques, however, poured concrete can be made to look like flagstone, brick, or cobblestone at a fraction of the cost of the real thing. Embedding the surface with aggregates increases your design possibilities even further and can create a dazzling concrete surface.

Designing with concrete
In one sense, concrete has unlimited design potential, which makes it a useful material in both formal and informal design schemes. The material itself is considered design-neutral. Coloring, forming, and stamping or texturing give it its final surface quality. Concrete is also a perfect base for a variety of surface materials, partly because it conforms to variations in grade. Properly mixed and cured, it requires little maintenance.

A concrete installation, however, requires careful planning and, for large projects, heavy equipment and helpers. Most important, concrete has a specified working time, which is affected by weather conditions and can be altered to some degree with additives. Once that working time is up, you can't correct mistakes easily or inexpensively.

It is the substrate material of choice for all mortared paths and patios, providing a strong, level, and stable base for brick, tile, and stone.

Dressing up an old slab
Plain concrete slabs used to be the standard for a patio, and there was a time when almost every new home came with a concrete slab in back. Some still do.

If your house has one and you have thought about tearing it out, consider other solutions first. If the slab is in the right location and is structurally sound, with a surface in good repair, you have a ready-made base for a mortared brick, tile, or flagstone patio. Using the existing slab will save you money, time, and effort.

If the slab is structurally sound but its surface is chipped or cracked, you can resurface it and mortar on a finished paving material. If a mortared surface is not in your plans or budget, you can easily add color to it.

Concrete stain offers the quickest facelift. Most home centers carry a variety of stains, some which produce an attractive, mottled finish. These coloring agents hide other stains and blemishes, too, especially if you use darker colors. Darker hues also help blend in the patio or walk with the rest of the landscape and cut down on glare from the sun.

You'll need several coats to produce a rich color. To create a mottled effect to downplay minor imperfections in the surface, apply the first coat evenly; then dab on subsequent coats unevenly with a sponge. Some dyes will etch the concrete and are caustic. Protect your hands with rubber gloves and your eyes with safety goggles. You can apply stencils to create accents within the perimeter. If you want to go all out, have a pattern cut in the concrete surface with a diamond saw before you stain it. Look in the Yellow Pages for a professional who can do this for you.

You can dress up poured concrete with color and texture (above left and center). Stamped patterns, such as the flagstone effect (above right) and stenciled designs, make concrete look like other paving materials.

Installing a poured-concrete wall

Pouring concrete into prefabricated forms is a popular method for building both freestanding and retaining walls. You can rent the aluminum forms and assemble them yourself, but a small crew of helpers is recommended. Three or four workers can put up the forms for a 12-foot wall in less than a day. The forms have to come off when the concrete is cured, but that takes about half the time of assembly.

Poured concrete for walls is available in various colors as are forms that leave patterns imprinted in the face of the wall.

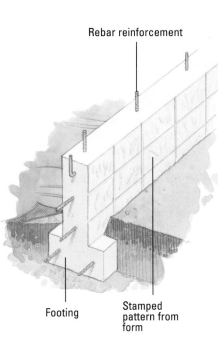

Rebar reinforcement

Footing

Stamped pattern from form

Open and closed concrete stamps

A concrete stamp with a closed top textures the surface, here giving the look of stone.

Open-top stamps impress a shape but not a texture into concrete. You can combine any stamp pattern with a color.

Concrete options

Mix the concrete from scratch, or order it ready to go. The choice is yours.

Bulk dry ingredients: You can buy the cement, sand, and aggregate separately and mix them with water in a mortar box, wheelbarrow, or rented concrete mixer. Mixing concrete is heavy work, but for medium-size jobs it's economical.

Premix: An easier but somewhat more expensive alternative is to buy concrete mix, i.e., bags with the dry ingredients already mixed in the correct proportions. You just add water, mix, and pour. Premix takes the guesswork out of mixing—but not the effort. It makes jobs under a cubic yard manageable (you'll need 40 or more bags for a cubic yard, depending on the weight of the bags), but for anything larger than that, order ready-mix.

Ready-Mix: Ready-mix relieves you of the mixing process but requires a quick and experienced work crew. Your site must be accessible to the mixing truck and ready for the pour as soon as the truck arrives. You can order ready-mix with additives that make it workable in a variety of weather conditions.

STANLEY PRO TIP

Buying concrete

Buy bags of premix concrete at hardware stores, home centers, lumberyards, or building-supply centers. Order bulk ready-mix concrete from a ready-mix concrete company. Buy dry ingredients (portland cement, sand, and aggregate) to mix it yourself at any of the above outlets.

To estimate how much you'll need, compute the volume of your project (multiply length times width times depth in the same units). Then add 5 percent to this amount.

A 40-pound bag of premix makes $\frac{1}{3}$ cubic foot.
A 60-pound bag makes $\frac{1}{2}$ cubic foot.
An 80-pound bag makes $\frac{2}{3}$ cubic foot.

A 4×20-foot walk that's 4 inches ($\frac{1}{3}$ foot) deep requires $26\frac{2}{3}$ cubic feet of concrete. (One cubic yard is 27 cubic feet.) For quantities over a cubic yard, order ready-mix.

STUCCO

Stucco first appeared thousands of years ago as a mud plaster baked by the sun. After several millennia, it came to be a mixture of gypsum and lime. Stucco has continued to improve, keeping pace with consumer styles and technological improvements. Its purpose, however, has remained the same.

Stucco is a finish application of three relatively thin coats of mortar designed to protect and beautify a surface. It's a good example of the design flexibility cement-based products offer.

Stucco can transform the appearance of a block wall—or any wall. Because it's flexible before it cures, you can mold and shape it to complement any style.

The first coat of stucco, about ½ inch thick, is called the scratch coat. That's because it's scratched with a scarifier or other tool to roughen the surface, thereby forming ridges for the second coat to bond into. The second coat is about ¼ to ⅜ inch thick and is called the brown coat. The third or finish coat is about ⅛ to ¼ inch thick and is sometimes called the color coat because it is often tinted with oxide pigments.

Although you can paint stucco, it is unwise to do so because it's difficult to repair damage to painted stucco. The mortar won't stick to a painted surface even with a bonding agent.

Stucco's application to a block wall requires little preparation. Simply mist the wall lightly with water; dry block would take moisture too rapidly from the stucco. Wood surfaces require an application of felt paper and metal lath to give the surface tooth for the stucco. Lath comes in three forms: paper-backed lath, with the paper already attached for quicker installation; self-furring lath, with a dimpled surface that holds it away from the wall; and galvanized metal lath, for use on exterior walls. You can install corner beads to strengthen the corners and prevent stucco from chipping.

In any case, when you're ready to start the job, wait for an overcast day if you can, especially when stuccoing walls that have a southern exposure. Excessive heat dries the stucco too quickly, causing it to shrink and crack. Cool temperatures, on the other hand, stiffen the stucco, preventing proper troweling. Do not apply stucco if nighttime temperatures will fall below freezing. The ideal temperature for installing stucco is between 50 and 80 degrees Fahrenheit.

Stuccoing is a slow-moving job. Although you will soon develop a knack for applying the stucco, this material, like all cement-based products, needs adequate time to cure properly. If codes allow, you can apply the brown coat to the scratch coat after the first coat has begun to set. Both coats must cure thoroughly before you apply the finish coat. Otherwise the stucco may crack.

Designing with stucco

The color range for stucco is somewhat narrow. You'll find white, browns, greens, reds, and blues, generally in muted shades. Texture varies depending on the tools you use to embellish the finish coat. Possibilities include whisk brooms, brushes, and natural objects such as leaves and branches. You can also use dowels or other objects as styluses to scratch designs into the surface.

One-coat stucco

A newer material is the one-coat stucco. Ingredients are proprietary to each

Making stucco

You can buy stucco at home centers in premixed bags. Manufacturers achieve a much higher degree of accuracy when mixing proportions than you can with the shovel-and-mixer method.

On the other hand, masons have been mixing stucco from scratch for years, and you can too. The basic ingredients are portland cement, lime, and sand. The only difference between coats is the proportion of sand, shown at right.

Scratch coat
1 part portland or masonry cement
1 part hydrated lime
2½ to 4 parts sand

Brown coat
(for brick walls)
1 part portland or masonry cement
1 part hydrated lime
3½ to 5 parts sand (1 part more than scratch coat)

Finish coat
1 part portland or masonry cement
1 part hydrated lime
1½ to 3 parts sand (1 part less than scratch coat)

manufacturer, but most include fibers and other performance enhancers that help resist cracking. One-coat stucco is intended as a base-coat application with a finish coat applied after curing. The material is available both in concentrated form, requiring the addition of sand and water, and in presanded versions requiring only the addition of water.

One-coat stuccos tend to go on faster, weigh less, and are more flexible than three-coat stuccos. While they are not as thick as three-coat stuccos, they are strong and durable.

Finish-coat products made with fibers in an acrylic solution are also available. These acrylic-base finishes are strong and flexible, and come in a wide range of colors that, because of the nature of the acrylic base, tend to be slightly more vibrant than the muted tones of the oxide pigments.

STUCCO TEXTURES

Wavy

Swirled

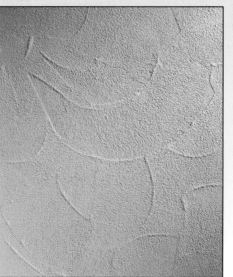

Stippled

Dashed travertine

Imprinted

LOOSE STONE

Loose stone, although seldom used to cover an entire patio surface, makes an excellent material for borders, paths, or patio sections in which you wish to provide contrasting textures. When selecting loose stone, take into account the appearance of the stone and whether it is smooth or rough.

Rough materials, such as crushed granite chips or lava rock, gradually compact and form a relatively solid surface. They may be hard on bare feet, however. Smooth stones, such as river rock or pea gravel, settle into a somewhat inconsistent base but they tend to migrate and are more resilient.

You'll find many types, sizes, and colors of loose stone. Crushed quartz and quartz pebbles range from white to light pink. Crushed granite and lava rock are red. Dolomite and limestones are white or blue-gray. Pea gravel and river rock display a variety of colors. Larger river rock isn't as comfortable to walk on as smaller stones, but it works well as an ornamental border for a path. For walking comfort, choose $\frac{1}{4}$- to $\frac{3}{8}$-inch aggregates.

Designing with loose stone

Perhaps no other paving material offers as many colors and textures as loose stone—certainly not at such a low cost. Stone textures vary considerably, depending both on size and whether the stone is crushed or rounded mechanically or naturally.

All kinds of stones suit formal and informal design schemes. But overall, loose stone lends a more casual character to a path or patio section and is better suited to informal themes. If you're looking for a product to define and separate flower beds and shrub plantings from surrounding lawn areas, any of these materials will do.

Loose stone is one of the least expensive landscape materials and is easy to install. It does, however, require a subbase of gravel and sand for proper drainage and stability, and most loose stone needs a border to contain it.

Stone conforms well to even severe variations in terrain, provides a flexible bed underfoot, drains quickly, and is not subject to heaving in freeze-thaw cycles.

Smooth stones wider than $\frac{3}{8}$ inch may prove difficult to walk on, and moving wheeled equipment over a loose-stone path is even harder. Small, smooth stone, such as pea gravel, displaces easily, making walking on it, especially on slopes, difficult.

Pea gravel

Lava rock

Decomposed granite

River stone

Crushed stone

Although stone is a hard material, its durability and maintenance requirements largely are determined by its size. Heavy traffic creates worn spots that require additional aggregate.

When considering loose stone for a path, you may be tempted to choose larger stone because it will cover the area more quickly. Larger stone will prove more difficult to spread, however.

Loose stone with
brick edging

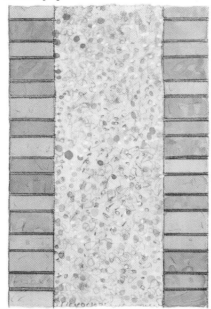

Loose stone with
cut-stone edging

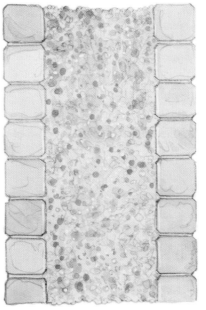

Loose stone with
flagstone edging

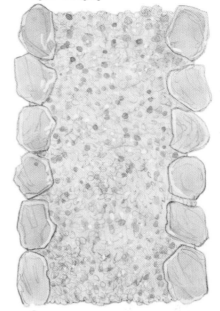

Design tips

First determine the route of the path, then decide what color and texture you'd like. Next choose the material you want to install as a border. If you want a borderless path (effective in woodland settings), path material will gradually spill out of the confines of the path, creating a natural-looking effect.

Decide if you want the color of the path to offset the predominant color scheme of your flower beds or complement it with a subtle change in hue.

Choose colors carefully. Bluestone may look enticing in the bag, but it might be too vivid when installed. White rock stands out in most landscapes and reflects moonlight, but wide white walks may overwhelm a nearby flower bed and glare harshly during the day. White rock also turns a dirty-looking gray over time.

 **STANLEY** PRO TIP

Buying loose stone

For small projects, you can buy loose stone by the bag at home centers, patio supply stores, or garden centers. Browse the Yellow Pages for "Building Materials," "Landscaping," "Quarries," or "Stone." It's also sold by the cubic foot or in bulk (truckload) by the cubic yard or ton.

Determine the volume of your path or patio section (multiply the length times the width times the depth) and order quantities to cover it. As a general rule, you can figure that a ton of loose stone spread 1½ inches deep will cover approximately 17 square yards.

Buying stone materials in bulk from a local quarry or sand and gravel yard will save money on a large project.

MORTAR

Mortar is the glue that holds masonry units together, and although all mortars (with the exception of some thinset tile mortars) are composed of the same ingredients—portland cement, hydrated lime, sand, and water—not all mortars are the same. They vary in the proportion of ingredients and, therefore, what kind of material they are used with and how you use them. Mortars are similar to concrete but have more compressive strength and are formulated to bond masonry units, seal them, and account for small differences in their sizes. Lime is added to increase the water-retention properties of the mix and to make it more workable.

Types of mortar

Mortar is classified in the following types:

Type M: This mortar has the highest compressive strength. It is the best choice for masonry that's below grade, subject to frost heave, or in contact with the earth, such as retaining walls and walks.

Type N: This medium-strength mortar is the type most commonly used. It is suitable for general use in above-grade exterior masonry, such as freestanding walls and nonloadbearing structures such as planters.

Type S: This medium-strength mortar is used where lateral strength (the ability to resist bending) is more important than compressive strength, as in structures subject to high winds or other side loads.

Type O: This low-strength mortar is suitable for interior use only.

Thinset Mortars: These mortars are used for tile installation. Some are cement-based, others are epoxies or organic mastics. Use latex-modified thinsets and grouts when tiling outdoors.

Making your own mortar

You can mix your own mortar, using the proportions shown in the table at the bottom of the page, but bagged factory mixes, though more expensive, are better in two respects: Their proportions are more accurate than on-site mixes and their ingredients are more thoroughly distributed throughout the mix. For most do-it-yourself projects, prebagged mortar proves more cost-effective. If you do mix your own, clean sand and clean water are essential.

Selecting the right mortar

No matter what kind of masonry material you're working with, make sure you have the right mortar and that you mix it properly. For example, the lime in most mortars stains stone so their mortars are lime-free but rich in cement. Mix the mortar for a stone wall a bit on the dry side so it's able to support the weight of the stones. Mix brick mortar a little wetter than block mortar. For tuck-pointing, start by mixing type N mortar with half the recommended amount of water. Let it stand for an hour, then mix in the remaining water. Always ask your retailer for the mortar that meets the requirements of your project.

Mortar is caustic
Wear work gloves, long sleeves, a respirator, and safety glasses when mixing or spreading mortar.

Estimating mortar

Use these general guidelines to estimate how much mortar you'll need to set brick and concrete block for structures. Because different mortars have different weights per cubic foot (for example, 70, 75, and 80 pounds for Types N, S, and M, respectively), check the specifications on the bag before you complete your order.

Here's what you'll need for a wall with ⅜-inch joints:

■ Concrete block: 6 cubic feet of mortar for 100 square feet of 8×16-inch block.

■ Brick: 4.2 cubic feet of mortar for 100 square feet of 4×8-inch brick.

If you're making ½-inch joints, you'll need just under one-third more mortar.

Most brick walls are built with two faces (wythes), each one brick thick, as shown on *page 176*. So figure out how much mortar you'll need for one wythe, then double it.

Mortar proportions

Type	Cement	Lime	Sand
M	1	¼	3¾
S	1	½	4½
N	1	1	6
O	1	2	9

EDGING

The edging on your patio or path contributes greatly to its overall appearance. Use edging materials that match or tastefully contrast with the paving materials. For example, brick is naturally a great complement to brick, but it also provides striking contrast to a loose-filled or poured concrete surface.

Common edging materials are shown on this page, but you can use almost anything. River rock (both the large and small varieties), whole or broken sea shells, broken brick or block, and even reclaimed roofing tiles or broken-up concrete make attractive and functional edging.

Edging is more than an aesthetic element. It also helps contain the surface material. Although not required for flagstone and mortared surfaces, edgings are a must for dry-set brick and concrete pavers. Without it, maintenance chores increase greatly.

Types of edging

■ **Brick:** Brick set as soldiers (upright and on edge) and sailors (flat and perpendicular to the pattern of the paving) enhance both formal and informal designs. Set bricks into a trench on an angle for an attractive sawtooth edging. Brick works well for edging curved patterns as well.

■ **Poured concrete:** You can color and texture poured concrete to match or contrast with the patio or path. Installed in curbs, it requires strong forms and a little extra effort, but if properly installed, it will outlast many other edgings.

■ **Plastic and steel:** Plastic edging is flexible and affordable and conforms to almost any curve, though it isn't strong enough to contain heavy materials. Anchor it with spikes driven through lugs. Use commercial-grade steel edging to contain precast concrete pavers and in any installation where you need edge restraint but don't want a visible edging material. Both plastic and steel edgings are buried below the edge of the surface materials so they don't show.

■ **Wood:** Lumber (2×4, 2×6, or 2×8) and landscape timbers (4×4 or 6×6) make a pleasant contrast with brick or concrete paving. Stake timbers in place and backfill with topsoil to hide the stakes. Or predrill timbers and drive ½-inch rebar through the holes into the soil.

■ **Stone:** Both flagstone and cut stone make excellent edging. You can purchase precut stone or cut the pieces yourself. Make sure to select stones of roughly the same width so the border doesn't look haphazard.

■ **Precast edging:** Precast pavers come in straight or curved shapes, many with sculpted designs. You can use them to match or set off your paver pattern. Some styles pair well with sand-set brick.

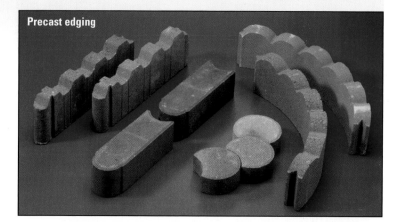
Precast edging

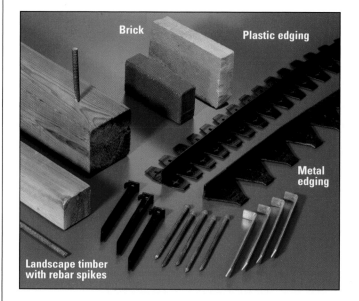
Brick

Plastic edging

Metal edging

Landscape timber with rebar spikes

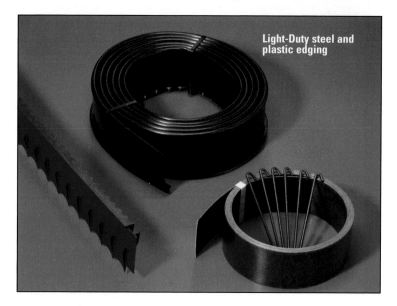
Light-Duty steel and plastic edging

TIPS, TRICKS & TECHNIQUES

Whether you're building a patio, wall, or walkway, it helps to remember that construction follows a certain order for all structures—usually from the ground up. The best way to keep your project moving smoothly usually comes down to doing all the steps in the correct order.

There are, however, critical steps that precede construction. If you haven't done so already, you should make a construction schedule that lists and organizes all the tasks you have to complete. Make sure you include everything. At a minimum, your list will look something like this:

■ Research and decide on materials
■ Conduct site analysis and determine location of patio, wall, and paths
■ Have underground utilities marked
■ Draw plans and elevations
■ Estimate quantity of materials needed and costs; develop budget
■ Apply for building permit and schedule inspections as required
■ Modify plan if necessary to meet code; resubmit permit application
■ Order materials
■ Grade site and install drainage lines
■ Organize materials and set up on-site work station

■ Strip sod and prepare site
■ Set batterboards and lay out site
■ Pour footings as necessary

Once you've made your list, add expected completion dates and jot down the names of prospective helpers. Make notes about any plans you have for contingencies, such as weather delays.

When you finish each day's work, put everything away. Keeping the project site orderly lets you get right to work the next time without having to hunt for the tools and materials you need. Make a note of what you need to start with next time.

CHAPTER PREVIEW

Preparing and laying out the site
page 74

Excavating
page 76

Building forms
page 78

Providing drainage
page 82

Installing edging
page 84

Building a sand base
page 86

Remove the sod before you lay out the site with batterboards. Drive temporary stakes at the approximate corners of the footprint of the patio and tie mason's lines between them. Mark the ground with upside-down spray paint. Remove the sod. Now you're ready to start work on the patio.

Working with concrete
page 88

Working with brick
page 92

Working with concrete block
page 96

Working with stone
page 100

Working with tile
page 104

Working with stucco
page 108

PREPARING AND LAYING OUT THE SITE

Laying out a site so the perimeter is perfectly square relies on the simplest of homemade tools—batterboards. You'll need two batterboards for each corner (unless you drive stakes close to the house). Make them from 2-foot pointed 2×4 legs and an 18- to 36-inch 1×4 crosspiece.

Start your layout by outlining the edge of the structure with temporary stakes, mason's lines, and upside-down spray paint (it sprays upside down so you can mark lines on the ground; get it at your home center). Remove the sod within the outline to make the job easier. Place the batterboards, keeping the crosspieces level (check them with a level).

Then follow the rest of the steps to lay out the site. The steps shown here pertain to patio layout, but they are essentially the same for a wall footing or walk. If you're laying out a freestanding patio, you won't have the side of the house or the doorway to use as a guide, but the rest of the steps will be the same.

PRESTART CHECKLIST

☐ **TIME**
About 6 hours for a 12×16-foot patio or 25-foot walk, excluding sod removal and preparation

☐ **TOOLS**
Tape measure, cordless drill, small sledgehammer, plumb bob, mason's line, line level, wooden stakes, spray paint, rototiller

☐ **SKILLS**
Measuring, leveling, driving stakes, making simple calculations

☐ **PREP**
Prepare dimensioned plan

☐ **MATERIALS**
Scrap 2×4s and 1×4s, deck screws, masking tape, stakes

Preparing a patio site

1 Drive a stake close to the house about 1 foot beyond your actual project perimeter. Using your scaled plan, measure and stake the other three corners, also about a foot beyond the final dimensions. (The stakes are temporary so their locations don't have to be perfect). Measure the diagonals and adjust the outside stakes until the diagonals are roughly equal. Run mason's lines between the stakes—a couple inches off the ground—and pull the lines tight. Then spray-paint the grass along the lines. Remove the lines, slice the sod in strips, and roll it up. Save enough to resod the edges of the project when you've completed it. Loosen the soil with a rototiller to make the excavation easier.

LAYING OUT A PATIO SITE

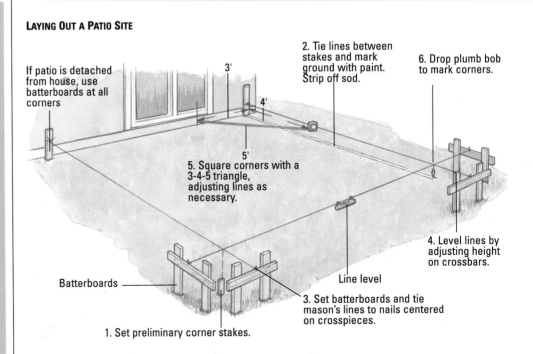

If patio is detached from house, use batterboards at all corners

2. Tie lines between stakes and mark ground with paint. Strip off sod.

6. Drop plumb bob to mark corners.

3'

4'

5'

5. Square corners with a 3-4-5 triangle, adjusting lines as necessary.

4. Level lines by adjusting height on crossbars.

Line level

Batterboards

3. Set batterboards and tie mason's lines to nails centered on crosspieces.

1. Set preliminary corner stakes.

2 Make batterboards from 2-foot pointed 2×4s and 18- to 36-inch 1×4 crosspieces fastened to the stakes with 1½-inch screws. Drive the batterboards perpendicular to each other 2 to 3 feet beyond the corners of the bare soil and deep enough to support tightly stretched lines.

3 Reset the stakes against the house so they represent the exact location of the outside edges of the forms (1½ inches more on each side than the size of the patio or walk). Tie mason's line to one of the stakes against the house and run it to the approximate center of the opposite batterboard. Repeat the process for the remaining batterboards. Adjust the line parallel to the house so it is equidistant from the house along its length. Pull the lines tight and level them by driving in the batterboards. Make sure the lines touch at their intersections. Then square the corners.

SQUARE THE CORNERS

To square the corners, measure 6 feet along one line and mark the spot with a piece of tape. Measure 8 feet along the perpendicular line and mark it also. (Make sure you remember which edge of the tape indicates the exact spot.) Measure the distance between the marks; if it is 10 feet, the lines are square to each other. If not, adjust one line. With this method you can substitute any multiples of 3, 4, and 5; for example 9, 12, and 15 or 12, 16, and 20. The larger the numbers, the greater the accuracy.

Mark the crosspiece

Mark exact string location

Once you have squared the corners, mark the new location of the mason's line on each crosspiece. Then wrap the line tightly on the mark. This way, you can remove and restring the lines as necessary without disturbing the dimensions.

EXCAVATING

Digging is hard work, even if you've loosened up the soil with a rototiller. If you think the work is beyond your abilities or will exceed your available time, hire a contractor or other willing laborers. Consider this option especially if your local codes require you to dig down to undisturbed soil, as many do.

The procedures illustrated on these pages assume that your project requires forms and the working room to install them. That's why the batterboard mason's lines are set a foot beyond the actual perimeter of the project. If your structure doesn't need forms, you won't need the trench.

Be sure to excavate your site to a depth that will accommodate all of the materials needed—for example, 4 to 6 inches of gravel, 2 inches of sand, and 3 to 4 inches of concrete (or whatever the thickness of the finished surface will be).

Because the weight of a concrete slab is distributed over many square feet, it usually doesn't need footings. A slab floats; that is, it moves up and down with the surface as the ground freezes and thaws. But a footing is required to support most walls (except dry-laid stone walls), spreading the weight so the wall doesn't sink. Most codes require footings that are twice the width of the wall and as deep as or deeper than the frost line. Be sure to check your local codes before you pour the concrete.

PRESTART CHECKLIST

☐ **TIME**
About one day for one person to dig 100 square feet 6 inches deep

☐ **TOOLS**
Round-nose shovel, spade, small sledgehammer, mason's line, plumb bob, chalk line, marking paint, sand, garden hose, level, tape measure, stakes, wheelbarrow

☐ **SKILLS**
Digging, laying out, leveling

☐ **PREP**
Lay out and square the site

Excavating for a patio or walk

1 To mark the outside corners of the forms, drop a plumb bob from the intersections of the lines. Drive 2-foot stakes at the intersections. Remove the lines but leave the batterboards.

2 Tie mason's lines between the stakes to represent the height of the finished surface. If excavating for a patio, the lines will be level with the patio line on the house. For both a patio and walk, excavate a 1-foot-wide trench outside the lines to the depth your installation requires.

PATIO LINE ON THE HOUSE

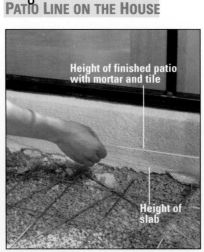

Height of finished patio with mortar and tile

Height of slab

If the patio will abut the house, you need to snap a chalk line under the door at the height of the patio surface. Put it about 1 to 3 inches below the threshold to keep snow and rain out of the house. The line marks the finished surface of the patio. Use it to set the excavation depth for the entire site.

Laying out a curve

Where your patio or walkway plan calls for a curve, lay a charged garden hose (water turned on, nozzle shut off) to mark the curve. Pour sand over the hose (you can use marking paint if you don't mind having a painted hose). Lift off the hose and you'll have an easy-to-follow curved line.

3 Use a tape measure to periodically measure the depth of the trench. That way, it will remain consistent and you'll have a constant reference point when you excavate the interior of the site.

4 Remove the lines but not the stakes. Excavate the interior, removing the soil to the depth of the perimeter trench. To keep the entire excavation at a consistent depth, check it periodically with a 4-foot level or a slope gauge (see *page 79*). If you remove too much soil in some places, fill the dips with sand or gravel— not loose soil. Use a flat spade or square shovel to dig the final inch of soil from the bottom and sides of the excavation.

WHAT IF...
You're excavating a wall footing?

1 Drive temporary stakes to mark the approximate location of footing corners. Drive layout stakes (or batterboards) beyond the temporary stakes. Then tie mason's lines and square the corners with a 3-4-5 triangle *(page 75)*. Drop a plumb bob at the intersection of the lines and redrive the temporary stakes under the plumb bob. Tie mason's lines between the stakes, and paint the ground along the lines.

2 Using your painted lines as a guide, slice the sod about 6 inches outside the perimeter of the footing and strip away the sod, saving enough to fill in the bare edges of the footing after you've finished it. Then excavate the footing trench to the depth required by local codes, measuring down from the mason's lines to keep the depth consistent.

BUILDING FORMS

Strong, straight forms make the best slabs. Slabs that bulge, tilt, or otherwise display sloppy construction mar the beauty of your project. There's no easy, inexpensive way to correct faults in concrete once it sets.

Inspect each piece of form lumber before buying it. Look for knots, splits, and other defects that could affect its strength. Wet concrete will push the form with a tremendous amount of force, so the forms need to be structurally sound.

Make your 2×4 stakes long enough to put at least 8 inches into the ground when the stake is driven to 1 inch below the top of the forms (this keeps the stake out of the way when you screed the concrete). Slabs wider than 8 feet require control joints. These cuts in the surface of the slab keep cracks from spreading randomly across the surface. You'll cut them after the concrete is poured, but you'll mark their location on the forms before you make the pour.

After you build the forms, pour and tamp a gravel base to the depth required by code. Then lay reinforcing wire mesh on dobies or bolsters on the gravel.

PRESTART CHECKLIST

☐ **TIME**
About 4 to 6 hours to build forms for a 10×10-foot slab with curves

☐ **TOOLS**
Sledgehammer, circular saw, hammer, carpenter's level, mason's line, cordless drill

☐ **SKILLS**
Measuring, cutting, leveling, driving stakes, fastening

☐ **PREP**
Lay out and excavate the site

☐ **MATERIALS**
Deck screws or nails, bender board, expansion strip, construction adhesive, 2×4 and 2×6 lumber

Staking forms for a patio or walk

1 Lay out and excavate the site as shown on *pages 74–77.* Then restring the mason's lines between the corner stakes. If you're going to use the top of the forms as a screed guide, restring the lines level with the top of the slab (for a structure with a slab base) or the sand base (for a sand-set installation). Then drive 2×4 stakes at about 2-foot intervals along the mason's lines, keeping their tops just below each line. Make sure the interior face of each stake falls directly under the mason's line.

STANLEY PRO TIP

Don't forget the expansion strip

If you've designed your patio to abut the foundation of your house, the foundation becomes one of the forms for the slab. The foundation and the slab, however, expand and contract at different rates and need some kind of cushion between them. Here's where you need an expansion joint—a ½×4-inch piece of compressed fiber made especially for this purpose. Once you have all the forms in place, cut expansion joint material to length and apply it to the foundation with a generous bead of construction adhesive. (See illustration, *page 122.)*

WHAT IF...
The project requires curved forms?

If your patio or walk design incorporates curves, form the curve from 3½-inch-wide strips of ¼-inch hardboard or plywood. For strength, use two or three plies. Tack one end of one board temporarily with two 4d nails. Spring the material against the stakes on the curve, mark its length, and cut it. Cut the remaining pieces, then fasten them in place.

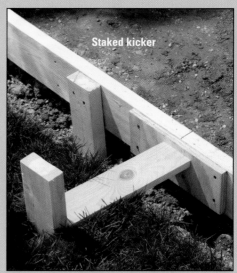

Staked kicker

2 Place a 2×6 against the interior face of the stakes and, keeping it level with the mason's line (or a carpenter's level), fasten it to the stakes with 2½-inch screws. When you add the gravel subbase, the 2×6 will let some gravel seep under its bottom edge but not as much as a 2×4 would. The wider form will be more stable.

3 Continue fastening 2×6s to the stakes. Butt-join them and reinforce each joint with a 1× or a ¾-inch plywood cleat screwed across the joint.

4 Screw and stake 1× kickers to each joint and at 4-foot intervals on the outside of the forms. Concrete is very heavy and without the kickers, its weight would push the forms out of alignment or snap them. If you are dividing a large patio with internal forms, now's the time to anchor them.

DIVIDING A LARGE PATIO

If you pour a large patio slab or driveway in sections, one of your crew can start screeding one section while the next is poured. If the dividers will be temporary, you can use any straight length of lumber that's the same dimension as your perimeter forms. If the dividers are part of the design and will remain in the slab, use redwood, cedar, or pressure-treated lumber. Brush sealer on permanent forms and tape the top edge to keep wet concrete from staining the wood and to minimize scratches when you screed. Support the dividers with stakes driven 1 inch below the top so they will not be visible once the concrete is poured.

Getting the slope right

The surfaces of all outdoor hardscapes must slope ¼ inch per foot to allow water to drain off freely. Build a slope gauge to get the right slant on your project. Put a ½-inch dowel or drill bit under one end of a 2-foot level taped to an 8-foot 2×4. This gauge will set the slope at 2 percent. The slope is correct when the bubble is centered in the vial.

Forming and pouring a wall footing

1 Lay out and excavate the footing as shown on *pages 74–77*. Drive corner stakes and tie mason's line between them, with the line indicating the top of the forms. Then drive 2×4 stakes at 2-foot intervals, keeping their tops just below the line and the interior faces under it.

2 Fasten level 2×8s to the stakes. (Use 2×8s even if the footing will be deeper than 8 inches because excess concrete that flows underneath the form only makes the footing stronger.) Clamp the forms to the stakes to make them easier to fasten. Reinforce joints with 1× scrap or ¾-inch plywood.

3 Lay a level across the form to make sure both sides are at the same height. Adjust them by hammering the stakes (not the forms), if necessary. Fasten 2×8s to the ends to complete the form. Then add 4 to 6 inches of gravel, tamp it, and reinforce the footing as local codes require.

REINFORCE THE FOOTING

Rebar strengthens

Depending on your local codes, you may need to reinforce a slab or footing with rebar, especially if you live in an area subject to earthquakes or hurricanes. Most codes also require rebar reinforcement for walls taller than 3 feet.

The rebar most commonly specified is #4 bar (½ inch in diameter). Placing two parallel runs along the entire length of the form is standard practice. Support the rebar by wiring it to bolsters or dobies made for this purpose. They hold the rebar in the middle of the slab. Overlap the ends of the rebar by at least a foot, and tie the overlaps with wire. If vertical reinforcement is required, drive rebar into the ground, spacing it as local codes require.

STANLEY PRO TIP

Use a form-release agent

Before pouring concrete for the slab or footing, coat the forms with vegetable oil or a commercial release agent.

Once the concrete has set, you'll remove the forms. This job will be remarkably difficult if you don't coat the forms with a release agent before pouring the concrete.

Without the agent, the boards will stick to the concrete. Separating the forms from the concrete can require much effort, and some of the slab may break away as you pry the forms. With the release agent, the forms come off easily.

4 Reinforce the forms at 2- to 3-foot intervals with 1×2 spreaders tacked to the top edges. Then, starting at one end of the form, pour in the concrete, consolidating it by working a 2×4 up and down along the mix. To screed the concrete, lay a 2×4 (about 8 inches longer than the width of the form) across one end of the form and pull it along the length of the footing, using a seesaw motion as you go. Remove the spreaders and rescreed the concrete. Then let the concrete cure.

5 When the footing has cured, remove the forms and backfill the soil around the edges. After shoveling in about 4 inches of soil, tamp it with a 2×4. Continue backfilling and tamping until the soil is level with the surrounding soil. Resod the area after completing the wall.

How deep is deep enough?

Footings need to be twice the width of the wall, but how deep into the ground should they go?

Footing depth depends on the frost line. The bottom of the footing should be at least 6 inches below the frost line. Check your local building codes to find out how deep that is in your area. In deep-frost areas, pour the footing, then build a foundation wall on top of it after the footing cures.

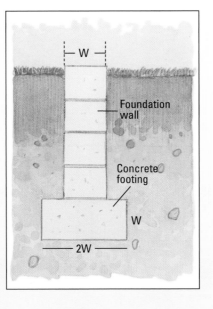

W

Foundation wall

Concrete footing

W

2W

WHAT IF...
The footing is on a slope?

Footing forms for sloped sites are built using the same techniques used for straight footings—except they're stepped down the slope. Use 2×8s and overlap the ends of the steps by at least 2 feet, as shown. Make sure the step rises no more than 2 feet. Assemble the forms as you would straight forms and add reinforcement and gravel as required by local codes.

PROVIDING DRAINAGE

Many yards have areas that collect water, a problem that a new patio or path can actually make worse. Water doesn't soak through the hard surface of a patio or path, so it runs into the yard. This runoff can create problems if you don't correct it before you start construction. Easy-to-install solutions can carry the water away.

A swale or French drain channels the water away from the site to a place where it won't cause problems. You can divert water only to another place on your own property, however, not onto the neighbor's yard. If you can't divert the water to a good location, you'll have to run a French drain to a dry well.

A dry well collects water and lets it seep slowly into the surrounding soil. Look to local codes for the required dry-well size for your area. The size could be subject to conditions of your property or neighborhood. Even if your yard doesn't have runoff problems, you can avoid creating them by installing a gravel-lined trench around the patio.

Be sure to check the location of underground utility lines before you install any kind of drainage system.

PRESTART CHECKLIST

☐ **TIME**
Four to six hours for a 10-foot trench and dry well

☐ **TOOLS**
Round-nose shovel, slope gauge, spade, scissors

☐ **SKILLS**
Excavating, lifting light loads, using a slope gauge

☐ **MATERIALS**
Gravel, 4-inch perforated drainpipe, couplings, landscape fabric, concrete patio block

Building a French drain and dry well

1 Using a spade, slice the sod along the path of the line—about 2 feet wide. Remove the sod, roll it up, and save it. Dig out the trench about 6 inches deep all along the line, using a slope gauge to slope it ¼ inch per foot *(page 79)*. At the low end of the trench, dig a dry well about 2 to 4 feet wide and 3 feet deep. Line the trench with landscape fabric and gravel. Then lay in 4-inch perforated drainpipe with the holes facing down. Continue running pipe a few inches into the dry well. Connect the pipe sections with fittings and without glue.

Where does the water go?

A swale is a shallow trench dug along the low edge of a portion in the landscape that collects water. To dig a swale, first slice a foot-wide section of sod along its path. Then remove the sod in rolls and excavate a shallow trench in the soil (about 3 to 4 inches deep), throwing the soil in a wheelbarrow. Replace the sod and use the soil elsewhere.

SWALE

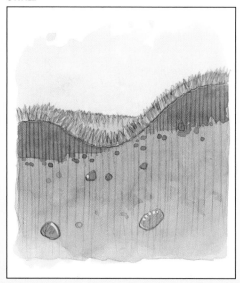

2 To keep the gravel from settling into the soil, line the well with landscape fabric, leaving about 2 feet of surplus fabric on each side. Cut a hole for the drainpipe. Then fill the trench and the well with gravel, leaving enough clearance over the well for a 2- to 3-inch-thick patio block cover.

3 At the well, fold the surplus landscape fabric over the gravel and cover it with a patio block. Backfill the trench and the well, tamping the soil lightly.

4 Cover the patio block with at least 3 inches of soil, tamping it lightly with a garden rake. Then replace the sod.

FRENCH DRAIN

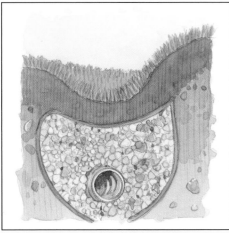

A French drain is a swale lined with gravel and a drainpipe which carries the water to an inconspicuous location or a dry well.

OPEN DRAIN TO DAYLIGHT

Your drainage systems can daylight onto an out-of-the-way place in the lawn—but only on your own property. Check local codes for restrictions on any drainage system you build.

DRY WELL (CROSS-SECTION)

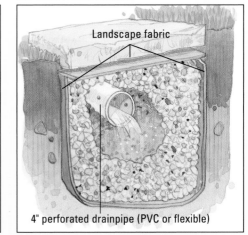

Landscape fabric

4" perforated drainpipe (PVC or flexible)

A dry well isn't dry at all. It is a hole in the ground, about 2 to 4 feet wide and 3 feet deep lined with landscape fabric and gravel. The gravel controls the drainage of water into the surrounding soil, preventing erosion.

INSTALLING EDGING

Edgings do more than keep patio and path materials inside their boundaries. They also become an integral part of the design, adding color, form, and texture. Here are some common edging materials:

Brick: Brick is set as soldiers (standing upright and on edge), sailors (flat along the edge), or at an angle. Set brick in a concrete footing for increased stability.

Poured concrete: You can color poured concrete during mixing to match or contrast the paving material. You can also give it texture with the techniques shown on *pages 64–65.*

Plastic and steel: Flexible plastic edging will conform to almost any curve. It's easy to install by anchoring it to the ground with spikes driven through integral lugs. Use steel edge restraints for precast pavers and any time you want to restrain the edging material without the restraint being visible.

Wood/Landscape timbers: Use only wood edging made of naturally resistant species or pressure-treated stock rated for ground contact. Backfill the edges with topsoil to hide the stakes.

Stone: Both flagstone and cut stone make excellent edging, especially for wide walks. You can purchase precut stone or cut the pieces yourself from paving stones. When cutting your own, keep the width consistent so the stones don't look mismatched.

Precast edging: Many manufacturers make precast edging or tiles to match paver patterns. They come in straight or curved shapes, many with sculpted designs. You can also use precast blocks by themselves as borders for planting beds.

Staking curved edging

Benderboard or 1×4 kerfed to allow bending

Gravel base

Lay out the site using a hose and chalk to mark the curve. Excavate a trench along the curve to the depth required for the base and paving materials. Then drive stakes along the trench and prepare the edging by sawing kerfs in ¾-inch stock at 1-inch intervals. The kerf depth should be about half the thickness of the stock. Fasten the edging to the stakes and excavate the remainder of the site. Spread and tamp gravel and sand, then install the edging and paving.

STANLEY PRO TIP

Edging first

Loose materials such as bark and stone will migrate off the path if there's no edging to keep them in. Sand-set surfaces also require edging to keep them in place.

In most cases and for most materials, you should set the edges before the paving, but if you're edging a concrete slab, you'll have to set the edging after the slab has cured and you've removed the forms.

Wherever your design permits it, set the edging slightly below the lawn surface or no more than an inch above it. Doing so makes mowing neat and easy.

Installing a concrete curb

Lay out the site, including the width of the concrete curbs, and excavate it to the depth codes require. Install the staked forms and spread and tamp the gravel subbase. Pour the concrete, screed it on the forms, and finish the edge. When the concrete has cured, remove the forms, lay the sand and paving, and backfill the trench.

Installing timber edging

Lay out the site and excavate it to the depth local codes require for the combined thickness of paving and gravel. Include the width of the timbers in your layout. Predrill 4×4 or 6×6 landscape timbers for ½-inch rebar at 3-foot intervals. Spread gravel and set the timbers on it along the edges of the excavation. Drive rebar through the gravel into the soil, then spread the sand, tamp it, and lay the paving.

Installing brick edging

Lay out the site and excavate it to the depth required for your materials. Drive 2×4 stakes every 3 to 4 feet. Attach 2× forms to the stakes below ground level and spread the gravel base. Then spread the sand base and tamp it. Install the brick edging, setting one or two rows of paving as you go. Then backfill the edges of the site.

Installing plastic edge restraints

Lay out the site and excavate it to the depth required for your materials. Spread the gravel base and tamp it. Set the edging along the contours of the site and anchor it with landscape spikes driven through the tabs. Then spread and tamp the sand bed, lay the paving material, and backfill the trench.

Installing flagstone edging

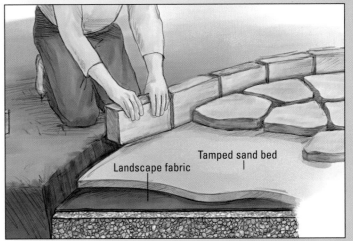

Lay out and excavate the site. Spread and tamp the gravel base and the sand bed. Set the edging and paving as you go. As an alternative, you can excavate the site with trenches on the perimeter and set the edging in the trenches, followed by the gravel base and sand.

BUILDING A SAND BASE

When not secured with mortar, patio and path paving—brick, flagstone, and precast pavers—must be set in a sand base over a gravel subbase. Sand provides a solid base for the pavers, and the gravel ensures good drainage.

Sand-set (sometimes called dry-laid) installations are much easier to build than mortared surfaces. They don't require specialized skills, and because there's no concrete required, they are less expensive. A properly bedded sand-set patio will last for years and require little or no maintenance.

Take your site measurements with you when you're ready to order the paving. Your dealer will help you convert those measurements to gravel, sand, and paving quantities. Remember to buy extra pavers to cover breakage and mistakes, and to store in case a paver or two needs replacing in the future.

Soil conditions will influence the construction of your project. Sandy soils drain very quickly but are soft. Clay is hard and doesn't drain well. Contact your extension office or building department for tips pertinent to your locality.

PRESTART CHECKLIST

☐ **TIME**
About 3 days to lay out and excavate a 12×14-foot site

☐ **TOOLS**
Round-nose shovel, tape measure, spade, mason's line, batterboards, carpenter's level, small sledgehammer, screed, garden hose

☐ **SKILLS**
Measuring, leveling, laying out square lines

☐ **PREP**
Plan site, choose materials, draw plans

☐ **MATERIALS**
Landscape fabric, edge restraints and spikes, gravel, sand, PVC pipe or 2-inch lumber strips

1 Lay out the site with batterboards and staked lines *(pages 74–75)*. Slope the lines to provide drainage, slice the soil at the perimeter, and remove the sod. Excavate the site for the thickness of your materials: typically 4 to 6 inches of gravel, 2 inches for a sand bed, plus the thickness of the pavers. Measure from the mason's lines for consistent depth. Shovel in the gravel or crushed stone base 3 inches at a time, spreading it evenly. Compact each layer until it reaches the proper thickness. A crushed rock base with an abundance of fine particles will compact firmly and create solid support.

Sizing the site exactly

If patio or path dimensions equal multiples of tile or modular materials, you'll have less cutting to do at the edges. Save yourself time and effort by making the site dimensions the same as an even number of pavers. Lay out the paving in both directions on a flat surface, and measure the lengths. Then lay out your site to these dimensions.

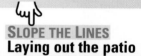

SLOPE THE LINES
Laying out the patio

Patios and paths must slope ¼ inch for every lineal foot to provide proper drainage. Measure the length of the mason's line between the stakes in feet, then multiply by ¼. On the low stake, move the level line down by that much.

2 Spread landscape fabric over the gravel—it will help kill the weeds and prevent the sand base from sifting into the gravel. Overlap the edges of the fabric by at least 6 inches. Install the edging around the perimeter, following the manufacturer's instructions. The easiest edge restraints to install are those with wide supports and closely spaced holes for the anchor spikes. Make sure you drive the spikes through the gravel into the soil.

3 Set 1½-inch PVC pipe (or 2-inch boards ripped from 2×4s) on the landscape fabric, parallel with the edges of the excavation and at about 5-foot intervals. They provide a built-in depth gauge and screeding tool for the sand base. Shovel sand over the entire surface, dampen it, and tamp it. Then screed the sand level.

WHAT IF…
The patio has curves?

For curved and rounded patio edges, use plastic edging with notches in the outside flange. This material conforms to almost any arc. Drive spikes through the holes in the flanges, making sure they penetrate the soil below the gravel.

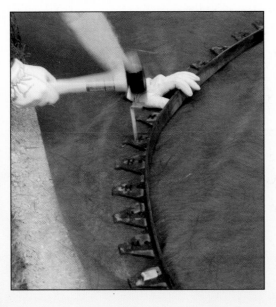

SCREED THE SAND
Use a 2×4 to level the sand

Screed the sand to a consistent level by setting a long 2×4 on the edge forms and the PVC or wood inserts. Pull the screed across the surface in a seesaw motion—you'll need a helper for large areas. Then fill in depressions, dampen the sand, and tamp it. When the site is level, remove the pipes or boards, fill the recesses with sand, and tamp again.

WORKING WITH CONCRETE

Concrete is a mixture of sand, coarse aggregate, portland cement, and water. Here are some things to consider if you are mixing your own concrete rather than using premix or ready-mix.

The sand used in concrete should be sharp sand, not builder's sand, which is used in mortar. It should also be clean—free of vegetation and dirt, which will weaken the mix.

The coarse aggregate—gravel or crushed stone—must also be clean and no larger than one-quarter the thickness of the pour. Most residential projects call for concrete with medium-size, ¾-inch aggregate. The water you mix with the concrete should be clean enough to drink.

Portland cement is composed of clay, lime, and other ingredients that have been heated in a kiln and ground into a fine powder. Choose Type 1 cement.

Additives

Concrete additives modify the concrete in specific ways. They can accelerate or retard the concrete's setup time, prevent deterioration of a surface due to freezing and thawing, or make the concrete mix workable in extreme heat or cold.

Before mixing or ordering concrete, ask your supplier for advice on what additives to use to adjust the concrete to the specific conditions under which you're pouring it.

Reinforcements

Concrete has great compressive strength but little tensile strength—it doesn't stretch or bend well, so it cracks easily. Steel reinforcing bars, rebar, or wire mesh are used to add tensile strength. Rebar comes in 20-foot lengths; ½-inch bar is adequate for most home projects.

If your design has curves, you can bend rebar by hand. Have a helper stand on a board placed over the bar. Slip a pipe over one end of the bar to where you want the bend, then lift up on the pipe. There's also a tool designed to cut and bend rebar. Rent one if you have a lot of rebar to install.

Reinforcing a concrete slab

After you have installed the forms and braced them, lay reinforcing wire mesh in the excavation, leaving about 1 inch between the forms and the ends of the wire mesh. Support the mesh on dobies or wire bolsters (made for this purpose) or small chunks of concrete, tying the supports to the corners of the mesh with soft wire. The dobies or bolsters should approximately center the mesh in the thickness of the slab.

STANLEY PRO TIP

How much will you need?

Area	Slab Thickness			
	3"	4"	5"	6"
10 sq. ft.	.10	.14	.17	.20
25 sq. ft.	.25	.34	.42	.51
50 sq. ft.	.51	.68	.85	1.02
100 sq. ft.	1.02	1.36	1.70	2.04
200 sq. ft.	2.04	2.72	3.40	4.07
300 sq. ft.	3.06	4.07	5.09	6.10
400 sq. ft.	4.07	5.43	6.79	8.15

This chart is a quick calculator to help you estimate how much concrete you'll need. It's based on the simple math formula for calculating the volume of a structure: multiply length times width times thickness in feet to find cubic feet. Then divide this figure by 27 to find the volume in cubic yards. Add an extra 10 percent to allow for variations in grade and waste.

Score some control joints

No matter how carefully prepared and finished, all concrete will crack because of internal stresses. Most cracks in the surface do not constitute a structural problem, but they mar the appearance of the project. Control joints are the solution.

Control joints are grooves cut partway through the slab after it begins to set. They give the concrete a place to crack, rather than having cracks spread like spiderwebs across the surface. The cracks follow the joints.

Control joints differ from expansion joints. Control joints are the lines you see on a sidewalk. Expansion joints are placed between pours to allow large sections of concrete to expand and shift with the climate. These joints usually incorporate another material as a cushion between paving sections.

Coat the forms

Paint the forms with a commercial release agent or vegetable oil. This will make the forms easier to remove after the concrete has cured.

Build a ramp

Mix the concrete near the work site and protect the lawn with a 2× ramp. Start dumping the concrete in the corner farthest from the mixing site. Place each subsequent load against the preceding one so fresh concrete mixes with what's already there.

Get a crew together

Pouring ready-mix is a team effort, and it's best to engage the help of some friends or neighbors who have done it before. The driver may run the chute, but you'll need screeders, shovelers, and finishers.

Mixing concrete in a wheelbarrow

1 If you're mixing concrete in a wheelbarrow, get a large one—a lot of concrete will spill from a small wheelbarrow as you mix it. Pour the contents of a premix bag into the wheelbarrow (never mix a partial bag) or measure in the dry ingredients with a shovel. Mix the dry mix together with a hoe, then mound it into the center of the wheelbarrow and make a depression in it.

2 Add about one-half of the total water into the depression and work the mix into the water with a hoe. Then work the mix back and forth the length of the wheelbarrow with the hoe, scraping up dry material from the bottom. Add water as necessary, working it into the mix before adding more. When the concrete clings to a trowel turned on edge, it's ready.

Power mixing

If using premix, empty full bags into the mixer. Partial bags often result in an improper mix. If using dry mix, measure the right proportions of cement, sand, and aggregate into the mixer in shovelfuls. Turn the mixer on to mix the dry materials thoroughly. Then add about one-half the prescribed water and mix thoroughly. Continue mixing, adding water a little at a time, until the mix clings to the side of a shovel turned on edge.

Screeding the mix

Screeding is another word for leveling and smoothing. The forms provide you with a reference surface. You'll need a 2×4 (a metal stud is excellent) long enough to span the forms. With a helper, pull the screed along the top of the forms with a side-to-side motion. Screed again to remove any humps in the mix. Fill low spots with concrete; then screed again. Remove any temporary guides, fill the cavities they leave behind, and screed once more.

Floating the surface

Floating pushes the aggregates below the surface of the concrete. If you can reach the entire surface from outside the area, use a darby. Hold the darby flat as you move it across the surface in wide arcs. Then tilt it slightly and work in straight pulls. For large jobs, use a bull float. While one or more people float a section, the finisher can work right behind them, rounding the edges with an edger and cutting control joints, as needed.

Infinite textures

Finishing a concrete slab with exposed aggregate can bring unusual textures to your patio design—and there's almost no limit to your choices. Each aggregate will create a design effect all its own.

STANLEY PRO TIP

Working with bleed water

You'd think that after a material as heavy as concrete is poured, that would be all there is to it. But even after the pour, there's a lot going on beneath the surface. The heavy materials gradually sink and they leave a thin layer of water, called bleed water, on the surface. The bleed water must dry before you move on to other steps.

Timing is the key to an attractive finish. Here's what you should do and when you should do it:

■ Settle and screed the concrete and control joints immediately after pouring and before bleed water appears. If you wait, crazing, spalling, and other flaws can develop.

■ Let bleed water dry before floating or edging. Concrete should be hard enough that pressure from your foot leaves an impression no more than ¼ inch deep.

■ Do not overfloat the concrete. You may cause bleed water to reappear. Stop floating if a sheen appears and resume when it's gone.

Cutting control joints

To cut straight control joints, tack a straight 2×4 guide to the forms at both ends. Cut control joints every 8 feet by sliding the side of a jointer along the guide. Tip up the leading edge of the tool slightly as you move it back and forth. Make the depth of the control joints about 20 percent of the thickness of the concrete (for example, ¾ inch on a 4-inch slab).

Curing concrete

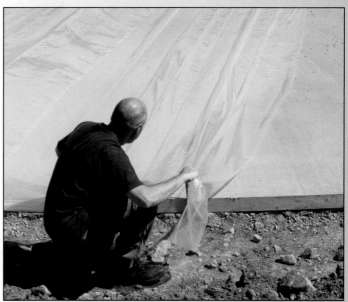

Concrete goes through two hardening processes. The first is when chemical reactions in the mix cause it to set up. The concrete hardens, but not completely. Concrete sets up within a short time after the pour. Curing, the final hardening, takes longer, at least a week for a patio slab. During this time, you must mist the surface periodically with a lawn sprinkler or cover it with plastic or straw to keep it from drying too quickly. Premature drying causes cracking and other weakness.

WHAT IF...
You want a flagstone look?

To make the surface look like flagstones or to break it up into regular geometric shapes, score the surface soon after you finish it and after water has evaporated. A concave striking tool works well for creating undulating lines.

Stamping a brick pattern

To create a brick pattern in your concrete walk or patio, you can rent a stamping form, which you push into the wet concrete, or several fill forms like the one shown. These forms are available at your home center and work great on small jobs.

Set the form on top of the gravel and fill each section to the top of the form but no higher. Finish the concrete with a trowel. After water has evaporated from the concrete surface, wiggle out the form carefully so clean-looking lines remain. Flick away any excess and carefully trowel the surface. Once the concrete cures, fill the gaps with mortar.

WORKING WITH BRICK

A certain romance comes with building with brick. Not only because of the beauty of the material but because bricklaying techniques haven't changed much over time. Gaining command of the technique takes a little time. It's not something you learn overnight, but with practice you'll get the hang of it.

It will help to understand bricklaying terminology. A **stretcher** is a brick laid so its long edge faces out. A **header** is a brick turned so its end faces out. A **course** of bricks is one horizontal row. **Wythe** refers to how many bricks thick a wall is (freestanding walls are usually two wythes thick). **Bond** does not refer to the bond mortar makes between two units but to the overall pattern in which the bricks are laid. Three common bonds are the English bond, Flemish bond, and running bond. **Workable** is a mason's word for a mortar that is mixed just right.

Working with mortar

Mortar is the critical element in bricklaying. If mortar is the wrong consistency, laying brick is difficult and the faces of the courses will be erratic.

Select the correct mortar strength for your project *(page 70)*. Although you can mix the ingredients yourself, it's best to buy premix. The key to making mortar workable is getting the right amount of water in it, and premixed bags take the guesswork out of mixing it. Simply use the amount of water specified on the bag.

Always mix the dry ingredients thoroughly before adding water, then add the water a little at a time.

Mix enough mortar in a mortar box for an hour's work—perhaps ¼ cubic foot for 20 or so bricks to start. As you get faster at laying brick, mix bigger batches. Put the box at a height you won't have to bend to reach.

After about 30 minutes, the mortar will start to thicken because some of the water has evaporated. You can retemper the mortar by adding more water, a little bit at a time, until it resumes the proper consistency.

Depending on the weather, this may occur a few times. But after about 2 hours, mortar starts thickening as the chemical reaction of the cement causes it to harden. If this happens while you're still working, mix a new batch.

You can usually retemper the mortar mix safely within the first 1½ hours, though hot weather can shorten the time. Always replace mortar that's more than 2 hours old.

Laying the brick

If you've never done this before, there's no getting around the need for practice. You'll save yourself a lot of time and frustration if you practice on a mock-up wall rather than the real thing. Set out a row of three or four bricks on a plywood square and practice throwing the mortar until you can get it to stick correctly on at least two bricks.

This will get you started. From there, your skills will increase with repetition. Speed is not critical in amateur bricklaying. Straight courses and clean joints are.

If you set a brick too low, lift it out, add new mortar, and lay it again. Don't simply adjust its position; doing so could leave a gap in the mortar where water could enter and cause damage.

Testing the mortar

Mix the dry ingredients thoroughly, then carefully mix in clean water a little at a time. Pick up a small amount of mortar with your trowel and quickly turn the trowel upside down. If the mortar sticks, it is the correct consistency.

Getting mortar on the trowel

With a brick trowel, cut off a section of the mortar at the edge, shaping it so it's roughly the length and width of the trowel. Then slide the edge of the trowel under the mortar in one quick motion. Once the trowel is under the mortar, pick it up. Then flick your wrist in a snapping motion so the mortar moves onto the trowel; this bonds the mortar to the trowel. You will have enough mortar on the trowel to bed about three bricks.

Throwing mortar

1 Once you have the hang of getting the right amount of mortar on the trowel, don't try to lay the mortar on the brick. Throw it. Tilt the trowel, and sling the mortar onto the brick bed, pulling the trowel toward yourself in the same motion. You want the mortar to slide off the edge of the trowel and land firmly along the brick. Throwing helps adhere it to the bed. In the beginning, try to cover two bricks with one throw. Then try for three or four bricks.

2 Spread the mortar to an even thickness of about 1 inch, and trim the excess from the edges with the trowel. Then lightly furrow the center of the mortar bed with the tip of the trowel. Don't make a deep furrow, which may leave an air gap under the brick. Set the corner brick in place, tap it gently, and check it for level.

3 Butter the end of the next brick by holding it in one hand and tipping the end at a 45-degree angle. Place a small amount of mortar on the trowel and slap it onto the end of the brick with a sharp downward scraping motion. Form it with the trowel into a four-sided pyramid.

4 To set a brick, place it on the mortar bed and push it firmly against the adjacent brick. When done correctly, mortar will push out at the sides and top of the joint, and the joint will be about ⅜ inch thick.

5 Skim off the excess with the trowel, and butter the end of the next brick with it. Rap the placed bricks with the end of the trowel handle to set and level them.

Adding color

Coloring the mortar can help set off the brick. Or it can make the mortar disappear if it's the same, or similar, color to the brick. Like most masonry practices, there's a certain art to coloring mortar. This time you add the pigment to the dry mix before you add the water. What's most important is that you keep the color of each batch consistent. Measure the pigment carefully, and record the proportion. Make a test batch and let it dry. If you don't like the color, change the mix. When you find one you like, use that proportion consistently.

You can't retemper colored mortar because the additional water changes the proportions and therefore the color. It's best to mix colored mortar in small batches so you don't have to throw much away.

Cutting brick in batches

1 Any place in the layout where several bricks must be cut the same, use a framing square to mark several of them at the same time. Clamp the bricks with bar clamps to keep the marking accurate and prepare them for cutting.

2 You won't be able to cut clear through standard brick with a circular saw equipped with a masonry blade (the blade won't cut that deep), but you can score several bricks at the same time. Use a rip guide to get a more accurate cut.

Give your brick a wet-test

Before you begin laying your brick, you need to know something about its absorbency. Bricks that are very absorbent wick water from the mortar so fast that they weaken the joint. Test your bricks before laying them.

Select a brick, and pencil a circle about the size of a quarter on its face. Pour ½ teaspoon of water onto the circle and time how long it takes for the water to soak in. If the water absorbs in 90 seconds or less, wet the bricks before laying them.

Spread out several dozen bricks and spray them on all sides with a hose. Let the surfaces dry before using them—wet surfaces will not bond with mortar.

Bonds

STACKED BOND

1	2	4	7	11
	3	5	8	12
		6	9	13
			10	14
				15

RUNNING BOND

1	2	3	4	5
6	7	8	9	10	11
12	13	14	15	16

HALF BASKET WEAVE

BASKET WEAVE

LADDER WEAVE

HERRINGBONE

When choosing brick patterns, consider the aesthetic effect, the relation of your project to its surroundings, how many bricks you'll have to cut, and how difficult the pattern will be to lay. Follow the diagrams above to minimize the amount of time you'll spend moving from one place to another to set the pattern (use for a patio or path surface).

Cutting brick with a brick set

A brick set is a cold chisel with a wide face made for masonry work. Mark the cut line clearly, then score all faces of the brick with a brick set. Don't make cuts that intersect the hole (the core) of the brick. Then, holding the brick set firmly on the line, strike it with a sharp blow and the brick will split.

To cut an angle, you'll have to work in stages. Mark the final cut line first, but don't score it. Then mark and score the first cut line about ⅛ inch from the final line. Cut the brick on the first line. Repeat the process until you have cut the angled line.

Using a brick splitter

One of the advantages of using a brick splitter is that you don't need to score the brick. Just mark the cut line, set the brick with the line under the cutting blade, and pull down sharply on the handle.

Reinforcing brick

Though a two-wythe wall is the preferred width, your wall will be even stronger if you tie the wythes together with either of the two metal reinforcements shown here.

Corrugated fasteners or Z-shape ties will help strengthen a wall. So will rebar inserted in the cores of modular brick made with holes.

None of these reinforcements, however, is a good substitute for strong, well-thrown mortar joints.

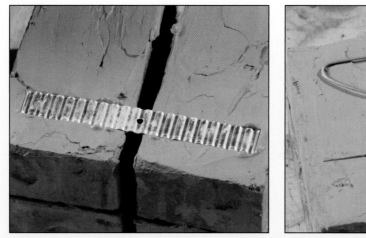

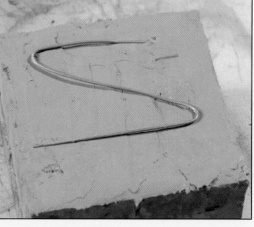

WORKING WITH CONCRETE BLOCK

Concrete blocks are five or six times larger than bricks, so you might think that setting blocks would be about that much easier. But the blocks are heavier than bricks—about 40 pounds—and require more mortar, so there's little time or effort saved.

Have the blocks delivered as close as possible to the work site, then set them along the footing so they're readily accessible. You can build a block wall by yourself, but one or two helpers will make the job easier.

Before you start, become familiar with block terminology. The concrete that forms the block is called the **web**. The cavities within the block are called **cores**. A **stretcher block** is the common block with **ears**, or flanges, on the ends. Stretcher blocks make the middle of a wall between end blocks and corner blocks. **Leads** are the built-up corners of a wall, and are three or four courses high. You'll build leads first, then fill in between them.

Preparing the job

Block walls require careful planning, just like any other masonry structure. If possible, plan the length of your wall so it's divisible by 16 inches (the length of a standard block and mortar joint) to minimize cutting. Since most block walls are later faced with brick or another material (the block won't show), use a standard running bond. It's easy and strong (page 94).

Build the wall on a concrete footing that's twice as wide as the block and as deep as local codes require. Even if reinforcement is not required, embed 32-inch lengths of rebar vertically in the footing at 32-inch intervals. The rebar extends into the cores when you set the blocks.

Laying the blocks

Before you apply mortar, lay the first course of blocks in a dry run, spacing the blocks with ⅜-inch plywood. Since you'll need some method for keeping the block square to the footing, either snap a chalk line on the footing along the edges of the block or 1½ inches away from the edges. Once you've set the block, you can use a 2×4 to keep the first course spaced on this line. Or you can set stakes with mason's line to align the outside faces.

Concrete block webs are wider on one side. The wide side should face up because it provides a larger bed for the mortar. This reduces waste, minimizing the amount of mortar that falls off the web. It's also easier to handle the blocks when you grip the wide side. To save time, distribute the blocks along the job site with all the wide sides up.

Do not wet the blocks before installing them. Wet blocks expand, then shrink when they dry. If it rains or rain threatens, cover the blocks.

Spread mortar only on the outside edges of the block (a technique called **face-shell bedding**), not on the cross web. Applying mortar to the cross web is difficult, wasteful, and not necessary when building a wall in the landscape. An exception is when laying reinforcements, as shown on *page 99*.

On ends without corners, every other course after the first one should start and end with a half block.

STANLEY PRO TIP

Getting the low-down

High walls consume more time and materials than low ones. They are also more likely to fall down. Make sure your wall is only as high as it needs to be. A 3-foot wall might be all you need to separate one space from another.

Local building codes, too, may restrict the height of the wall. Be sure to have your building department approve your plan before the wall goes up. If you need a higher structure, install a lattice panel on a low wall to add interest, increase privacy, and filter breezes.

A CONCRETE FOOTING
Build a solid base

Block walls must be built on a solid base. Poured concrete footings for walls should be twice the width of the wall, flush with the ground, and as deep as local codes require. Building codes may also call for concrete reinforcement *(page 80)*.

Make a story pole

A story pole helps you space the courses more quickly. To make one, cut a piece of straight 2×4 to the height of the finished wall. Then mark the courses on the board, separating them by ⅜ inch for mortar joints.

Take a trial run

1 Set a block at each end of the footing and center the width of each block on the width of the footing. Mark the edges of the block on the footing and snap chalk lines on the surface of the footing. Make sure your chalk lines extend to the ends of the footing.

2 Starting at one end of the footing with either an end block or half-corner block (depending on the length of the wall), set blocks without mortar. Place the edges on the chalked lines, spacing them with ⅜-inch-wide plywood. When you set the last block, snap perpendicular chalk lines to mark the ends of the row.

3 If your wall turns a corner, establish the corner with your layout lines. Then start the second leg of the trial run with a full corner block. Check the corner with a framing square. Lay out the rest of the blocks along the chalk lines.

ESTABLISH THE CORNER
Make the corner square

Use your batterboards and mason's lines to mark the corners of the wall on the footing. Drop a plumb bob from the intersection of the lines and mark the footing clearly. Then snap a chalk line between your marks. Check the corners for square using a 3-4-5 triangle *(page 75)* or framing square, and adjust as needed.

Surface-bonded block

Surface bonding, an alternate method for laying concrete block, saves time, effort, and material costs. It doesn't require the application of mortar between courses.

With this method, you mortar the first course of blocks to the footing and stack the rest of the blocks on that course without mortar. Then you trowel on a surface-bonding agent made of portland cement and fiberglass.

The result is a strong wall. The bonding agent makes the seams invisible when it is properly applied. Check your local building codes before you decide to use this method. Some localities do not approve of surface bonding.

Laying concrete block

1 Start the first course by laying a mortar bed on the footing. Make it 1 to 1½ inches thick and about three blocks long. The mortar bed will cover the chalk lines, but you can still line up the first block with the lines that extend to the edges of the footing.

2 Carefully push the corner block into the mortar bed, lining it up with the ends of the chalk lines on the footing.

3 Check the height of the block with your story pole, and push the block down until the top is even with the mark. If the block is low, pull it out, place more mortar on the bed, and replace the block. Then place a level on top of the block and level it along its length and width.

Cutting concrete block

Concrete block is made in so many configurations that you may not need to cut it at all. But if you do need to cut a block, place the block on sand or loose soil and use a brick set and small sledgehammer to score both

sides of the block. Then set the block with its web up and place the brick set on the scored line. Strike the brick set until the block breaks cleanly. Wear eye and ear protection.

You can also cut block with a circular saw equipped with a masonry blade. Wear eye and ear protection.

4 To prepare the second block, set it on end and butter its ears with a downward swiping motion of the trowel. Then press down on the mortar on the inside edge of the ear. This will keep the mortar from falling off when you set the block. If the mortar does fall off, start over with fresh mortar.

5 Set the second block in place, pushing it against the first block, making sure you leave a ⅜-inch joint space. Using the same techniques, butter the third block and set it. Don't remove the excess mortar on the footing until it has set up a bit.

6 With three blocks laid, set a level on top and tap the blocks into place with the end of the trowel handle. Repeat the process on the width of the block. Check for plumb by holding the level against the side of each block. Then build the other corner and the leads as shown on *pages 184–186*.

WHAT IF...
You need to reinforce the concrete block?

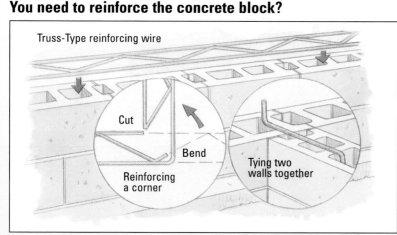

Retaining walls and other walls subject to substantial lateral pressure (sideways pressure pushing against the face of the wall) require reinforcement. Embed reinforcing wire in the mortar of every other course, overlapping the ends by at least 6 inches. At a corner, cut and bend the wire 90 degrees.

To tie intersecting walls together, bend rebar into an S shape and embed it into the mortar as shown.

Tying walls together

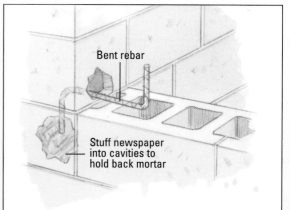

Walls built perpendicular to each other must be tied together, and if you're putting up a new wall next to one that's there already, you can't place metal ties between the courses. Knock a hole in the core of the existing wall, stuff newspaper into the cavities, and place an S-shape piece of rebar in the hole. Then fill the holes with mortar and lay the next course.

WORKING WITH STONE

Stone is one of the most artistic materials in masonry and setting it requires planning, a knowledge of the materials, and the ability to use the tools correctly. A stone structure may be formal, informal, or even rustic. Stone masonry requires practice and creativity, but is one of the most satisfying masonry endeavors.

Gathering your own stone

You can order your stone from a local quarry or stone distributor, but if you own, or have access to, an open landscape, you can gather your own materials.

Doing so requires a long pry bar, a crowbar, and an understanding of leverage. Bring along something to transport the stone—a garden cart or a child's wagon for small stones, a hand truck with inflatable rubber tires for larger stones, and some 2×12s for ramps in case the wheels get bogged down. You can probably rent a "stone boat," a sled with iron runners.

When loading up a garden cart, tip it and roll the stone inside instead of lifting the stone and dropping it into the cart. If you need the 2×s on soft ground, alternate moving the equipment on one board and setting another in front of the first one. If you're using a wheelbarrow, concentrate the load toward the back to keep the weight off the front wheel. A stone boat is handy because it's low to the ground and all you have to do is roll the stones onto it. You can also hitch it to a car or truck and drag it across the field.

Use a low trailer to bring your stones to the project so you won't have to lift the stones too high. Roll the stones up a ramp made of 2×12s or flip them end over end.

Tips for stone masonry

In general a stone wall should be about 2 feet thick for every 3 feet of height. (A 6-foot wall should be 4 feet thick, for instance). For every 6 inches of additional height, add 4 inches to the width of the base. Local building codes may specify dimension requirements for stone walls.

A mortared wall requires a footing; a dry-laid wall does not. If you're building a stone retaining wall or planter, install weep holes—either unmortared gaps in the base or sections of ½-inch PVC pipe.

Handle stone safely

Save time and stress by organizing your material. Set out the stones in piles or sections by size, keeping bondstones in one, fillers in another, and the remaining stones in a third. These categories will help you pick the right stones and will also help you prepare yourself when you need to lift the heavy ones.

The sheer size and weight of some stones makes them difficult to place properly on your wall. A ramp made from 2× stock can make the job easier. Push the stone up the ramp or flip it end for end. Consider renting a portable crane and chain for larger stones.

Protect your back when lifting stone. Wear a back support belt and always keep your knees bent. To be safe, enlist the aid of a helper or use one of the mechanical methods shown to assist you.

For boulders too large to lift, rent a boulder cart. These are made to handle any size boulder you or two people can pull or push.

Planning a mortared wall

1 Lay out the footing, then excavate and pour it *(pages 74–81)*. When the footing has cured, measure the width of one of your bondstones and snap chalk lines that distance apart on the footing to mark the front and rear faces of the wall. Snap lines to mark the ends of the wall as well.

2 Choose bondstones of equal width (or cut them to the same size) and lay one at each end of the footing, lined up on your chalk lines.

3 Make a trial run by dry-laying the first course of both wythes. Choose stones based on both aesthetic and practical considerations. Vary the length of the stones on each wythe to add visual interest, cutting stones to fit as necessary.

Battering the walls

A stone wall is narrower at the top than the bottom. Slant (batter) both faces of the wall slightly and at the same angle—about 1 inch per 2 feet of height. Increase the batter for fieldstone and retaining walls. Build two batter gauges following the directions at right.

Cut four pieces of 1×4 as long as the height of the wall and two more pieces as long as the base width. Compute the width of the top based on the amount of batter you want, and cut two 1×4s to this length. Nail the boards together as shown above. Add a diagonal crossbrace, and set the gauges at the ends of the wall.

As an option, cut two 1×2s to the finished height of the wall and fasten them together at one end with 1¼-inch screws. At the other end, insert a spacer to separate the boards by the amount of batter you want. Fasten the boards with the spacer, and tape a level to the gauge. The wall is battered correctly when the level shows plumb.

WORKING WITH STONE (continued)

The key to building a sturdy, pleasing wall is stone selection. Carefully select and fit each stone before applying mortar. Use stones that nest comfortably against the surrounding ones. Wedge small stones between large stones to fill any voids.

Work with a few shovelfuls of mortar on a piece of plywood, and keep it on the ground beside you. Mist the mortar with water to keep it well tempered.

You don't need to be delicate when mortaring a wall. Throw mortar from the trowel onto the stone. Rap the stone firmly with the end of the trowel handle to seat it and to force out any air bubbles. Scrape off the excess mortar and throw the excess into the center of the wall.

To keep the stones clean as you work, have a bucket of water with a large sponge handy to immediately wipe off any spills.

After cutting a stone, dress the edge (remove sharp irregularities) with a pointing chisel. Place the point of the chisel at the base of the bump and rap the chisel sharply with a small sledgehammer.

You can cut stone with a cold chisel and hammer as shown on *page 103*. Or you can split large, flat stones, 3 or 4 feet across, with tools called feathers and wedges, made for breaking stone.

First chalk a cutting line. Then, using a power drill and a masonry bit the diameter of the feather-and-wedge assembly, drill a hole every 8 inches along the line. Insert a feather and wedge into each hole. Gently tap each, starting in the middle, then working alternate sides. The pressure should split the rock along the line. If it doesn't, redrill holes at 4-inch intervals and try again. Take care not to jam the wedges into the feathers so tightly that you can't pull them out. If they do get stuck, pry them out with a crowbar. Place a wood block under the crowbar so it doesn't mar the stone.

Every two or three courses, lay bondstones that span the thickness of the wall to tie it together. Place these about 4 feet apart horizontally and about halfway up the wall (more often on higher walls).

Throwing mortar

You need not be gentle in applying mortar to stone. Load up the trowel and throw the mortar into the joint.

Tying wythes and filling gaps

Bondstones are longer and wider stones that tie the front and rear wythes together. You'll need one of these stones every 4 to 6 feet. From time to time, you may need to insert chinks to level the front edges of the stones.

Cut chinks from larger stone and shape them with a mason's hammer. Fill gaps in the center of the wall with similar small stones chipped from larger ones.

Planting a stone wall

Instead of trying to create perfect rock courses without gaps, put plants in the pockets. Crevices create a favorable environment for plants and may actually extend their hardiness zones. The rocks create a warmer environment for the plants than what exists out in the open—a perfect place for cascading plants and herbs.

Plant the crevices as you build the wall, lifting off the ill-fitting stone and filling the gap with loamy soil. Vary the size of the plants and the color assortment. You can use plants with large root systems, but be careful not to damage the roots.

Cutting thick stones

1 Mark the stone where you want it to fracture. With the stone on a soft surface such as grass or sand, score the top face of the stone with a stone chisel. Strike the chisel, moving it along the line.

2 Extend the marked line to the opposite face of the stone and score this line using the same techniques. (For thin stone, you can score just one face.)

3 Place the stone on solid material, such as a length of 2×4, making sure the scored line extends beyond the support. Then hit the unsupported section with a solid blow of a small sledgehammer. Not all stone will crack. If it doesn't, choose another and repeat the process.

WHAT IF...
You put the wrong stone in the wall?

If you put a stone in the wrong place or decide to select one that looks better, take up the stone and remove the mortar with a wet brush before repositioning it.

Pack and scrape

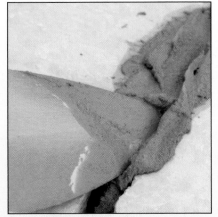

As you set the courses of the stone, pack mortar into the joints between them. Excess mortar will squeeze out of the joint—scrape it off with a pointing trowel. Sometimes it's easier to remove the mortar after it has begun to set.

Make thin joints

Keep the joints between courses as thin as possible—thin joints are stronger than thick ones. Joints in ashlar walls should be ½ to 1 inch thick.

WORKING WITH TILE

If you have an existing slab and it's in good shape, the right size, and in the right location, you can tile over it. If you don't have a slab, you'll need to pour one.

To tile an old slab, lay out tiles without mortar first to center the pattern so the edge tiles will be the same size. If you're tiling a new slab, plan the slab size so that it won't require any cut tiles.

In either case, use thinset mortar mixed with a latex additive—it is stronger than water-mixed thinset. Mix only as much thinset as you can use in half an hour. Use a drill with a ½-inch chuck equipped with a mixing blade and mix the mortar in a 5-gallon bucket. Mix thoroughly, let the mortar stand (slake) for 10 minutes, then mix it again. Work in sections small enough that you can lay all the tiles within a section before the mortar sets up.

When installing tiles, insert spacers to ensure even joints. Drop each tile in place, then give it a slight twist to ensure the thinset adheres at all points. Stand back every few minutes and inspect the joints. Make any adjustments to each section before the mortar starts to set.

WHAT IF...
The tile goes on a new slab?

If you're tiling a new slab, you can lay it out in such a way that you won't have to cut the edge tiles. This means the dimensions of your slab must be equal to a length of tiles and joints without cuts. On a flat area such as a driveway or garage floor, lay out tiles and spacers in lengths approximately the size of your proposed patio. Measure the lines in both directions. The measurements will become the dimensions of the slab. If the slab has control joints, place them so you can start the layout lines on the joints. That way tiles won't span a control joint, which could lead to breakage.

Laying out an existing slab

1 Prepare the surface of the slab, making any critical repairs *(pages 122–123)*. If the slab doesn't have control joints, mark the center by snapping chalk lines at the midpoints of opposite sides. If the slab has control joints, start your layout at Step 4. (See *page 128* for additional information)

2 Check the chalk lines for square using a 3-4-5 triangle *(page 75)*. Measure and mark 3 feet on one line and 4 feet on the other. If the diagonal distance between the two marks is 5 feet, your lines are square. If not, adjust the lines.

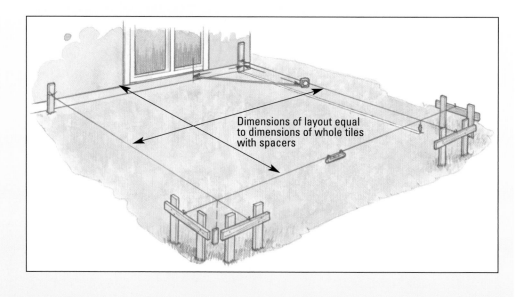

Dimensions of layout equal to dimensions of whole tiles with spacers

3 Adjust the lines until they are square by moving the chalk line slightly and resnapping the lines. If the diagonal measured more than 5 feet, move the line slightly clockwise with reference to the center point. If it was less than 5 feet, move it counterclockwise.

4 Dry-lay a row of tiles along both axes—from one end of the slab to the other. Adjust the lines of tiles until the edge tiles are at least half a tile wide and the same width. Repeat the adjustment on the other axis until you have even borders.

5 Measure from the chalked lines a distance equal to an even number of tiles and joints, and snap layout lines at these points in both directions. Use these lines as a layout grid for sections when you lay the tile. Snap additional lines if you need them to help keep your tiles straight.

STANLEY PRO TIP

Choose the right trowel

The size of the notches in the trowel you use determines the depth of the ridges made in the adhesive. Use a trowel whose notches form ridges that are about two-thirds the tile thickness.

For 6- to 8-inch floor tiles, use a ¼- to ⅜-inch square-notched trowel; for large tiles (more than 12 inches), use a deep (½-inch) square-notched trowel. Your tile retailer can recommend the right trowel.

To comb the adhesive so it forms ridges of the proper depth, you must hold the trowel at the correct angle (see box, *near right*). If you have trouble making ¼-inch ridges with a ¼-inch trowel, switch to a ⅜-inch notch and hold the trowel more perpendicular to the surface.

Combing the mortar

Pour enough mortar to cover a layout grid. Holding the straight edge of the trowel at about a 30-degree angle, spread the mortar evenly, about as thick as the depth of a trowel notch. Spread the mortar to the layout line and comb it with the notched edge at about a 45- to 75-degree angle.

Testing the mixture

Properly applied thinset forms ridges that compress to cover the entire back of the tile when it is embedded. If thinset is applied too wet, it won't hold these ridges. A dry thinset application won't compress and will result in the tile adhering to the top of the ridges only.

Test a thinset mixture by pulling up a tile and examining the back. If the thinset completely covers the surface as shown above, the mixture is correct.

Laying the tile

1 Spread thinset on the first layout grid on your slab up to, but not covering, the grid lines. Set the first tile on the grid lines and lower it into the mortar. Give it a slight twist. Continue laying the tiles and spacers, checking them as you go. If you need to straighten a tile that is out of reach, kneel on a 2-foot square of ¾-inch plywood to distribute your weight. Cut at least two pieces of plywood so you can position one while kneeling on the other.

2 Periodically check to make sure the tile conforms to the layout lines in both directions. Lay a long metal straightedge or 4-foot level on the edge of the tile. This edge should align itself with the layout lines. Each joint within the pattern should be straight as well. Scrape off any excess thinset that may have spread over a layout line. Adjust the tiles to straighten the joints, if necessary.

Setting spacers

When laying tiles, use plastic spacers to keep them spaced properly. Insert the spacers vertically in the joint after you set each tile. That way the tile will move into the correct placement after it is embedded in the mortar.

Once you reach a point where tiles form corners, flip down the spacer into the corner. Remove the spacers before grouting, even if the manufacturer's instructions indicate that you can leave them in place. Spacers may show through the grout.

Straight cuts with a wet saw

Set the tile securely against the fence with the cut line at the blade. Turn on the saw and feed the tile into the blade with light pressure. Increase the pressure as the saw cuts the tile and ease off as the blade approaches the rear of the cut. Keep the tile on the table at all times.

Leveling the tile

When you have finished laying one section or grid of tile and checked all the tiles for correct alignment, set your level on the surface and look for tiles that are higher or lower than the rest. Make a beater block out of a 12- to 15-inch 2×4 covered with scrap carpet. If a tile is high, tap it into place using the beater block and rubber mallet. If a tile is low, lift it out, back-butter the tile with thinset, then reset it.

Grouting

Let the mortar cure overnight. Then spread grout in one section at a time with a grout float, holding the float at an angle and forcing grout into the joints. Once you have grouted a section, hold the float almost perpendicular and scrape off the excess. Let the grout set and clean the surface as specified by the grout manufacturer. See *pages 136–137* for more about grouting.

Making curved cuts

1 Using a wet saw, make several relief cuts from the edge of the tile to the curved cut line. Relief cuts do not have to be exactly parallel to each other, but make sure they stop just short of the curved line.

2 Place the jaws of tile nippers about an inch away from the curved line and carefully snap out the waste at the relief cuts.

3 Working the nippers on the cut line, snap away the remaining excess. Don't try to bite through the tile with the nippers. Instead, grasp the tile with the tool and use a prying motion.

WORKING WITH STUCCO

One of the characteristics of stucco is that no two walls finished with it look exactly alike. Stucco allows you to create a one-of-a-kind surface. Applied properly, it will be maintenance-free for years.

Because it's a form of cement mortar, stucco dries to a gray color, but you can tint it by adding oxide pigment to the finish coat. To make white stucco, use white portland cement and white sand.

If you're going to stucco a house with siding, remove the siding and install felt paper and metal lath. To stucco a masonry wall, wire-brush any loose material and fill holes with patching concrete.

Some manufacturers recommend using a latex bonding agent so the first coat adheres more strongly to masonry. Be sure to use the bonding agent if it's recommended.

Apply the finish coat with a concrete finishing trowel, using long strokes. Keep the leading edge of the trowel only slightly raised for a uniformly smooth finish.

Trowel the scratch coat

1 Hold a batch of stucco on a hawk—a square platform with a handle on the bottom—and apply it to the wall with a square mason's trowel. Apply the mortar with an upsweeping motion, working from the bottom up. Spread the mortar on the wall to a consistent thickness of ⅜ to ½ inch. Work in sections. Apply stucco to each section of the wall in the same way, always starting from wet mortar. Once you begin a wall, always complete it to avoid start-and-stop lines (called cold joints).

STUCCO ON BLOCK

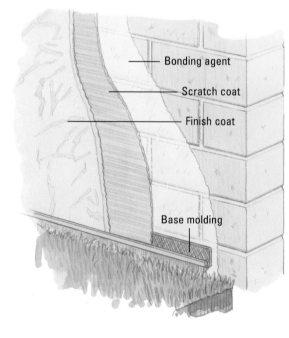

- Bonding agent
- Scratch coat
- Finish coat
- Base molding

WHAT IF...
The stucco goes on wood?

To apply stucco over plywood sheathing you'll need to give it something to grip onto. Staple 15-pound roofing felt to the sheathing, then cover it with metal lath. Cut the lath with aviation snips and fasten it with galvanized roofing nails. Lath has a top and a bottom. Install it so the metal vanes are angled up. Trowel on a ¼- to ½-inch coat of mortar, forcing it into the lath.

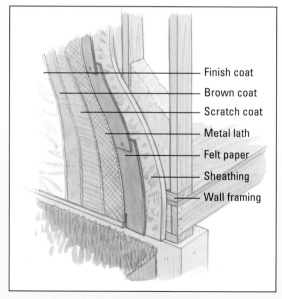

- Finish coat
- Brown coat
- Scratch coat
- Metal lath
- Felt paper
- Sheathing
- Wall framing

2 Allow the scratch coat (the first coat) to set up slightly, then ridge it with a plasterer's rake or a homemade scarifier, made by driving 4-penny galvanized nails through a 2-foot length of 2× stock at 1-inch intervals. Scratch the entire surface horizontally to a depth of about ⅛ inch.

Apply the brown coat

Let the scratch coat cure. If local codes allow, you can apply the next coat (the brown coat) while the mortar is still wet. If the mortar has cured, mist it lightly. Using a flat trowel, apply a ¼- to ⅜-inch-thick coat. Allow the stucco to cure for several days, misting the surface occasionally to slow the curing process. After it cures, apply the finish coat and texture it (see below and *page 67*).

Texturing the finish

When the brown coat has cured, apply the finish coat ⅛ to ¼ inch thick. Let it set up a little before you start any texturing.

Texture makes a more interesting surface. To start, experiment on an inconspicuous part of the wall to make sure you like the texture.

Begin texturing the finish coat as soon as it begins to set. Your texturing technique need not be complicated. You can create a coarse, uniform texture simply by making passes with a wood float. For a rougher finish, dab the stucco with a piece of carpeting that has a thick pile.

Textured or not, mist the finish coat frequently for several days in order to minimize cracking as it cures.

For a marbled look, push a stiff brush into the surface. Then flatten the high spots with a metal trowel, moving the tool back and forth in even strokes.

To get a spattered finish, load a paintbrush with stucco and strike it against a wood block, creating a stucco spray. To make the surface more uniform, spatter it again in an hour.

For an old-time overlayed finish, dab the stucco with a pointing trowel held flat on the surface. Pull up the trowel at an angle and twist it slightly to create edges across the surface.

SAND-SET & MORTARED PATIOS

This chapter includes step-by step instructions for building a variety of patios made with brick, stone, and tile, both those set in sand and those mortared to a slab. If you've completed your planning and are ready to build, turn to the pages for the type of patio you have chosen, and start building. If you haven't decided what kind of patio to build, browse each project to get an idea what each method involves.

If you're ready to build, schedule a delivery date for your materials, allowing plenty of time to prepare the site. That way the materials will not be in your way while you are laying out the site,

excavating, and building forms. With the site prepared, you can have materials dropped close to the work area rather than in your driveway, which would require you to move them again later.

If you do need to store materials, make the storage safe for both the materials and your neighbors. Store bags of concrete or mortar mix where they won't get wet; cover them if they're out in the open. Mark off a pile of flagstone with yellow construction tape so children and visitors won't stumble into it—a pallet stacked with stone looks very inviting to young children looking for a place to play. Keep brick and stone on the pallets, and

don't cut the steel bands until you're ready to lay the material. Also, don't leave an excavation without marking it: String fluorescent marking tape between rebar posts driven into the ground so it's immediately visible.

Consider the size of the project and recruit a crew of helpers if possible. This is especially important when pouring ready-mix concrete. Although you can take your time with concrete you mix yourself, ready-mix won't wait. Once the truck arrives, you have to get the concrete into the forms quickly. Above all, work safely. Use common sense, wear protective gear, and take your time.

CHAPTER PREVIEW

Brick-in-sand patio
page 112

Sand-set flagstone patio
page 118

Precast paver patio
page 120

Preparing an existing slab for mortar
page 122

Pouring a new concrete patio
page 124

Mortared brick patio
page 130

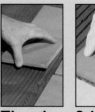

Mortared flagstone patio
page 132

Tile patio
page 134

Saltillo tile patio
page 138

Pouring a concrete landing pad
page 142

Building an outdoor kitchen
page 144

Pouring a concrete walk
page 146

Brick or precast-paver walks
page 150

Flagstone walks
page 154

Stepping-stone paths
page 156

Poured concrete steps
page 158

Steps with timbers and bricks
page 164

Finishing steps with mortared brick
page 168

Tiling outdoor steps
page 172

BRICK-IN-SAND PATIO

Abrick-in-sand patio is about the easiest patio to build. It requires just a few basic skills and minimum effort, and it's a job you can leave and pick up again according to the dictates of your time and family schedule. A mortared installation is not that flexible.

The key to a long-lasting sand-set installation is the quality of the bed. Most building codes require both a gravel subbase and a sand bed. Both of these materials should be installed in layers. Shovel in about half the gravel required, then tamp it thoroughly. Then shovel in the rest and tamp again. Use the same technique when laying the sand bed, but mist both layers of sand with a fine spray before tamping them.

No matter what size your patio, tamp it with a rented power tamper. Getting the tool to the work site requires some heavy lifting, but it is the best tool for the job. Some rental outlets will deliver such heavy items to you.

PRESTART CHECKLIST

☐ **TIME**
Several days to dig and lay a 10×10-foot patio

☐ **TOOLS**
Round-nose shovel, spade, line level, hose, carpenter's level, hammer, brick set, small sledgehammer, screed, circular saw with masonry blade, broom, rubber mallet, power tamper

☐ **SKILLS**
Measuring, leveling, laying out square lines, cutting bricks, setting bricks

☐ **PREP**
Lay out site and prepare sand bed

☐ **MATERIALS**
Bricks, bedding and mason's sand, gravel, landscape spikes, landscape fabric, edging, plywood for spacers

1 Lay out the site and prepare it for a sand bed as shown on *pages 86–87*. When you excavate, make sure the depth of the bed will leave the brick about 1 inch above grade. This will provide drainage and permit you to mow around the edges easily. Set in any edge restraints you're using *(pages 84–85)*, then lay the border brick in the pattern of your choice. Starting at one corner, lay the first row, spacing the bricks about ⅛ inch apart and keeping the courses straight with a mason's line.

TYPICAL BRICK-IN-SAND INSTALLATION

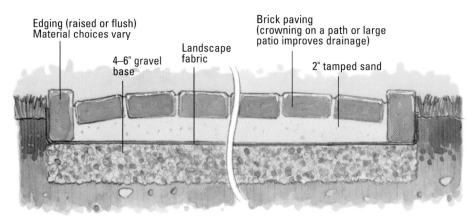

Edging (raised or flush)
Material choices vary

4–6" gravel base

Landscape fabric

Brick paving (crowning on a path or large patio improves drainage)

2" tamped sand

2 After laying six to eight units, bed the bricks in the sand bed, tapping them with a rubber mallet. As you progress across the site, use a slope gauge to make sure the surface will drain correctly. When you have to kneel on the laid bricks, use pieces of plywood to distribute your weight.

3 As you complete about a 4×4-foot section, lay a straightedge on the surface to make sure none of the bricks are too high or too low. Seat any high brick with the rubber mallet. If a unit is low, pull it out, add sand, and replace the brick. Continue laying bricks using the same techniques.

4 Once you've finished setting all the brick, spread out a thin layer of fine mason's sand over the surface. Put on enough to fill the joints ¼ inch deep. Using a soft-bristle broom, sweep the sand into the joints, but don't fill them completely. Mist the surface to bed the sand.

Staying the course(s)

Bricks and pavers are modular but may vary slightly in finished size. To keep the installation straight and the bricks at the same height, tie mason's line to two bricks and station them at opposite ends of the site. Pull the brick until the line is tight, and use the line as a guide.

BED THE SAND
A solid surface takes time

You'll bed the sand a little at a time. After the first sweeping, mist the surface and sweep in more sand. Repeat this process until the joints are full. Filling the joints gradually and misting them between layers creates a virtually immovable surface.

STANLEY PRO TIP

A weighty decision

Before you take the family car to pick up your bricks, calculate their weight. One standard brick weighs about 5 pounds. It takes 4½ bricks to lay a square foot, or 450 per 100 square feet, and at 5 pounds a brick, your 10×10-foot patio (100 square feet) will weigh about 2,250 pounds—more than a ton, and more than your car, or even a small pickup, can carry.

On the other hand, a lift of bricks (the quantity in which they are shipped) contains 500 bricks—just enough for a 10×10-foot patio, including some extra for waste. If you order a lift from a distributor, you might be able to arrange free delivery.

Setting a running bond pattern

1 Prepare the site for a sand bed as shown on *pages 86–87*. When you excavate, make sure the depth of the bed will leave the brick about 1 inch above grade. Set any edge restraints and border pavers. Tie mason's line to two pavers and set them at the beginning and end of the first course.

2 Using the mason's line as a guide, lay the first row. Cut pieces of ⅛-inch plywood for spacers, moving them as you go. Start the next row with a half brick to offset the joints and alternate half and full starter bricks on the remaining rows. Using the techniques illustrated on *page 113,* set the brick with a rubber mallet, level the surface, and finish with swept sand.

RUNNING BOND PATTERN

A running bond is often called a two-over-one pattern because all the joints are offset by a half brick. This means that every other row starts with a cut brick. Plywood spacers keep the joints straight and even.

WHAT IF…
You have many bricks to cut?

Even a 10×10-foot patio requires 30 half bricks on alternating rows. Scoring 30 bricks with a brick set and splitting them will take a substantial amount of time and effort. Instead rent a wet saw to cut the bricks more quickly.

Clamp several bricks with pipe clamps and mark them at their midpoint using a framing square *(page 94).* Unclamp the brick and set each one on the saw table. Start the saw and push the brick into the blade.

Setting a basket-weave pattern

1 Prepare the sand bed and install edging. Snap a chalk line at the midpoint of the sand bed. Set the first brick in place against the edging, abutting the centerline. Lay six bricks in a basket-weave pattern on each side of the line. (See *page 94* for an alternate setting order.)

2 Before you finish the first row, start the second row on the centerline, reversing the pattern and keeping the bricks spaced with ⅛-inch plywood spacers. In this row, lay four bricks on each side of the line.

3 In the third row, lay only two bricks on each side of the centerline, reversing the pattern. This will create a stepped pyramid pattern, which keeps subsequent bricks aligned and square.

4 For each subsequent row, work up the sides of the pyramid until you reach the edge restraints on the other side of the patio. At the edges, cut the brick to fit between those already laid and the edge restraints. Continue laying in a stepped pattern, and finish the site with swept sand.

BASKET-WEAVE PATTERN

If you lay out your site so its dimensions correspond to the dimensions of whole brick, you won't have any brick to cut.

Setting a parallel herringbone pattern

1 When you lay out the site, either set its interior dimensions (inside the border brick) to correspond to the dimensions of the pattern or install edge restraints and the borders on two adjacent legs only. When you reach the other side, you can lay the last brick and borders, then the edge restraints. Spread brick along the site so they're readily at hand as you lay the pattern. Starting at one corner, lay a pair of full bricks at right angles, then a half brick next to each full brick. (See *page 94* for alternate bond patterns.)

2 Inside the first legs of brick, lay two full brick at right angles and two full brick perpendicular at their ends. Once you've laid a leg of the pattern, bed the brick with a rubber mallet.

PARALLEL HERRINGBONE PATTERN

A herringbone pattern is fancier than a running bond and creates a stunning effect. It looks more difficult to lay than less complicated patterns, but the job goes quickly once you establish a rhythm for laying the bricks. You'll have to cut many bricks, so plan to rent a wet saw. This pattern works only when the real, not nominal, length of the brick is twice the real width.

3 Continue laying stepped legs, spacing them as necessary and bedding them with a rubber mallet. Check the surface for units that may be too high or low and correct them. Then sweep sand into the joints, alternately misting and sweeping until the joints are full *(page 113)*.

Setting a herringbone on the diagonal

1 To gauge the starting point of the pattern, mark a 45-degree angle on the corner of one brick. Then set out nine bricks. Line up the leading corners of the brick with a straightedge. Then measure the distance between the 45-degree line and the straightedge, and note it.

2 Using the measurement from Step 1, stake a line inside and parallel to the edge restraints. Lay the first two bricks so the outside corner of one and the inside corner of the other fall on the line. Lay two more bricks and square them.

3 Continue laying bricks on this starter row, making sure their inside and outside corners are lined up as in Step 2. Continue the starter row to the other end of the site.

DIAGONAL HERRINGBONE PATTERN

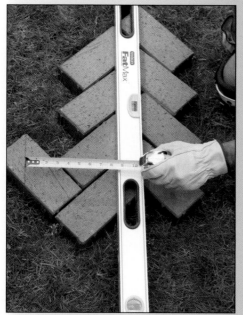

A diagonal herringbone pattern is one of the most difficult to lay, not so much because the pattern itself is complicated, but because it's difficult to keep the units properly in line. It requires a substantial amount of cutting to fit into a rectangular space.

4 Starting at the beginning of the starter row, lay the second brick of this row against one leg of the starter row, then lay the first brick against the edge restraint. Lay the remaining bricks in this row; do not lay the next row until you finish this row.

5 After you've laid two more single rows as in Step 4, stretch a line along the corners. They should line up. Reposition them if they don't. Continue laying and checking the bricks, then cut bricks to fit the edges and finish the site with sand.

SAND-SET FLAGSTONE PATIO

A flagstone patio lends its rough-hewn character and country quality to an outdoor design, and looks at home in almost any landscape.

One aspect of its construction sets it apart from other materials—its pattern. No two flagstone installations are the same because of the variety of the stone. Your best bet is to dry-lay the stone on the grass beside the site, selecting pieces from the pile and moving them around until the pattern satisfies you.

Purchase a variety of sizes and shapes. An entire site set with flagstones of approximately the same size looks unnatural. A variety also provides options when you're looking for the right stone to fill a space.

When you lay out your trial pattern, try to set stones with corresponding outlines next to each other—concave next to convex. Cut them if necessary (*page 103*).

Stonework is not easy. Work slowly and make breaks part of the schedule.

PRESTART CHECKLIST

☐ **TIME**
About 8 to 12 hours to excavate and set a 10×10-foot patio

☐ **TOOLS**
Round-nose shovel, rototiller, spade, garden rake, 2×4 lumber, small sledgehammer, power tamper, rubber mallet, brick set, soft broom, garden hose, carpenter's pencil

☐ **SKILLS**
Cutting stone, laying stone, laying out square lines

☐ **PREP**
Prepare site

☐ **MATERIALS**
Stones, bedding sand, mason's sand, gravel, landscape fabric

1 Lay out and prepare the site *(pages 86–87)*. To set stone paving for the best visual effect, lay out the stones next to the patio site. This leaves the bed undisturbed and gives you more working room. Start with large stones on the perimeter and fill in with smaller stones, cutting to fit or for the best aesthetic effect.

2 Once you devise an attractive layout, place the stones in the same relative positions on the sand bed, keeping the joints about ½ inch wide. Bed the stones with a rubber mallet. To work with your weight on the surface, kneel on a 2-foot plywood square.

TYPICAL SAND-SET FLAGSTONE INSTALLATION

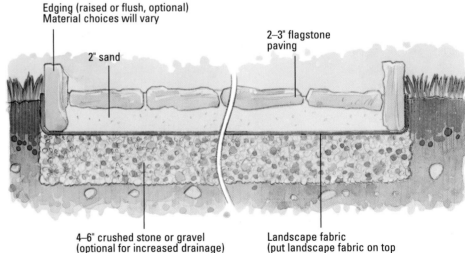

Edging (raised or flush, optional)
Material choices will vary

2" sand

2–3" flagstone paving

4–6" crushed stone or gravel (optional for increased drainage)

Landscape fabric (put landscape fabric on top of gravel if not using crushed-stone base)

3 After setting a 6-foot square, use a straightedge or level to check the stones for level. If a stone is too high, pick it up and dig out sand beneath it. Add sand to raise low stones. Test each stone to make sure it doesn't rock.

4 **(Option A)** If you want to put low-growing plants between the stones, shovel soil into the joints. Spray the surface to clean it and wash the excess soil into the joints. Fill in low spots, spray again, and repeat until the soil is about $\frac{1}{8}$ inch below the edges. Plant the gaps with grass, moss, or a groundcover to discourage weeds.

4 **(Option B)** You can finish the patio with sand. Spread a thin layer of sand on the stones and sweep it into the joints with a soft-bristle broom. Mist the surface and sweep in more sand. Repeat misting and sweeping in sand until the sand in the joints is level with the stones.

WHAT IF...
You're installing cut stone?

Cut stone is a formal version of flagstone—the same stone with the edges cut square and straight. Use it to create a far more symmetrical effect than standard flagstone, but the methods for installing it are virtually the same. The stones are not uniform in size, so make a trial layout beside the site to determine the most pleasing arrangement. Cut stone looks best with tight joints; space the stones about $\frac{1}{8}$ inch apart, using plywood spacers to keep the lines consistent. Finish the joints with fine sand.

STANLEY PRO TIP

Designing patterns

Flagstone is natural and informal looking, so it might seem you could set the stones randomly and have a gorgeous patio. That isn't the case, however. If you don't take care in planning a layout, a flagstone surface can look busy, complicated, and far too random.

The trick to laying a professional-looking flagstone surface is to keep the gaps between stones consistent. Test the gaps with a scrap piece of wood; a piece of $\frac{1}{2}$-inch plywood works well.

Mix the sizes of the flagstones. Before you start laying out the job, make piles of small, medium, and large stones. Select from the piles alternately so you won't end up with all small stones in one corner of the patio and all large ones in another.

Move stones around until you have a pleasing pattern. You may have to cut some stone for the best pattern and to make consistent joints.

PRECAST PAVER PATIO

Precast concrete pavers fall into three categories: rectangular, multiweave, and keyed. Almost all concrete pavers are cast with lugs that space them for a sand-set installation. Most manufacturers sell half pavers so you won't have to cut your own. They cost more but are worth the cutting time saved.

Rectangular pavers install the same way bricks do *(pages 112–117)*. Multiweave and keyed pavers require different techniques.

Multiweave pavers have sinuous edges that fit against one another. For many patterns, they make installation easier, though the edges are hard to square with a straightedge. Any pattern that works for rectangular pavers works for multiweave pavers. The sinuous edges imply a more intricate pattern.

You can install multiweave pavers using the open-field method: Install edging on two adjacent sides and lay the pavers to either meet or go past your layout lines on the opposite sides. Snap lines on the pavers and cut them before installing edging.

PRESTART CHECKLIST

☐ **TIME**
At least 2 days to lay out, excavate, and lay pavers for a 10×10-foot patio

☐ **TOOLS**
Round-nose shovel, rototiller, spade, garden rake, 2×4 lumber, small sledgehammer, power tamper, rubber mallet, brick set, soft broom, garden hose, carpenter's pencil, wet saw

☐ **SKILLS**
Cutting stone, laying stone, laying out square lines

☐ **PREP**
Prepare site

☐ **MATERIALS**
Pavers, bedding sand, mason's sand, gravel, landscape fabric

Installing perpendicular keys

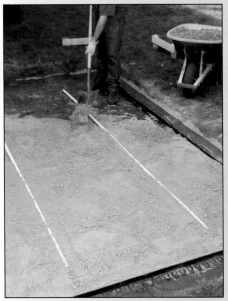

1 Lay out the site and excavate it so the final paver height will be about an inch above grade. Prepare the sand bed as shown on *pages 86–87*. Install edge restraints on two adjacent sides only.

2 Starting in the corner, lay border pavers or other border material of your choice. Lay the border against the edge restraints. Cut two octagonal pavers and set them next to each other in the corner, with their keys pointing in opposite directions.

TYPICAL SAND-SET PAVER INSTALLATION

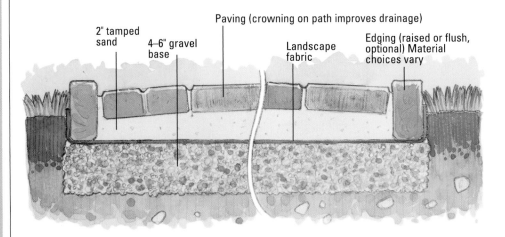

2" tamped sand

4–6" gravel base

Paving (crowning on path improves drainage)

Landscape fabric

Edging (raised or flush, optional) Material choices vary

Installing diagonal keys

3 Cut the key of the third paver and install it. Then install the fourth cut paver and set it. What you are doing is creating a second border of cut pavers and filling in diagonally across the surface with full pavers. Continue laying cut pavers and full pavers diagonally between them, with alternating keys in opposite directions.

4 Continue laying pavers until you have filled the site. Snap chalk lines on the surface of the pavers at the other sides. Remove each marked paver, cut it with a wet saw, and reinstall it. Install the border on these edges and the edging, then sweep the surface with sand.

Lay out a row of pavers on a flat surface and measure the dimensions of the row from one edge to the cut line opposite. Set up edge restraints on all four sides at this distance. Lay the pavers, cutting the keys on the opposite side. Insert corner blocks and sweep with sand.

The shape is a key

Octagonal pavers are really key shapes. A square key extends from the octagon. Laying these pavers requires a lot of cutting. Use the open-field method. Some manufacturers make half pavers that simplify trimming.

Working with multiweave patterns

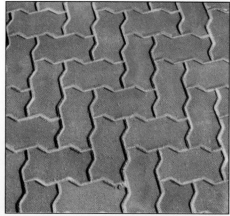

Alternate basket-weave pattern. This is another pattern that works best when the site size equals some multiple of the brick dimensions. If it's any less, you'll have to trim many blocks to fit along the edge.

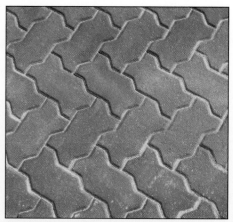

Diagonal herringbone is another pattern that works well with the open-field method. Such an installation requires many cuts.

PREPARING AN EXISTING SLAB FOR MORTAR

It's easy to mortar a concrete patio or walkway that is solid, smooth, and level. If you plan to mortar your present slab, check its condition before you start the job.

First check for large cracks and sagging sections. If you find such conditions, the base is not adequate—you'll need to remove the slab and pour a new one.

Even if your present slab appears to be good, you need to make sure it will stay that way. Dig along the perimeter of the slab and look for a 4-inch gravel base and 3 to 4 inches of concrete. If an adequate subbase is present, check the surface for drainage. A slab must slope at least 1 inch for every 4 feet and should not contain spots higher than 1/8 inch in 10 feet.

A surface crowned in the center for drainage will work as long as the crowning is gradual. You can repair minor holes or flaking with the techniques shown.

PRESTART CHECKLIST

☐ **TIME**
From 30 to 45 minutes per square yard

☐ **TOOLS**
Repair surface: level, hammer, cold chisel, trowels, grinder, vacuum cleaner, sanding block, brush
Repair structural defects: sledgehammer, crowbar, wheelbarrow, rented concrete saw or jackhammer

☐ **SKILLS**
Leveling, troweling, grinding

☐ **MATERIALS**
Repair surface: hydraulic cement, thinset, self-leveling compound
Repair structural defects: gravel, reinforcing wire, epoxy bonding agent, concrete mix, 2×4 lumber

1 Working in 6-foot-square sections, check the surface with a 4-foot level. Mark any cracks, high spots, and other defects with a carpenter's pencil. Cracks may be a sign of structural problems. Some may be repairable. Others may require professional help.

2 Use a small sledge and a cold chisel to open small cracks so you can fill them. Angle the chisel into each side of the crack to create a recess wider at the bottom than the top. Doing so helps hold the patching cement more securely.

TYPICAL OUTDOOR SLAB CONSTRUCTION

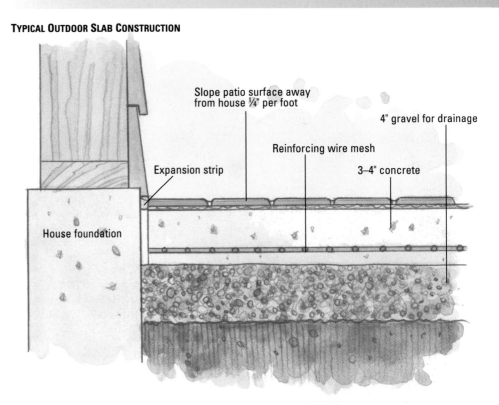

Slope patio surface away from house 1/4" per foot

4" gravel for drainage

Reinforcing wire mesh

Expansion strip

3–4" concrete

House foundation

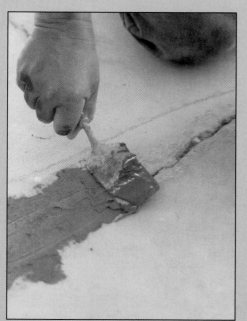

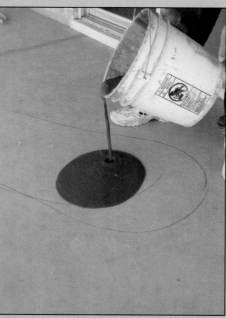

3 Wash out the crack with water and fill it with quick-setting hydraulic cement or thinset. Use a margin trowel or mason's trowel to feather out the edges until the patch is level with the surrounding surface. When the patch has cured, install an isolation membrane.

4 To fill depressions in the slab, pour a small amount of self-leveling compound into the depression or trowel on a skim coat of thinset. Add thinset or compound until the surface is level. If you're using thinset, feather the edges even with the floor. Self-leveling compound will do this on its own.

5 Grind down high spots with an angle grinder fitted with a masonry-grit abrasive wheel. Hold a vacuum cleaner hose near the grinder to remove the dust as you work. Vacuum and damp-mop the surface thoroughly.

STANLEY PRO TIP

Repair damaged edges

If a slab has extensive edge damage, chip away the loose concrete, then clean and wet the edge. Set a 2× form that extends about 1 inch above the surface against the edge. Fill the damaged area with fresh concrete, smooth it, and let it cure.

Cutting control joints

Slabs wider than 8 feet require control joints to prevent the slab from cracking. If an existing slab has no control joints, snap chalk lines at 8-foot intervals, perpendicular to the edges. Cut control joints ¾ inch deep with a concrete saw (you can rent one). After setting the tile, fill the joint with foam backer rod (page 135).

WHAT IF...
You have to remove a slab?

If your existing patio slab is not good enough, you'll have to remove it. You'll need at least a 10-pound sledgehammer—heavier is better, if you can handle it—and crowbars. If the slab is thicker than 4 inches or you have a large area to remove, rent a masonry saw or jackhammer.

Start at a corner and crack small sections. Pry out the section with a crowbar and carry it away in a wheelbarrow.

Work your way across the surface, cracking and prying. Let the crowbar do most of the work—it's easier to pry up concrete than to pound it into smaller pieces. For a large slab, rent a roll-off refuse container for the rubble.

POURING A NEW CONCRETE PATIO

The first step in installing a slab for a mortared patio is laying out its perimeter. For small jobs, such as a pad for a new barbecue, use an uncut sheet of plywood to mark and square the corners. Anything larger than 4×8 feet calls for batterboards *(pages 74–75)*. After you've laid out the site, cut the batterboards into kickers for the forms.

Plan for drainage before you pour a slab. Slope the surface 1 inch every 4 feet. Let the runoff pour into a mulched flower bed or shrub border. You also can dig a trench around the slab and fill it with gravel. For really wet sites, embed a perforated drainpipe in the trench *(pages 82–83)*.

When you reset the lines for the excavation in Step 4, set their intersections to fall on the inside or outside edge of the forms. When you make the forms, make sure you set the 2× stock on the correct side of the stakes.

PRESTART CHECKLIST

☐ **TIME**
About 15 hours for a 10×10-foot patio

☐ **TOOLS**
Shovels, rototiller, plumb bob, tape measure, power tamper, 4-foot level, hammer, small sledgehammer, trowels, screed, hand float, edger, broom, pliers, wheelbarrow, mortar box, cordless drill

☐ **SKILLS**
Measuring, cutting, assembling forms, excavating, laying tile

☐ **PREP**
Lay out site on a dimensional plan

☐ **MATERIALS**
Gravel, 1× and 2× lumber, nails, decking screws, concrete, expansion joint material, reinforcing wire mesh, dobies, tie wire, plastic tarp

Laying out and excavating the site

1 Set temporary stakes about a foot out from the corners of the slab and drive batterboards 3 to 4 feet beyond the stakes. Tie mason's lines to the crosspieces so they intersect at the dimensions of the slab plus a foot on each side. Then square the site with a 3-4-5 triangle *(page 75)*.

2 At each corner, suspend a plumb bob at the intersection of the mason's lines (hardly touching). Move the temporary stakes to the spot where the point of the plumb bob comes to rest. These points represent the outside corners of the excavation.

WHAT IF...
You can't drive batterboards close to the house?

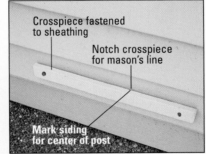

Crosspiece fastened to sheathing

Notch crosspiece for mason's line

Mark siding for center of post

If you can't drive batterboards close to the house, attach a crosspiece to the siding. Notch the back edge of the crosspiece so you can wrap the mason's line around it. Fasten the crosspiece securely with screws that penetrate the sheathing. For masonry, use self-tapping masonry screws. Caulk the holes when you remove the piece.

Laying out a small job

To lay out a small project, such as a concrete landing pad for stairs, you can use the corners of a 4×8-foot sheet of plywood instead of batterboards. Make sure the plywood is square to the rest of the site, then drive landscape spikes at the corners.

3 Remove the mason's lines from the batterboards, and tie a line between the stakes at ground level. Mark the ground along the line with powdered chalk or upside-down spray paint. Remove the lines from the stakes to get them out of your way, and take up the sod. Push the shovel about 2 inches under the roots to dislodge them. Store the sod in the shade for later use or replant it.

4 Retie the mason's lines to the batterboards so they intersect at the dimensions of the slab or at a point 1½ inches out on each side (to allow for the thickness of the forms). Excavate the perimeter of the site to the depth required for your materials; use a slope gauge to slope the site for drainage. Then excavate the remainder of the site, keeping its depth the same as the perimeter excavation.

Marking the patio height

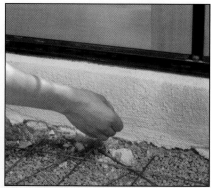

If the patio will abut the house, snap a chalk line under the door at the level of the patio surface. Put it about 1 to 3 inches below the threshold to keep snow and rain out of the interior. Remember to include the thickness of the surface covering. Use this line to set the excavation depth along the house.

STANLEY PRO TIP

Loosen the soil

Excavating a patio is easier if you loosen the soil with a rototiller before you dig.

Remove the sod first, then set the tiller to the depth of the substrate and tile. Take a couple of passes across the site with the tiller and remove the soil with a shovel.

USE A SLOPE GAUGE
Slope surfaces for drainage

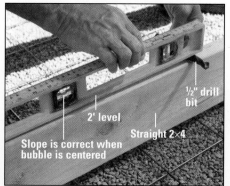

½" drill bit

2' level

Straight 2×4

Slope is correct when bubble is centered

All hardscape surfaces must slope slightly to allow rainwater to run off. A slope of 1 inch every 4 feet is all you need. A homemade slope gauge like the one shown above helps slope the site correctly. Set the gauge on the soil periodically as you dig and adjust the excavation to keep the bubble level.

Preparing the base

Set stakes 1" below top of forms to avoid interfering with screed

Form slopes 1" every 4 linear feet

Dobie supports reinforcing wire

Install kickers every 4 feet

1 Pound stakes into the soil at the corners and every 2 to 4 feet. Then set the forms using 2×s with the inside or outside edge directly under the mason's line (depending on how you set up the stakes). Assemble the forms with deck screws, splicing sections with plywood cleats.

2 To slope the forms, use the slope gauge or start at the house and measure the distance from the top of the form to the mason's line. Then measure at the lower edge of the form. Adjust the forms until the lower measurement is an inch less for every 4 feet of length.

3 Spread a gravel base, then pack it with a power tamper until the surface is smooth, solid, and consistently 4 inches thick. Lay 6×6-inch 10/10 reinforcing wire mesh on 2-inch dobies, overlapping the ends of the wire by 4 inches and tying the dobies to it.

Pouring a large patio

Temporary screed guides

A patio larger than 8×8 feet is difficult to pour and screed all in one shot. Simplify the job by dividing the area into sections and installing temporary screed guides to partition the work.

WHAT IF…
Codes require a footing?

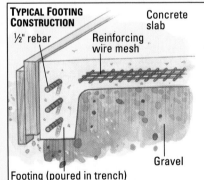

TYPICAL FOOTING CONSTRUCTION

Concrete slab

½" rebar

Reinforcing wire mesh

Gravel

Footing (poured in trench)

Some patio installations (especially those including a wall) may require a footing on the perimeter of the slab. Footings are extra-thick sections of concrete reinforced with rebar. Dig the footing trench at the same time you excavate the site, and pour the footing and slab at the same time.

TYING THE DOBIES

You can lay reinforcing wire on dobies and leave it untied, but tying it down will keep the wire at the right level. Wrap the bottom of the dobie with soft stove wire and twist it snug with pliers. You can also use wire supports, sometimes called chairs, to hold up reinforcing wire.

Making the pour

Put next load of concrete where previous load ends

1 Start pouring in the corner farthest from the truck or mixing site. Fill the excavation to the top of the forms and push concrete into the edges of the site. Don't throw the mix. Then consolidate, or settle, it by working a shovel or 2×4 up and down in it. You may have to recenter the wire mesh with a garden rake. Add the next load of concrete as soon as you've spread the first one. Pour it where the first load ends.

2 Level the concrete with the top of the forms using a long, straight 2×4 or steel stud as a screed. With one person at each end of the board, pull it along the top of the forms with a side-to-side sawing motion. If there are humps in the surface of the concrete after the first pass, screed again. Fill low spots with concrete; then screed again. Remove any temporary guides, shovel concrete into the cavity they leave behind, and screed once more.

Mixing your own concrete

If the site is 10×10 feet or smaller, it might be cost efficient to mix your own concrete from dry ingredients. Here's a recipe.
- 1 part portland cement
- 2 parts sand
- 3 parts gravel or aggregate
- ½ part water

Combine the dry ingredients in a mortar box or wheelbarrow and stir in the water a little at a time.

The moisture in the sand and the atmospheric humidity will affect how much water you need to add. To test the sand, squeeze a handful, then relax your hand. If the mix holds together, add just ½ part water. If it crumbles or leaves your hand wet, use less water. An ideal consistency resembles thick malted milk.

STANLEY PRO TIP

Handling a concrete pour

- A wheelbarrow is a valuable concrete tool. Protect your yard from wheel ruts with a ramp of 2×12s.
- If your concrete forms will be permanent, use redwood or cedar or pressure-treated lumber rated for ground contact. Cover the top edges with duct tape to protect them from concrete stains.
- If the forms for your patio slab will be temporary, coat the inside edges with a releasing agent so you can pull the forms away after the concrete has cured.
- Don't pour new concrete against concrete that has already set up. Doing so creates a cold joint, which fractures easily.

Concrete additives

Plain, unmodified concrete works well in moderate weather, but extremely hot and cold temperatures can make a mix unworkable and cause it to cure improperly. Engineers have developed additives for less-than-perfect weather.
- Air bubbles (air entrainment) in the mix helps keep concrete from freezing when pouring in extreme cold.
- Accelerators help concrete set up faster in cold weather.
- Retardants slow the curing process when the weather gets too hot.
- Water reducers make the mix more workable, reducing time and labor on large jobs.

Finishing the surface

1 For small areas that you can reach from the edges of the slab, use a hand float or a darby that extends your reach about 2 feet. Hold the darby flat as you move it across the surface in wide arcs. Then tilt it slightly and work in straight pulls. If you have to work on the surface, spread your weight with 2×2-foot pieces of plywood. While one or more people float a section, have the finisher work right behind them.

2 Cut control joints every 8 feet by sliding the side of an edger along a guide board (1× or 2× stock that's as long as the surface you're jointing and fastened to the forms at either end). Don't try to cut a control joint without a guide; the joint will look sloppy. Slightly tip up the leading edge of the tool as you move it forward and back. The desired depth of the control joints is about 20 percent of the thickness of the concrete (for example, ¾ inch on a 4-inch slab).

CONTROL JOINTS
Match grout lines to control joints

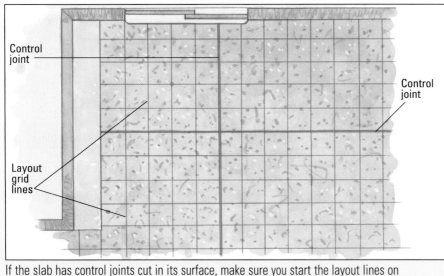

Control joint

Control joint

Layout grid lines

If the slab has control joints cut in its surface, make sure you start the layout lines on the control joints. That way you'll know a grout joint and not a tile, brick, or stone falls on a control joint.

WHAT IF...
The site is too large to float with a darby?

For any site too large to float with a darby, use a bull float—a smooth board or plate attached with a swivel joint to a long handle. Push the float away from you with the leading edge slightly raised so it doesn't dig into the concrete. Pull it back in the same manner. Overlap each pass until you've gone over the entire surface.

Curing the slab

3 If you're preparing the new slab for mortared tile, brick, or stone, give it a slight tooth to increase the adhesion of the mortar. Brooming the surface is a good way to do that. First trowel the concrete; then drag a dampened, stiff garage broom across it. After brooming the surface, you may need to touch up the edges and control joints.

Cover the concrete with plastic so it cures properly. Use black plastic only in cool weather—it absorbs heat from the sun. Weight the edges and seams with stones or boards. If you are able to attend to your slab regularly, it is better to sprinkle it with water occasionally than to cover it. Cover the slab with old blankets or burlap and keep them wet. Don't use a curing agent—most mortars will not stick to treated concrete. Snap layout lines when the slab has cured.

When to begin the final finish

Wait until the sheen of water on the concrete's surface disappears before you attempt to broom-finish the slab. As a test, step on the surface—your foot should leave an impression no deeper than ¼ inch. Finishing a slab while water remains on the surface risks concrete that is dusty, that spalls, or that has other problems after it cures.

   Evaporation can take minutes in hot, dry weather or more than an hour when it's damp and cool. If you notice that the concrete is beginning to set up before the sheen has disappeared, sweep off the water with a push broom, soak it up with burlap, or drag the surface of the concrete with a length of hose. Whichever method you use, don't step on wet concrete.

Release the forms

Concrete sticks to untreated wood like glue, and even with a release agent, the forms are hard to remove. As soon as you have floated a section, separate the concrete from the forms by slipping a mason's trowel between the two and drawing it along the form.

WHAT IF...
You're tiling a pool deck?

If you're tiling the deck around a swimming pool, have a pool contractor tile the pool's interior and cope the edge. Tiling the deck, however, is a good do-it-yourself project. Follow the steps for tiling a patio, with only a couple of adjustments. First wait until the pool is installed and tiled before starting the slab. Then make sure the excavation is deep enough for the gravel base and slab; the deck tile should be flush with the edge tiles. The finished deck should slope at least 1 inch per foot away from the pool.

   Install an expansion strip around the edge of the pool and build forms, setting the perimeter forms about ¾ inch higher than the yard or allowing for a finished cap tile to keep soil from backwashing onto the deck.

MORTARED BRICK PATIO

When mortaring brick on a patio, one of the first questions is where to start laying the brick. The answer depends on the pattern you intend to use, whether your slab is the same size as a multiple of whole brick, and whether the slab has control joints.

If the slab is the same size as a multiple of whole bricks (including mortar joints) lay the border first, then start setting brick at the border, as shown on these pages. If the slab has control joints, start along the control joints and work toward the edges.

Joint width depends on the relation of the brick's actual size to its nominal size. Generally if the actual size of a brick is ½ inch shorter than its nominal size, you'll make ½-inch joints. If it's shorter by ⅜ inch, you'll space the bricks at ⅜ inch. You can adjust spacing for aesthetics. Cut plywood of the desired thickness for spacers.

PRESTART CHECKLIST

☐ **TIME**
About 10 hours to 2 days to lay an 8×10-foot patio

☐ **TOOLS**
Layout tools plus mason's line, 3-pound sledgehammer, mixing tub, mason's trowel, rubber mallet, circular saw and masonry blade, brick set, mortar bag, striking tool, cordless drill

☐ **SKILLS**
Laying out square lines, excavating, basic masonry skills

☐ **PREP**
Lay out and prepare site

☐ **MATERIALS**
2× lumber, gravel, deck screws, mortar, bricks

Guide brick with mason's line.

1 Start the installation by setting the edging material of your choice *(pages 84–85)*. Then trowel a ½-inch coat of mortar on about a 4×4-foot section of the slab and comb it with the notched edge of the trowel. Apply only the amount of mortar you can use before it sets up.

2 Tie mason's line to two bricks and set them outside the site, with the line pulled tight and parallel to the border. Use the line to guide your installation, repositioning it at least every three or four courses. Set each brick in the mortar with a slight twist, lining it up with previous bricks.

MORTARED BRICK INSTALLATION

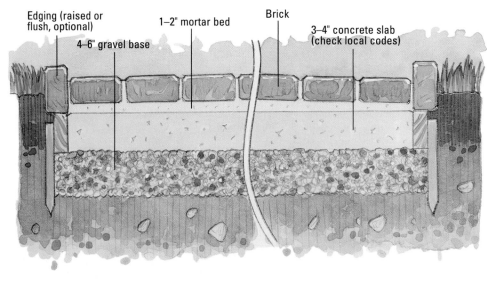

Edging (raised or flush, optional)

4–6" gravel base

1–2" mortar bed

Brick

3–4" concrete slab (check local codes)

3 As you lay each brick, set a short piece of 2×4 on it and tap it with a rubber mallet. Check each row with a straightedge, to make sure all the surfaces are on the same plane. Pull up low bricks, back-butter them with additional mortar, then reset them. Reseat those that are too high by tapping them with the mallet again. Before spreading the next section of mortar, recheck the section you've just completed.

4 After you've set the entire surface, let the mortar cure. Then go back and fill the joints with mortar, squeezing them full with a mortar bag. (You can mortar the brick with a trowel, but you might get more mortar on the bricks than between them.) Shape the joints with a striking tool.

WHAT IF...
You're mortaring borders to the slab?

If you're mortaring your borders to the surface of the slab instead of setting them on the side of the patio, build forms to contain them. On a new slab, remove the slab forms and reset them ½ inch higher than the surface. This small edge will keep the border material in place. For an existing slab, dig a trench around the slab and install new forms.

5 Let the mortar set up a bit, then lift off any excess from the surface with a pointing trowel. As a final cleanup, scrub off remaining mortar with a piece of wet burlap. Let the mortar cure for three days to a week before using the patio.

MORTARED FLAGSTONE PATIO

Flagstone is fractured or cleft into flat slabs of various lengths, 2 inches or more thick, with random edges. The flagstone most commonly used for patios includes bluestone, limestone, redstone, sandstone, granite, and slate. Irregular shapes suit flagstone to both casual free-form and formal geometric design schemes.

Cut stone is flagstone finished with straight edges and square corners. It ranges in size from about 1 foot to 4 feet across and comes in different thicknesses.

Whatever type of flagstone you choose must be at least 2 inches thick to avoid breakage. A ton of stone covers about 120 square feet; order 5 percent more for breakage. Large stones cover a surface more quickly than smaller pieces but may prove harder to move, cut, and design.

Unlike ceramic tile, you can set flagstone in a sand base. A mortared installation, however, will give you years of maintenance-free service. A mortared patio requires a slab to provide a solid base. Cleft stone installations require an exterior mortar, generally Type M (which has high compressive strength) or Type S (high lateral strength).

PRESTART CHECKLIST

☐ **TIME**
About 16 to 20 hours for a 10×10-foot patio, not counting slab installation

☐ **TOOLS**
Hammer, small sledgehammer, brick set, carpenter's pencil, mason's trowel, rubber mallet, mortar box, sponge, shovel, mortar bag, height gauge

☐ **SKILLS**
Troweling mortar and setting flagstone, using a mortar bag, cutting stone

☐ **PREP**
Install new slab or repair an existing one

☐ **MATERIALS**
Flagstone, mortar, 2× lumber

Setting the stone

1 Lay out your pattern as you would for a sand-set patio *(pages 118–119)*. Mix enough mortar for about a 3×3-foot section, and trowel a 1-inch thickness on the slab. Then lift your stones from your trial run and set them in the mortar in the same pattern.

2 Set the larger stones first, keeping them in the pattern and using a height gauge to set them at consistent height. Push the stones down; don't slide them. Fill voids with smaller stones, cutting the stones to fit and leveling them with a rubber mallet.

TYPICAL MORTARED FLAGSTONE INSTALLATION

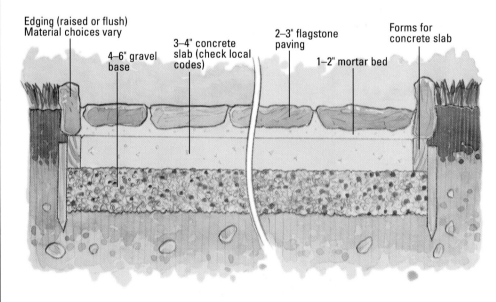

Edging (raised or flush) Material choices vary

4–6" gravel base

3–4" concrete slab (check local codes)

2–3" flagstone paving

1–2" mortar bed

Forms for concrete slab

3 Check the stones for level—pull out low stones, add mortar, and reset them. Tap down the high stones. If tapping them down won't level them, lift them and scoop out just enough mortar to make them level. Clean off any mortar spills with a wet broom before you lay the next section. Don't wait until you've finished the patio—the mortar will set on the first sections and you won't be able to get it off. Let the mortar cure three to four days, then mortar the joints.

4 Mix mortar in a mortar box and fill the joints using a pointing trowel or mortar bag. The bag squeezes mortar through a spout into the joints—it's less messy and will reduce cleanup chores. Clean spilled mortar right away with a wet sponge. When the mortar holds a thumbprint, finish the joints with a striking tool. Cover the surface with plastic or burlap (keep burlap wet) and let it cure for three to four days.

CUTTING THE STONES
Shaping stone to fit

1 Mark a cut line on the stone. You can freehand the line or set an adjoining stone on top of the stone you want to cut. Score the line with a brick set. Tap and move the brick set a bit at a time along the line.

2 Set the stone on a pipe or another stone, then break the stone with a single strong blow. Remove any excess stone along the contours of the cut line, shaping it with the sharp end of a mason's hammer.

Make a height gauge

The thickest stone sets the height of the entire patio. If you set the large stones first, a height gauge will help you level each stone as you go. Make the gauge long enough to span the widest stone. Augment your leveling efforts with a 4-foot level.

TILE PATIO

Before you set the tile, test the layout. You should have full tiles in the field of the site and as few cut tiles as possible on the edges.

Snap chalk lines between the midpoints of each side. If your slab has a control joint, snap chalk lines between the midpoints of the sides parallel to the control joint. Starting at the center point or the junction of the chalk line and control joint, dry-lay tiles and spacers on both axes, extending the tiles to the edge of the slab.

If one side ends with a full tile and the opposite side has only a partial tile, move the chalk line so both sides will have tiles of the same size. Adjust the tiles on both chalk lines but not on the control joint. When the layout fits the slab, snap reference lines at intervals equal to the tile dimensions.

Ideally you should apply mortar when the temperature is 60 to 70 degrees F. Don't work in direct sunlight—the mortar will set up too quickly. Start with enough mortar to lay just a few tiles. Work in sections you can complete in 10 minutes. As you set the tiles, mortar will squeeze up between them. If the mortar is more than half the tile thickness, you're using too much.

PRESTART CHECKLIST

☐ **TIME**
About 18 to 24 hours for a 10×10-foot area

☐ **TOOLS**
Five-gallon bucket, ½-inch drill, mixing paddle, chalk line, snap cutter or wet saw, square-notched trowel, beater block, rubber mallet, straightedge, grout float, caulk gun, wide putty knife, nippers, grout bag, sponge

☐ **SKILLS**
Mixing mortar; setting, cutting, and grouting tile

☐ **PREP**
Repair existing slab or install a new one

☐ **MATERIALS**
Latex-modified thinset, grout, tile, foam backer rod, caulk, spacers, sealers

Setting the tile

1 Start at the center of the slab (or at the center along a control joint), and spread a thin coat of mortar with the flat side of the trowel. Lay the mortar up to but not covering the layout lines. Rake the mortar with the notched side of the trowel. Set each tile in place with a slight twist and tap it with a rubber mallet and beater block. Place the covered side of the beater block on the tile and tap it a couple of times to seat the tile in the mortar, leveling it with the rest of the tiles.

REFRESHER COURSE
Cutting tiles

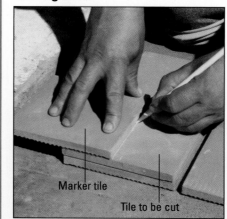

Marker tile

Tile to be cut

Place the tile you want to cut on top of the last set tile. Set another tile against the wall on the first tile and mark the cut line with a china marker.

A wet saw makes quick work of cutting a large number of tiles. Even for a small patio, renting one is worth the cost. Set the tile against the fence so the cut line is in line with the blade.

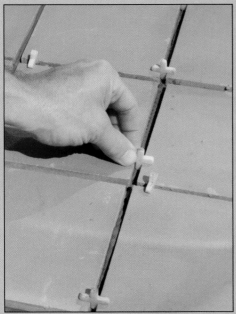

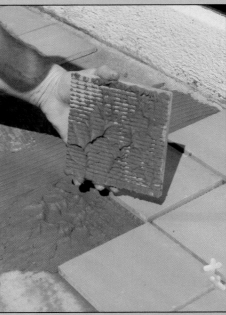

2 Use spacers to keep the tiles properly spaced. Set the spacers on end so you can remove them easily. As you work, remove the spacers from tiles that have had a few minutes to set up. It's much easier to remove the spacers before the mortar has hardened completely.

3 Pick up a tile occasionally to make sure the mortar is adhered evenly. Apply more or less as needed. Check each section with a straightedge. If a tile is too low, pull it up, apply more mortar, and reset it. If a tile is too high, scrape off excess mortar and reset it.

4 Continue spreading mortar in both directions away from the intersection of the layout lines. Leave yourself room to work. Use a spacer to remove excess mortar before it hardens. Finish cleaning the joints with a pointed trowel. Let the mortar cure and caulk the joints where necessary.

STANLEY PRO TIP

Have cut tiles on hand

As you get close to an edge, have a supply of cut tiles ready so you can set them in place without searching for them or having to cut new ones.

SAFETY FIRST
Save your knees

Don't subject your knees to possible injury or the discomfort that can come from working on a hard concrete slab. Wear knee pads—they're less expensive than surgery.

CAULK THE JOINTS
Filling control joints

After the mortar has set, use a wide putty knife or margin trowel to stuff the control joints with foam backer rod, leaving a recess of roughly two-thirds the thickness of the tile. Apply a high-quality silicone outdoor caulk, in the same color as the grout you will use.

Seal the joints where the patio meets the foundation of the house, making sure you apply enough to fill the gap all the way to the top of the expansion joint material. Smooth the caulk with a wet finger.

Grouting the tile

45° angle to surface

Almost perpendicular to surface

1 <u>Mix the grout</u> (latex-modified grout) to cover a small section. Scoop grout from the mixing container and set it on the tiles. Angle the grout float 45 degrees as you spread grout across the tiles, forcing it into the joints with the trailing edge. Move the float at angles to the tile pattern to fill the joints. Spread grout in alternating directions to force out air trapped in the joints. Grout the tile in sections and clean each section before grouting the next one.

2 When all the joints in the section are full, clean the grout float in a bucket of warm, clean water. Then use it to scrape excess grout from the tile. Hold the float almost perpendicular to the surface to remove the excess. Keep the float from pressing into the joints, or it will remove grout.

MIX THE GROUT
Power-mix the grout

Using a ½-inch drill and a mixing paddle, mix the grout slowly in a 5-gallon bucket. Follow the manufacturer's directions for mixing the grout and keep it in a container you can seal. For exterior applications, use grout that contains latex, which is easy to clean and needs little time to cure. If the grout you want to use doesn't come with a latex additive, ask your supplier if you can add it. If not, change brands.

Use the right drill

Power-mix mortar or grout with a heavy-duty ½-inch drill. Mortar and grout are stout mixes, and it takes a powerful drill motor to push the paddle through it. You might end up with an improper mix and a burned-out drill if you try to use a smaller drill for the job. If you can't rent or borrow a ½-inch model, buy one. You'll find plenty of other uses for it.

Estimating grout

The amount of grout you'll need depends on its composition, the size of the tile, and the width of the grout joints. Grout packaging is often printed with a chart that will help you estimate how much you'll need.

Study the chart before you make your purchase—it's better to have a little left over than to run out in the middle of a grout job. The table gives a rough idea of how much area a pound of grout covers.

Tile size (in inches)	Joint width	Coverage per pound
2×2×¼	¹⁄₁₆	24 square feet
4¼×4¼×⁵⁄₁₆	¹⁄₁₆	16 square feet
4¼×4¼×⁵⁄₁₆	⅛	8 square feet
6×6×¼	¹⁄₁₆	28 square feet
6×6×¼	⅛	14 square feet
12×12×³⁄₈	¹⁄₁₆	37 square feet

3 Scraping won't remove all of the excess grout. Test the grout to make sure it's set, then wipe the surface with a damp (not wet) sponge. The more often you change the water, the less haze you'll have to remove in the next step.

4 Use a clean soft cloth (old T-shirts work well) to wipe the haze off the tiles. In many cases the haze will be stubborn and you'll have to scrub hard, but doing so won't damage the tiles or the grout.

5 If the grout calls for damp curing, mist it lightly for a few minutes three times a day for three days. If the patio is in direct sunlight, cover the tile with clear (not black) plastic. After the grout has cured, seal the tile (if recommended by the manufacturer).

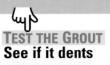

TEST THE GROUT
See if it dents

To make sure the grout has set up sufficiently to clean it (so it won't pull back out of the joints), press it with your fingernail or the tip of a pointed trowel. If one or the other doesn't leave a dent, the grout is ready.

WHAT IF...
Your design calls for wide joints?

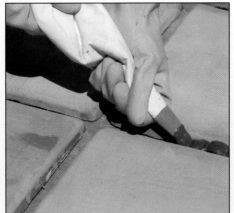

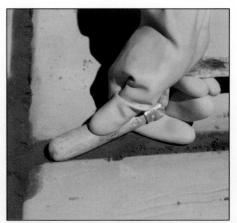

Some styles of tile look better with wide grout joints. For instance, saltillo tiles *(pages 138–141)* and other handmade materials look best with grout joints of at least ⅜ inch. At this width, a grout float will pull the grout out of the joints as you apply it, so you'll have to use a grout bag for such installations. Squeeze the bag as you draw its nozzle along the length of the joint. Stop just short of filling the joint completely, then tool the joints smooth with the rounded end of a trowel handle.

SALTILLO TILE PATIO

Saltillo tile takes its name from a region in Mexico which is known for its rich clays. The combination of raw materials and a hot climate ideally suit the area to the making of handmade tiles dried in the sun.

Saltillo tiles have an earthy, attractive quality unmatched by other materials. They also have drawbacks. Outdoors you can use them only in climates where they won't freeze. Also, their size, thickness, and consistency vary widely. This variety necessitates some special installation requirements, which are illustrated on these pages.

Saltillo tiles are porous and must be rinsed to keep them from absorbing moisture from the mortar too quickly. Rinsing also removes residual dust that otherwise weakens the mortar bond. Don't lay saltillo directly on layout lines as you would ceramic tile—set them back from the lines about ¼ inch to account for their irregular edges. Seal the tiles with a penetrating sealer before grouting them. Otherwise the grout will dry too quickly.

PRESTART CHECKLIST

☐ **TIME**
About 30 hours for a 10×10-foot area

☐ **TOOLS**
Five-gallon bucket, ½-inch drill, mixing paddle, chalk line, wet saw, square-notched trowel, beater block, rubber mallet, straightedge, grout float, caulk gun, nippers, grout bag, sponge, vacuum cleaner, tack rag

☐ **SKILLS**
Mixing mortar; setting, cutting, and grouting tile

☐ **PREP**
Repair existing slab or install a new one

☐ **MATERIALS**
Latex-modified thinset, grout, tile, foam backer rod, caulk, spacers, sealers

Preparing the tile

1 Sort the tiles into piles according to thickness and flatness. This will help you get an idea of how thick your mortar bed has to be, and how many domed tiles you'll have to back-butter as you layt them.

2 To slow the tile's absorption of moisture from the mortar, rinse the tiles in clean water and set them aside until the surface moisture dries or wipe off excess surface moisture. The tiles need to be slightly damp, not wet. Set them to dry in a homemade rack or against a wall.

Establish layout grids

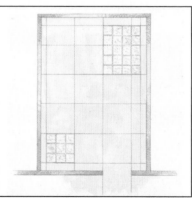

Setting saltillo tile takes more time than setting machine-made tiles because they are irregular. That means you might have to mix mortar in smaller quantities than you would for a ceramic project. To help organize your time, establish sections of nine tiles each and mix mortar in batches sufficient to cover that area.

WHAT IF...
A tile is domed?

Back-Butter domed tile

Boxes of saltillo tile usually contain several that have a domed surface. Don't throw domed tiles away—back-butter all of them at one time, starting in the center of each tile and working to get a level surface over the back, from edge to edge. Set the domed tiles aside and let the mortar dry before laying them.

Spreading mortar and setting the first tile

1 Snap layout lines and mix up enough latex-modified mortar to cover an area about 4 feet square. Spread it on the slab (just short of the layout lines) with the flat edge of a trowel to a uniform thickness of ½ to ¾ inch. Then comb it with a trowel with ½×¼-inch U notches.

2 Back-butter the tile with enough mortar to allow you to set it level with the other tiles. Comb the mortar with the notched trowel edge.

3 Set one corner of the tile in place about ¼ inch back from the layout line. Place the edge of the tile roughly parallel to the layout line and set it in place.

Working with uneven edges

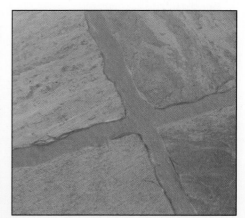

Tiles with irregular edges, such as saltillo and handmade pavers, are difficult to keep straight, and spacers aren't much help when it comes to aligning them.

To keep such tiles aligned, make your layout grids small—a nine-tile (three-by-three) layout

works well. Trowel adhesive one grid at a time, and set the tiles in place. Adjust the tiles until the appearance of the joints is consistent, and expect to make a few compromises.

Inserting a regular pattern of accent tiles into the corners of the pattern will also make the

layout easier. The alternate figures in the pattern of the tile will distract the eye and add to the informality of the design. When grouting the tiles, make sure you remove all the surface grout so the irregular edges are visible.

Continuing the pattern

1 Continue laying the tile in the first section, with the edges ¼ inch off the layout lines. From time to time, step back and look over the section. The tile should not look like it's lined up perfectly; if it does, it will look staged or contrived.

2 When you have finished laying a section, level the tile with a beater block made from plywood and carpet. The block should be wide enough to cover at least two tiles. Tap it with a rubber mallet. Because of irregularities, some tiles will rock. Take up the beater block and tap the high edge to even out the surface of those tiles.

Testing the mixture

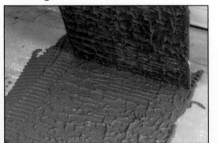

Properly applied thinset forms ridges that compress to cover the entire back of the tile when it is embedded. If thinset is applied too wet, it won't hold these ridges. A dry thinset application won't compress and will result in the tile adhering to the top of the ridges only.

   Test a thinset mixture occasionally by pulling up a tile and examining the back. If the thinset completely covers the surface, the mixture is correct, as shown above.

GROUT THE TILE
Using a grout float

1 Working from corner to open floor, spread the grout in a small section. Then, holding the grout float at a low angle (not quite flat) and working it diagonally across the tile, pack grout into the joints.

2 Go back over the section, this time holding the grout float almost perpendicular to the floor to scrape off the excess.

Sanding and sealing

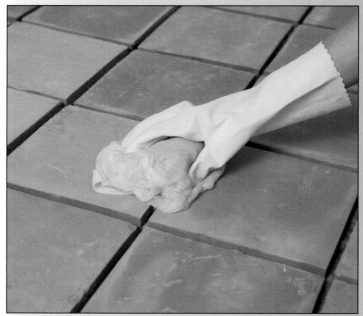

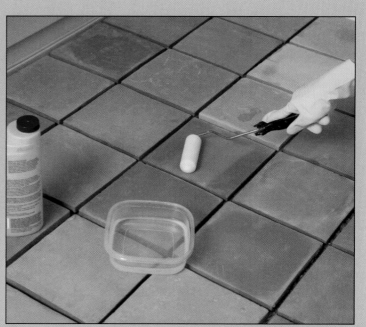

1 When the mortar has cured, grind down the edges of the tiles that are thick enough to disturb the smoothness of the surface. (Grind down any edge that would trip someone). Start with a masonry stone and finish the grinding with a sharpening stone (or start with 80-grit carbide sandpaper and work up to a 200 grit). Vacuum the tile, then wipe it with a tack rag to get all the dust up before sealing the tile.

2 If saltillo is not sealed, it will quickly absorb the moisture from the grout, causing it to crack. Seal the tile with a penetrating sealer—twice. If you've purchased presealed tile, seal it once before you grout. Apply the sealer with a brush, roller, or applicator recommended by the manufacturer. Then grout the tile.

3 When grout has set up (a fingernail will leave only a slight impression, see *page 137)*, use a barely damp sponge to remove the grout residue from the tile.

4 Smooth the joints with a barely damp sponge, rinsing out the sponge frequently. Let the surface dry, and seal the entire floor (or just the grout lines) according to the manufacturer's instructions.

POURING A CONCRETE LANDING PAD

Many concrete patios and sidewalks are less than 2 inches thick and lack metal reinforcing. In areas subject to freezing winters, such slabs usually crack. These pages show how to build a long-lasting pad for stairs or a ramp.

A concrete slab may be raised one step above the yard or an adjacent patio surface, or it can be set just above ground level. If the pad is 75 square feet or smaller, you don't need to worry about drainage. The pad shown here includes two piers to key into its sloped site. Omit the piers for a level site.

Though it may feel solid a few hours after pouring, concrete takes a week or two to achieve full strength. Wait at least three days before exerting heaving pressure on the pad.

PRESTART CHECKLIST

☐ **TIME**
About a day to excavate, build forms, mix concrete, pour, and finish the surface

☐ **TOOLS**
Level, tape measure, circular saw, sledgehammer, drill, hammer, wire cutters, concrete, wheelbarrow, hoe, concrete finishing tools (page 143)

☐ **SKILLS**
Measuring and cutting, checking for level and square, mixing concrete in a wheelbarrow, smoothing a concrete surface

☐ **PREP**
Determine the location for the pad and remove any sod

☐ **MATERIALS**
Two-by lumber for forms, stakes, gravel, bags of dry-mix concrete, reinforcing wire mesh

Drive stakes below the top of the form boards

1 Excavate topsoil and tamp down about 2 inches of gravel. Cut 2× boards to use as forms for the pad. Fasten them together to form a rectangle. Use a framing square to check the corners for square. Fasten the boards to stakes driven into the ground, and check for level and square.

Reinforcing mesh

2 Backfill with soil behind the form boards so too much wet concrete can't ooze out from the bottom. Cut wire reinforcing mesh to fit, then lay it on top of stones so it's near the center of the pad's thickness when you pour the concrete.

FORMING AND POURING A CONCRETE PAD

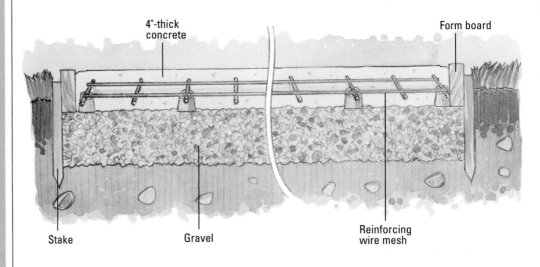

4"-thick concrete

Form board

Stake

Gravel

Reinforcing wire mesh

A solid concrete pad is 4 inches thick, rests on a bed of well-tamped gravel, and is reinforced with reinforcing wire mesh.

3 Mix the concrete and pour it into the forms. Using a board long enough to reach from form to form, screed the surface: Drag the board, using a side-to-side motion as you move it across the length of the pad. Repeat until the surface is level and has no low spots.

Screed board

4 Using a wooden, steel, or magnesium float (shown *below left*), smooth out the entire area. With the float held nearly flat, lightly scrape across the pad in long, sweeping arcs. As you work, water will rise to the top. Keep smoothing as long as the surface is wet. Once it has started to dry, lightly drag a broom across it to create a nonslip surface.

Concrete finishing tools

Magnesium float

Mason's trowel

Edger

All you need to finish a small concrete pad are these three tools. A magnesium float is easier to use than a steel or wooden float and is more than adequate for smoothing the concrete before you give it a broom finish (see Step 4 above).

5 Slip the point of a mason's trowel between the form and the concrete and slice all around the pad to a depth of 1 to 2 inches.

Edger

6 Run an edger around the perimeter to round off the corners. This will prevent chipping. Press lightly and repeat until the corners are smooth. Let the concrete set for a day, then pry away the forms.

BUILDING AN OUTDOOR KITCHEN

Outdoor barbecuing became a popular pastime in the 1950s, and since then the technology of grills and accessories has improved dramatically. If you've always been part of the outdoor cooking craze or are joining it for the first time, an outdoor kitchen is something you can use.

Like any landscaping project, the scope of an outdoor cooking area is best determined by answering the questions: How do you want to use it? For full-scale outdoor dining? For intimate gatherings with family or a few guests? Or merely for occasional weekend get-togethers?

At a minimum an outdoor kitchen requires a structure to house a grill. The unit illustrated here does just that, with little cost and effort. You can add a prep sink, under-the-counter fridge, rotisserie, and any number of storage areas. This design accommodates those features with the installation of additional bays.

1 Lay out and pour the slab and footings to meet local codes *(page 96).* Snap chalk lines to mark the location of the block walls. Using your dimensional plan, build the walls. Make sure the grill bay meets the manufacturer's specifications.

2 Cut ¾-inch exterior-grade plywood, metal lath, and backerboard to fit each section of the countertop. Fasten the plywood to the block webs with concrete screws (not anchors). Mortar the plywood, set the first piece of backerboard in the mortar, then install metal lath and the second backerboard.

PRESTART CHECKLIST

☐ **TIME**
About 24 to 30 hours

☐ **TOOLS**
Tape measure, shovel, hammer, rake, power tamper, cordless drill, hacksaw, concrete finishing tools, chalk line, mason's trowel, wire cutters, notched trowel, circular saw with masonry blade

☐ **SKILLS**
Installing a concrete slab, laying out and building with concrete block, setting tile

☐ **PREP**
Design layout, excavate, and pour concrete slab

☐ **MATERIALS**
Two-by stock for forms, deck screws, ready-mix concrete, mortar, concrete block, backerboard, metal lath, line blocks, ¾-inch exterior-grade plywood, thinset mortar, tile, grout, brick veneer

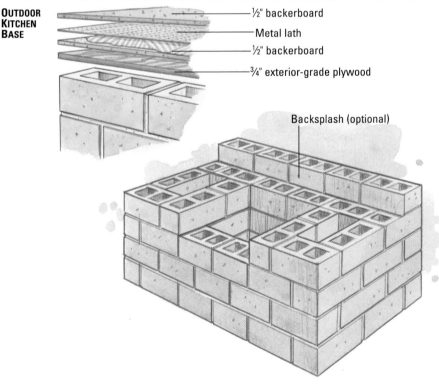

OUTDOOR KITCHEN BASE

- ½" backerboard
- Metal lath
- ½" backerboard
- ¾" exterior-grade plywood

Backsplash (optional)

3 Starting at the bottom, spread and comb thinset on a section of the block wall. Set each piece of brick veneer in the mortar with a slight twist. Level the veneer and keep it straight with a straightedge.

4 When the thinset has cured, fill a mortar bag with the mortar recommended by the manufacturer and squeeze the mortar into the joints. Let the mortar set up slightly, then tool it with a jointing tool.

5 Dry-lay the countertop tile to make sure everything fits. Then spread and comb a level coat of thinset on the backerboard and set the countertop field tile. Make sure all the joints line up, then set the edge tile. When the mortar cures, grout and clean the tile and install the grill.

Installing a concrete countertop

Nothing beats concrete as a substrate for tile. It's flat, stable, and won't bend under compressive loads. Concrete countertops are also ideal for outdoor kitchen installations, but for large cooking bases you may find their expense prohibitive. For small kitchens, however, there's a ready-made alternative—precast concrete stepping stones.

Poured in a 3-inch thickness and in 3×3-foot squares, these units are available at most home centers and certain Internet retailers (be careful of shipping costs, however). Besides providing an excellent base for tile, they offer an additional benefit—their 3-inch height makes it easy to set your countertop at exactly 36 inches.

To install this unit, use a circular saw with a masonry blade to cut it to 24 inches (the usual front-to-back depth of a counter surface). Apply mortar to the webs of the block walls

and set the slab in place. For additional stability, fill the block cores with concrete and drill the slab to accommodate $\frac{1}{2}$-inch rebar.

Installing undercounter storage

Installing an undercounter storage bay or recess for a refrigerator or other accessory means supporting the block above the bay. Lintels are made for this purpose. Using a hacksaw, cut the steel lintel to a length that extends over the opening by half a block on each side. Mortar the lintel in place, and cover it with lintel blocks as shown.

POURING A CONCRETE WALK

You can pour concrete as a stand-alone walk or as a base for other mortared materials such as brick, tile, or stone. The only difference is that a walk that will be a foundation for other materials must be put deeper into the ground so the finished surface won't be too high.

For a plain slab walkway, consider using any of the coloring, stamping, or texturing techniques illustrated on *pages 64–65.*

Concrete walks often abut an existing concrete or masonry structure—steps or another section of existing slab walkway. Anytime you pour concrete next to existing materials, you must install an expansion strip on the old structure. The strip cushions the expansion and contraction of the materials and prevents damage.

The procedures illustrated on these pages assume the proper layout and excavation of the site prior to working with the concrete. See *pages 74–77* for layout information.

PRESTART CHECKLIST

☐ **TIME**
About 20 hours to prepare, pour, and finish a 4×25-foot walk

☐ **TOOLS**
Layout and excavation tools *(pages 49–50),* wheelbarrow, tape measure, mason's line, cordless drill, circular saw, concrete mixer, mason's hoe, darby, edger, jointer, float, screed, broom

☐ **SKILLS**
Laying out square lines; form building; mixing, pouring, and finishing concrete

☐ **PREP**
Prepare and excavate the site

☐ **MATERIALS**
2¼-inch screws, 2× lumber for forms, expansion strip, gravel, wire mesh, dobies or wire balusters, soft-iron wire, form-release agent, concrete, construction adhesive, plastic sheeting or burlap

Prep and pour

1 Lay out the site and remove the sod, excavating to the depth of materials required by local codes. Set up the intersection of your batterboard lines (and ground stakes) to correspond with the outside edges of the forms. Drive 2×4 stakes at 2-foot intervals, with their inside edges under the lines. Fasten the 2× forms to the stakes with 2¼-inch screws, checking the slope of the forms with a slope gauge and adjusting the slope by raising or lowering the forms as you fasten them. If any stakes are higher than the top of the forms, cut them off level with the 2×s. If you've designed the walk to slope to the side, use a slope gauge *(page 125)* placed across the forms.

TYPICAL POURED-CONCRETE SLAB INSTALLATION

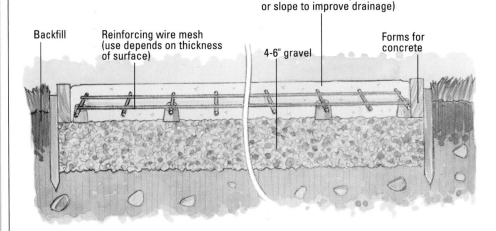

Backfill

Reinforcing wire mesh (use depends on thickness of surface)

3–4" concrete slab (crown or slope to improve drainage)

4-6" gravel

Forms for concrete

SAFETY FIRST
Concrete is caustic. Wear rubber boots and gloves along with eye protection.

2 Shovel in about 2 inches of gravel and level it with a garden rake. Then compact this layer with a power tamper. Shovel in the remainder of the gravel (for a total of 4 to 6 inches), level it, and tamp it. Lay 10×10-foot wire reinforcing mesh on the gravel, leaving about 1 inch between the ends of the wire and the forms, and overlapping sections by at least 6 inches. About every 3 feet, set dobies or wire balusters (also called chairs) under the intersections of the mesh and wire the mesh to these supports. The object is to raise the wire mesh to the approximate center of the slab.

3 Mix the concrete and use a wheelbarrow to move it to the work site. Don't load the wheelbarrow to the top; a full load is more likely to tip sideways as you move it. Start pouring in the farthest corner of the walk and then back to the mixing site. Work the mix against the forms with a shovel and garden rake.

STANLEY®   PRO TIP: **Mixing pigment**

1 Some manufacturers recommend presoaking the gravel base with water so the dry gravel doesn't pull the water from the concrete, thereby streaking the colors. This is generally done the night before you make the pour. Some pigments are added to the water before the dry ingredients, some are added during the mix but before the final water, and some manufacturers make dye in soluble bags—you throw bag and all into the mix, and the bag disintegrates as you mix the concrete. Follow the manufacturer's instructions.

2 The directions on the bag will tell you how much water to use. Whatever that amount is, add it a little at a time. If the mix is too stiff, add a bit more water until it becomes workable.

Screed and finish

1 Before you level the concrete, consolidate it by working a 2×4 up and down in the mix. Work a shovel along the edges to release any air bubbles, and tap the corners and edges of the forms with a hammer to help release trapped air. Then cut a straight 2×4 about a foot or so longer than the width of the walk and pull it in a seesaw motion down the walk. Work out bumps in the concrete, fill in low spots, and screed again.

2 To float the concrete, work a darby back and forth in wide sweeping arcs on the surface. Keep the leading edge of the darby slightly raised as you work the concrete. Stop when a water sheen appears on the surface.

STANLEY PRO TIP: **Roughing up the surface**

If you will lay a mortar bed over the concrete, scratch or scarify the surface to give the mortar a "tooth" that will make it stick better. Use a stiff broom or make a scarifier by driving 10d (3-inch) nails through a piece of 2×2. Work the tool over the wet concrete in arcs.

If you're not mortaring a finished material to the walk, you won't want to leave it smoothed by the darby. Smooth concrete will be slick. Brooming the surface creates a nonslip walkway. Float the concrete first, then pull a dampened stiff broom across the surface, perpendicular to traffic flow.

Finishing touches

After the concrete has cured, remove the forms. Then backfill the edges, tamping the soil with a 2×4. Replace the sod you removed earlier and water it thoroughly.

3 After you've finished floating the surface, run a pointing trowel along the inside edge of the forms to help break the bond between the wood and concrete (it'll be easier to remove the forms later). Then run an edger along the outside edges of the concrete to round them. Rounded edges will not chip as readily as square edges. Omit this step if you're going to mortar brick, tile, or stone to the slab.

4 Cut control joints in the slab with a jointer. To keep the joints straight, tack a 2×4 with 2-inch screws to the top of the forms—exactly perpendicular to the forms (use a framing square to measure the angle). Space control joints at intervals equal to 1½ times the width of the walk (every 6 feet for a 4-foot walk).

Curing concrete

Concrete must cure slowly for at least seven days to reach its full strength. (In fact, concrete keeps getting stronger for 28 to 45 days.) What's important during the cure is that the concrete does not dry too fast. Keep it wet with periodic misting from a lawn sprinkler. You can also cover the slab with plastic sheeting which will trap evaporating moisture. As an alternative, cover the slab with burlap and keep the burlap wet during the curing. Adjust the water flow so the water doesn't puddle on the burlap.

BRICK OR PRECAST-PAVER WALKS

Brick or precast concrete paver walks—whether laid on a sand bed or mortared to a slab—employ many of the same techniques used to build a similar patio. They offer the same potential for a varied, handsome surface, only on a smaller scale.

You will notice one difference, however, between a mortared path and a mortared patio. When building a paver path, you don't have to start in the center and work outward. All pavered walks start their paving in a corner.

Be sure to lay the base materials in layers and compact one layer before the next one. This is especially important if your walk will be subject to hard use, such as the movement of garden equipment. Base materials that shift under a sand-set path create ripples. In addition, improperly tamped slab bases can crack.

PRESTART CHECKLIST

☐ **TIME**
Between 20 and 40 hours to lay out and set a 4×25-foot walk, depending on your skill level

☐ **TOOLS**
Layout and excavation tools *(pages 49–50)*, concrete tools for a mortared structure *(pages 50–51)*, wheelbarrow, tape measure, mason's line, cordless drill, circular saw, concrete mixer, mason's hoe, screed, broom, wet saw

☐ **SKILLS**
Designing layout, form building, mixing, working with mortar

☐ **PREP**
Prepare and excavate the site

☐ **MATERIALS**
Gravel, sand, 2¼-inch screws, 2× lumber, brick or precast pavers, rubber mallet, 1×6, mason's line, stakes

Setting a paver-in-sand walk

1 Lay out the site *(pages 74–75)*, then remove the sod with a sod cutter or square shovel, pushing the shovel under the roots to lift it. If setting border materials in a trench, excavate the trench deeper than the rest of the site.

2 Install the edging *(pages 84–85)*. To set pavers in a side trench, stake lines at the height of the edging, dig out the sand from the trench, insert the edging, and backfill both sides of the paver to keep it straight. As an alternative, set a 2×4 on the outside of the trench.

Setting a running bond

1 Lay out and prepare the site to dimensions that equal a line of whole brick *(page 86)*. Install edge restraints and the first row of pavers. Start and finish the next row and every other remaining row with a half paver.

2 Periodically check the joints to make sure they run straight and perpendicular to the edge restraints or border. Make any corrections before going to the next section.

3 Tie mason's line to two pavers and set them outside the edging and parallel to the short side of the path. Use the line to help guide the edge of the pavers, spacing the units at about ⅛ inch. Continue setting the pavers, covering about a 4×4-foot section.

4 After completing a section, bed the pavers in the sand. Lay a 1×6 on the surface and tap it with a rubber mallet. Also check the slope of the section with a level or slope gauge. Lift out any low pavers, add sand, and reset. Tap down any high pavers. If this doesn't seat them properly, remove them, take out some sand, and reset them.

STANLEY PRO TIP

Bedding and setting sand

Like any other natural material, sand comes in different sizes, shapes, and grades. Sand grains (less than 5 mm) occur naturally or can be made by grinding larger rock and sifting it with screens for consistent size.

Not all sand works well for bedding pavers. The best one to use is bedding sand—coarse, hard sand with sharp edges. Limestone screenings, which are a common substitute, are too soft and will crumble with the weight of materials and the effects of water and usage.

On the other hand, sand for filling the joints between pavers needs to be smaller—very fine, actually, so it compacts in the joints. Ask for builder's sand or mason's sand, which is even finer.

WHAT IF...
Pavers are not prespaced?

Many precast concrete pavers are made with spacing tabs, which keep the units properly spaced for sand. Brick, however, and some pavers aren't. If your pavers aren't, use spacers cut from plywood.

5 Spread a thin layer of sand across the surface of the walk and sweep it into the joints with a soft broom. Mist the joints, add sand, sweep again, and repeat.

Building a mortared-brick walk

1 Lay out and prepare the site to dimensions that equal a line of pavers in the pattern of your choice *(page 86)*. If you plan to set the border material on the slab, build forms ½ inch higher than the slab. Pour and finish the slab. When the slab is ready, spread about ½ inch of mortar on a 2×2-foot section. You can set a 2×2-foot section before the mortar sets up. With some practice, you can set larger areas.

2 Cut a 2×4 slightly longer than the width of the forms and use it as a screed, pulling it across the forms with a seesaw motion. Fill any low spots with mortar and screed again. After screeding, comb the mortar with a notched trowel if desired.

5 Move the guideline and lay the second course. The technique is the same: Separate the pavers with spacers, move the spacers with each new course, and bed the paving with a rubber mallet.

6 After completing the first section, remove the spacers from the last course and check the section for level with a straightedge, resetting any high or low units. Continue laying the pavers in sections until you have finished the walk. Let the mortar cure, then mortar the joints.

3 Whatever pattern you choose, start by laying pavers in a corner. Set them up against the forms, and space them with a plywood spacer. Use ½-inch spacers for 7½-inch pavers; use ⅜-inch spacers for 7⅝-inch units. Tap the bricks with a rubber mallet to bed them in the mortar.

4 To help keep the layout straight and perpendicular to the forms, tie mason's line to two bricks and set them outside the site to mark the edge of the first course. Then lay the first course of pavers.

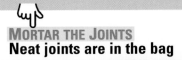

MORTAR THE JOINTS
Neat joints are in the bag

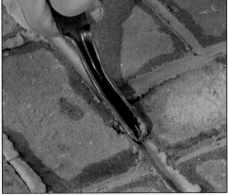

1 Mortar that gets on the pavers is a chore to clean. To minimize the amount of misplaced mortar, use a mortar bag to fill the joints. Make sure the bag's spout is thinner than the joints. Fill the bag with mortar and slowly squeeze it into the gaps.

2 Let the mortar set up until it just shows a thumbprint when you touch it with light pressure. Shape the joints by pulling a concave striking tool along them.

3 As you strike the joints, you'll leave some excess mortar on the face of the brick. Use a wet soft-bristle brush or piece of burlap to clean off this excess. Cover the walk with plastic while the mortar sets.

FLAGSTONE WALKS

When you're planning a flagstone path, remember that curved paths look best. Lay out any straight sections first with staked mason's lines. Then use a hose to lay out the curved sections, one at a time. To keep the sides evenly spaced, lay several 2×s cut to the length of the path width between the lengths of hose. Then mark the curve with chalk or sand, pull up the hose, and slice the sod.

Building a flagstone structure is always hard work—even experimenting with the pattern means lifting the stones and rearranging them, perhaps several times. Take breaks, even when you don't think you need one.

PRESTART CHECKLIST

☐ **TIME**
About 20 to 25 hours to lay out and set a 4×25-foot walk

☐ **TOOLS**
Layout and excavating tools *(pages 49–50)*, concrete tools for a mortared structure *(pages 50–51)*, wheelbarrow, tape measure, mason's line, cordless drill, circular saw, concrete mixer, mason's hoe, screed, broom, rubber mallet

☐ **SKILLS**
Designing layout, lifting and setting stones, mortaring slab for stonework

☐ **PREP**
Prepare site

☐ **MATERIALS**
Stones, bedding sand, mason's sand, gravel, landscape fabric

Setting flagstone in sand

1 Lay out straight path runs with staked lines. Mark curves with a garden hose (shut off the nozzle and turn on the water). Cut 2× stock to the width of the walk and lay it between the hose sections to keep the width consistent. Mark the hose with sand or chalk and remove it.

2 Slice the sod along the marked lines and remove it. Remove any large rocks and tamp sand into depressions deeper than the excavation depth. Spread sand in layers, rake it level, and tamp each layer with a power tamper. Install edging *(page 84–85)*.

Setting mortared flagstone

1 Prepare the site and set out the stones in a trial run *(page 155)*. To cut a stone to shape, mark the cut line on the stone and cut it as shown on *page 103*.

2 Spread mortar about ¾ to 1 inch thick to accommodate the uneven surfaces of flagstone. Comb it with a ½-inch notched trowel, if desired, making sure the notches don't reach the concrete base. Use long, sweeping strokes to comb the mortar.

3 Set the stones outside the walk site in the pattern of your choice. Usually it's best to start with large stones for the perimeter, then fill in the gaps with smaller ones. Pick stones so the contours of adjacent stones are similar—cut them to shape if necessary. Then set the stones on the sand in the same order. Check them for level, and reset units that are too high or low.

4 Shovel a thin layer of builder's sand onto the stones and sweep it into the joints with a broom. Don't fill the joints completely in the first sweeping. Wet the first layer, add more sand, and sweep again. Alternatively, you can use soil as a filler and put plants in the gaps *(page 119, Step 4, Option A)*. For a planted path, though, it might be easier to build a stepping-stone walk, shown on *pages 156–157*.

3 Pull the stones off the grass in order and push them into the mortar. Use a rubber mallet to bed the stones and use a straightedge to keep them approximately on the same level. Level any tipped stones—those with one edge higher than the other.

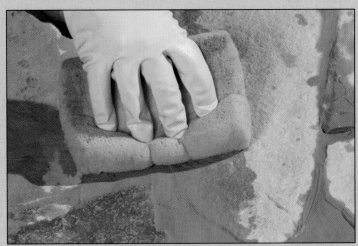

4 When the walk is completed, let the mortar bed cure. Allow the mortar to set; usually one or two days. Mix a sanded portland cement grout with latex additive, and push the grout into the joints with a grout float. Scrape off the excess with the float held nearly perpendicular to the tiles. Clean the grout and smooth the lines with a damp sponge.

STEPPING-STONE PATHS

Astepping-stone path is the most informal of paths and is best when it has as many curves as possible—stepping-stones look better laid along curves.

The outline of the path doesn't have to be precise. If the edges of some stones fall slightly outside the edge of the path, it merely adds to the appeal.

Stepping-stones are set individually in sand recesses, each excavated to conform to the shape of the individual stone. The path doesn't require a gravel base, just a 2-inch sand base in the recess dug in the soil.

Spacing for the stepping-stones depends somewhat on the purpose of the path and the speed at which you want the traffic to move. Spaced at 6 inches, the stones will slow the walk; at 10 inches, they will speed it up. Use a 1-inch spacing if you plan to run wheeled garden equipment over the path.

This installation is a fun weekend project for the whole family because it doesn't require heavy lifting.

PRESTART CHECKLIST

☐ **TIME**
About 8 to 10 hours to lay and set a 4×15-foot path

☐ **TOOLS**
Garden hose, 2× lumber, round-nose shovel, trowel, mason's line stakes, marking chalk, 4-foot level

☐ **SKILLS**
Laying out a path, digging, marking, setting stone

☐ **PREP**
Plan path dimensions and contours

☐ **MATERIALS**
Bedding sand, stepping-stones

Laying stepping-stones

2×s keep both hoses parallel.

Pour chalk over hoses. Removing the hoses will mark the edge of the walk.

1 Lay out the site, using staked mason's lines for straight sections and a charged garden hose for curved sections. (Turn the nozzle off and the water on to help the hose keep its shape.) You can cut lengths of 2× stock to the width of the walk and lay them between the hose sections to keep the width consistent, but a layout for a stepping-stone walk need not be as precise as for other walks. Mark the path with chalk and remove the hose.

STANLEY PRO TIP: **Path principles**

Following a few design and construction principles will make your stepping-stone path more enjoyable.

■ Stepping-stones usually make a one-person path; you can keep the scale small.

■ To start and stop the path or signal changes of direction, use stepping-stones about 1½ times larger than the average. Lay these junction stones first.

■ Try to pattern the stones so their shapes and contours relate to each other.

■ Lay long stones across the path, not parallel with its direction of travel.

■ Select stones with flat surfaces. Stones with recesses collect water, making the path slippery. In winter the water will freeze and could split the stone.

■ Stones that have an overall equal thickness ease installation. Stepping-stones should be at least 1½ inches thick. Thin stones break under little weight.

2 Pile the stones according to their general size. Then pick stones that will create the pattern you want as you lay them in place within the chalked outline of the walk.

3 When you are satisfied with the pattern of the stones, mark the outline of each one with chalk. Avoid using spray paint, which stains stones.

4 Remove each stone and set it aside. Use a round-nose shovel to dig out the sod along the chalk marks. Dig a recess deep enough for the stone thickness plus 2 inches of sand. Make adjustments in the excavation with a trowel as needed. Put 2 inches of sand into the recess; level it with a trowel.

5 Set the stone back in the recess and level it. After you've laid several stones, check them in groups to make sure they are at a consistent height at or slightly above grade. Take up any stones that don't conform and reset them, adding or removing sand.

POURED CONCRETE STEPS

Poured concrete steps provide a sturdy, long-lasting transition between an outdoor surface, such as a patio, and the entry to your house. One of the more confusing questions that arises, however, is how high and how deep (front to back) each step should be. The answer to this question is found in some simple math you can use to compute the unit rise and run.

When considering the total run of the unit, local codes often require the top landing to extend at least 12 inches beyond the door swing. Subtract the width of an outswinging door (usually 32 or 36 inches) from the length you measure between the foundation to the outside edge of the steps. If the remainder is less than 12 inches, you may need to change your plan.

Know the codes before you start planning steps. If you don't construct them according to code, a building inspector can make you tear them out. Codes may also have something to say about the placement of rebar or other reinforcements, as well as the concrete mix you use.

PRESTART CHECKLIST

☐ **TIME**
Two to three days to plan, lay out, and pour three steps (not counting curing time)

☐ **TOOLS**
Mason's line, level, framing square, circular saw, hammer, wheelbarrow, mason's hoe, shovel, edger, mason's trowel, broom, lawn sprinkler, tape measure, small sledgehammer, line level, plumb bob, powdered chalk, spade, 4-foot level, tamper

☐ **SKILLS**
Designing layout, assembling forms, pouring concrete

☐ **MATERIALS**
Two-by lumber, concrete, form-release agent

Laying out the site

1 Measure the rise and run of the site, and drive stakes to indicate where the base of the bottom step will be when poured. Compute the unit rise and run of the steps, and draw a dimensioned sketch.

2 Lay out footings 3 inches wider than the steps. Excavate the footings to the depth codes require, pour the concrete, and insert 12-inch lengths of rebar 7 to 8 inches into the footings. The top of the rebar should be about 2 inches lower than the finished height of the steps. Let the footings cure, then dig a 4-inch trench between them and fill it with tamped gravel.

MEASURE THE RISE AND RUN

Using straight 2×4s or stakes, measure the total rise and run of the steps as shown. The rise is the vertical distance from the ground to the landing, the run is the horizontal distance.

Consider the landing

When you calculate the total rise for your steps, subtract the height of any landing pad that will extend above ground level.

If you plan to build a concrete pad at the base of the steps and the surface of the pad will be 2 inches above grade, for example, reduce your total rise by 2 inches.

Local building codes may affect the construction of the landing, too, so check before you build.

Making the forms

1 Using your plan and the actual dimensions you have computed and sketched, draw the outline of your steps on a sheet of ¾-inch plywood. Draw the line for the landing so it slopes ¼ inch per foot. Clamp a second plywood sheet to the first, edges flush, and cut the outline of the step with a jigsaw.

2 Using a framing square to make sure the forms are perpendicular to the foundation of the house, set the forms in place, and drive supporting stakes alongside them. Make sure the forms are plumb and level with each other, then fasten them to the stakes with 2-inch screws. Cut off any portion of the stakes above the forms.

COMPUTE THE UNIT RISE AND RUN
Figuring the stairway

The unit rise and unit run of steps are the individual dimensions of each riser and each tread.

To compute the unit rise and run, first divide the total rise by 7, a standard step height. Round up fractional results to the nearest whole number. Then divide the total rise again by this number to get the unit rise.

For example, here's the math for a total rise of 20 inches: 20 inches÷7 inches=2.8, rounded=3 steps. 20 inches÷3 steps=6.6 inches. In this example, you'll need three steps 6⅝" high to climb 20 inches.

Next divide the total run (to the outside edge of the door sweep) by the number of steps to get the unit run. For example, if your total run was 48 inches, here's the math: 48 inches÷3 steps=16 inches per tread. However, a tread depth of 16 inches would feel too long. (See "Trip-Proof steps," *right*.) Adjust the tread depth to 13 inches, a more comfortable measure, and make the total run 39 inches.

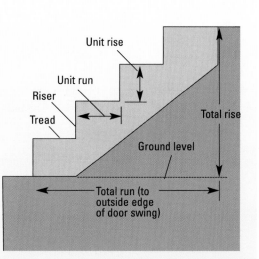

Unit rise

Unit run

Riser

Tread

Total rise

Ground level

Total run (to outside edge of door swing)

Trip-proof steps

Outdoor steps are configured differently from interior steps. They will be comfortable to climb if twice the riser height plus the tread depth equals a number from 25 to 27. That works out to a tread depth of 11 to 13 inches for a 7-inch rise (2×7=14; 25−14=11, 27−14=13). After you complete your preliminary calculations, adjust the rise and run of your stairs to comply with the formula. Using this formula virtually guarantees safe and comfortable landscape stairs.

Assembling the forms

2× riser form

2×6 keeps risers from bowing

Cut cleats to allow room for floating

1 For each step, cut a piece of 2× lumber to the width of the stairs and rip it to the height of the unit rise if necessary. Bevel the lower edge of each riser (except the bottom one) to make it easier to float the tread when you pour the steps. Fasten the top riser form to the outside of the side forms with three 2-inch screws. Then install the remaining riser forms.

2 Cut angled braces and fasten them to the side forms at the front edge of each step. Then drive 2×4 stakes at the bottom of the braces. Plumb the side forms and fasten the braces to the stakes. To keep the riser forms from bowing, drive a 2×4 stake 18 inches or deeper into the ground in front of the steps. Lay a 2×6 on the risers and fasten it to the stake and to cleats attached to the risers. Attach an expansion strip to the foundation with construction adhesive.

Shoring up your concrete steps

With an underlying grid of ½-inch rebar, poured concrete steps will give you years of low-maintenance service.

Some local building codes may require that you anchor concrete steps to the foundation wall. You can either drill at an angle into a poured concrete foundation, or through a concrete block wall and insert rebar in the holes.

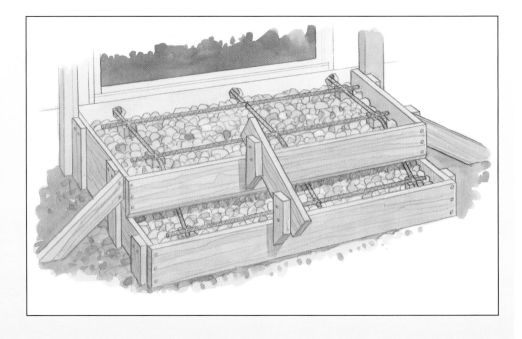

Filling the base

1 To save concrete, time, and money, shovel rubble—clean chunks of broken concrete, river rock, or any clean masonry—into the space inside the forms. Pile the rubble higher under the landing than the first step, but don't put in so much rubble that it will make the concrete in the steps too thin.

2 To strengthen the concrete, bend lengths of ½-inch rebar so it roughly corresponds to the shape of the rubble mound and lay it on the rubble at 12-inch intervals. Wire perpendicular lengths of rebar across the first pieces. Then raise the rebar up and support it on dobies or balusters that you wire to the rebar.

Building perpendicular steps

Steps can run either straight forward from an exterior door or at right angles to it. Forms for perpendicular steps go together in essentially the same way the straight steps illustrated on these pages do.

Strike a level line on the foundation to mark the height of the landing. Measure from this line to position the plywood forms for the rear and side. Brace the forms with stakes, cut beveled risers, hold them level, and mark their lower corner on the foundation. Then fasten the diagonal brace to the house and foundation and the risers to cleats. Brace the front edge of the risers as you would a straight stairs.

Pouring the steps

Insert rebar along front edge of each step

1 Coat the forms with a release agent. Mix the concrete and bring it to the site in wheelbarrow loads. Shovel the concrete inside the forms, starting with the bottom step and working up. Tap the sides of the forms and risers with a hammer and jab a 2×4 up and down in the mix to drive air bubbles out. Give the concrete enough time to settle between the rubble pieces, and add more concrete if needed.

2 To strengthen the front of each step, cut a section of rebar 4 inches shorter than the width of the step and work it into the concrete about 2 inches behind the riser forms. Then screed the concrete with a 2×4, working from the landing down to the first step. Float the steps from the top down also, working the front edge of the float under the bevel you cut in the riser. Insert J-bolts for your railing, if your railing requires them.

OPTIONS FOR OUTDOOR STEPS

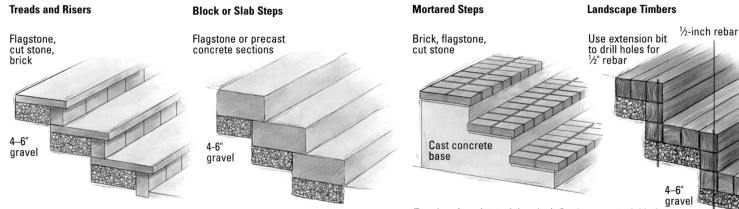

Treads and Risers

Flagstone, cut stone, brick

4–6" gravel

Block or Slab Steps

Flagstone or precast concrete sections

4-6" gravel

Mortared Steps

Brick, flagstone, cut stone

Cast concrete base

Landscape Timbers

Use extension bit to drill holes for ½" rebar

½-inch rebar

4–6" gravel

Tread surface (material varies). Set loose material below rear surface of tread and edged on the sides.

3 Run an edger along the inside edge of each riser form to round the front edge of each step to minimize chipping. If you're going to cover the steps with brick, tile, or stone, leave the edges square.

4 Let the concrete set up long enough to support its own weight, then remove the riser forms and finish the concrete with a trowel. Use a step trowel (a drywall corner knife works as well) to work the corners smooth. Broom the treads to roughen the surface, let the concrete cure, then install the railing. After 12 to 24 hours, remove the side forms and fill in any voids in the concrete.

Steps for a hillside

To build steps that run up a slope, measure the total rise and compute the individual rises and runs. Then remove the sod from the location of the steps. Dig two 3- to 4-inch-deep trenches in the slope, spaced the width of the steps. Cut two 2×12s to the length of the trenches, and set them as side forms in the trenches. Stake them parallel with each other.

  Excavate the soil in a series of stepped platforms between the forms. These don't have to conform to the finished steps, but they have to roughly correspond to the pattern on the 2×12s and be deep enough to allow for 4 inches of concrete.

  Rip riser forms to the correct unit rise and cut them to the width of the steps. Fasten them to the 2×12s and brace them with stakes. Pour the concrete and finish the steps as shown above. You can mortar brick, tile, or stone to the cured concrete *(pages 168–173)*.

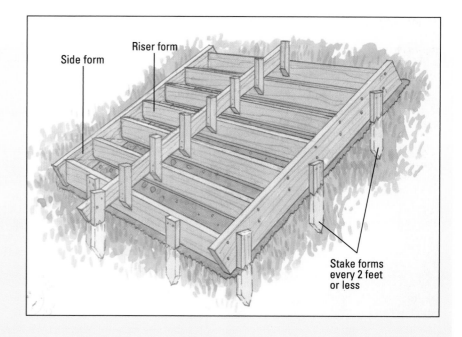

STEPS WITH TIMBERS AND BRICK

Brick treads framed with landscape timbers make attractive steps between different levels in your yard.

Timbers come in a variety of sizes, and the size of the timbers you use will affect both the dimensions of the steps and the possibilities for brick patterns within the frame. Find out what's available and use the actual measurements to draw a dimensioned plan (see "Timber tips," below). Most timbers come in 8-foot lengths, perfect for steps 4 feet wide.

When you design your steps (and before you start digging), decide on a brick pattern. Use a pattern composed of whole bricks so you can avoid cutting them. Choose the brick, purchase the correct quantity, and dry-lay it on a flat surface in the pattern of your choice. Use the dimensions of this mocked-up section to cut the timbers to fit.

The plan shown here uses rebar to anchor the timbers into the soil. If your soil is sandy, use a 2-foot length of ¾-inch pipe or steel conduit instead.

1 Make the steps with a riser height equal to the timber height and a comfortable tread length (see "Trip-Proof steps," *page 159*). Lay out the site with stakes and mason's line. Then dig rough recesses in the hill, with the first recess 6 inches longer (front to back) than the actual tread.

2 Lay out the brick tread on a flat surface, and measure the dimensions of the layout. Cut timbers to these measurements and test-fit them around the brick. Square the corners with a framing square.

PRESTART CHECKLIST

☐ **TIME**
About 1 to 1½ days to lay out and set a 4-step project

☐ **TOOLS**
Round-nose shovel, stakes, mason's line, circular saw, handsaw, level, drill bits and extension, small sledgehammer, 2×4 for tamping, rubber mallet, straightedge, screed, broom

☐ **SKILLS**
Designing layout, excavating, cutting, laying brick

☐ **MATERIALS**
Pressure-treated timbers, ½-inch rebar, 12-inch spikes, gravel, landscape fabric, sand, pavers

---

STANLEY PRO TIP: **Timber tips**

The nominal size of a board refers to the size before drying and planing; actual size means the size you actually get, and it's less than its nominal size in thickness and width.

Timbers are available in a variety of sizes—4×6, 5×6, 6×6, and 6×8—but these stated sizes are ½- to ¾-inch larger than actual sizes. Thus a 6×6 is actually 5½ inches on each side. The actual measure matters because the size of the timber you use will affect the dimensions of your steps. Timber with a 6-inch side (5½ inches actual) provides a convenient rise for outdoor steps. Be sure to include the dimensions of the other side of the timber when figuring the tread depth of each step.

Manufacturers widely used chromated copper arsenate (CCA) and ammoniacal copper arsenate (ACA) for pressure-treating lumber. Research, however, has shown that arsenic compounds are a potential health hazard, so production of such treated wood for residential use was halted in 2003. Still, you may find these products on the market today because the law allows suppliers to sell their existing stock. Check labels carefully. Lumber with newer treatment chemicals, such as ammoniacal copper quaternary (ACQ), is not considered hazardous. It is corrosive to metal fasteners and components, however. Buy hardware rated for use with treated lumber.

No matter what kind of pressure-treated wood you purchase, wear protective clothing, a dust mask, and safety glasses while working with it. Sweep up thoroughly and dispose of scraps. Do not burn pressure-treated waste. Call your local environmental agency and ask about proper disposal methods. Keep children out of the work area.

Rear timber

3 To assemble the timbers, drill pilot holes for 12-inch spikes completely through the front face of the outside timbers and about 2 inches into the side timbers. Drive the spikes with a small sledgehammer. At the corners of the rear timbers, center a mark on the top face, about 4 inches from the ends. Mark the middle of the timber also. Drill a ½-inch hole through the timber. (You'll drive rebar anchors through these holes when you set the frames.)

12-inch timber spike holds frames together

4 Set the frame for the bottom step in the lowest recess in the ground. Lay a 4-foot level across the sides of the frame and level it. Slope the frame from back to front at the rate of ¼ inch per foot. To get the slope right, lay a 2-foot level on the side timber with a ½-inch spacer under one end. The slope is correct when the bubble is centered.

Building timber-and-brick entry steps

1×4 tacked to rear of 2×4 creates flange that lowers edge of screed

1 Build and anchor timber forms with the proper rise and run and with interior dimensions that will accommodate your brick pattern. Excavate the recess if necessary to hold 4 to 6 inches of gravel, 2 inches of sand, and the paver thickness. Install the gravel and sand, then screed the sand in the recess.

2 Starting with the bottom step, lay the pavers, bed them with a rubber mallet, and level them. Spread fine sand on the surface and sweep it into the joints. Mist the sand with water, add more sand, and repeat the process until the joints are filled. The finished steps are shown on *page 167*.

5 When the first frame is correctly leveled and sloped, cut 24-inch lengths of ½-inch rebar and drive them through the holes in the rear timbers and into the soil.

6 Lay the second frame on the first. The front timber of the top frame lays on the rear timber of the lower one with their faces flush. Drill three pilot holes all the way through the top timber and partway into the bottom one. Then drive 12-inch spikes into the holes. Slope the second frame and anchor the rear timber with rebar driven into the holes you drilled in Step 3.

1×4 tacked to rear of 2×4 creates flange that lowers edge of screed

9 Make a recessed screed by nailing a 1×4 to a 2×4. The bottom edge of the 1×4 extends below the frame by the thickness of a paver. Screed the sand level and smooth.

10 Set the pavers in the frame in the pattern you used to determine the frame dimensions. Bed them in the sand with a rubber mallet, and level them as you would the surface of a brick-in-sand patio *(page 113)*.

7 Install the remaining frames, fastening and sloping them and anchoring the rear timbers with rebar. Make sure each frame is level from side to side before installing the next one.

8 Excavate the recess further until it's deep enough for a 3-inch layer of gravel, 2 inches of sand, and the thickness of your pavers. Tamp down the soil in each recess with the end of a 2×4, then lay landscape fabric on the soil. Shovel in the gravel, level it, and tamp it. Add the sand and tamp it as well.

11 Shovel a thin layer of builder's sand onto the brick and use a brush to sweep the sand into the joints. Mist the joints and brush on more sand, repeating the process until the joints are filled.

TIMBER-AND-BRICK ENTRY STEPS

Timber-and-brick entry steps are easier to install than poured concrete and give an informal look. The 5½-inch riser height may not be suitable in all instances, however. Lay out the steps, install the timbers, and set the brick as you would for steps in the landscape.

FINISHING STEPS WITH MORTARED BRICK

The method you use to finish concrete steps with mortared brick depends on whether you're pouring new steps or finishing existing steps. In both cases, the surface of the top step must be lower than the doorsill. If the surface will end up too high, you'll have to change the doorway or redesign the steps.

If you're pouring new steps, allow for the thickness of the brick and the mortar bed when you compute the unit rise *(page 159)*. A computed unit rise of 6½ inches, for example, finished with 2¼-inch-thick brick, would leave room for a 3⅜-inch-thick concrete base. This thickness is probably strong enough for mortared steps but may not satisfy local building codes. You may have to change the number of steps to provide a thick enough base.

If you're adding brick to existing steps, and they won't interfere with the door opening, use the technique illustrated here. The forms provide edges that will keep brick in line.

PRESTART CHECKLIST

☐ **TIME**
About 8 to 12 hours to finish four steps

☐ **TOOLS**
Hammer, mixing tub, mason's trowel, screed, level, rubber mallet, small sledgehammer, brick set, mortar bag, paintbrush, jointer, burlap rag, carpenter's pencil

☐ **SKILLS**
Building forms, screeding, laying brick

☐ **PREP**
Repair existing slab

☐ **MATERIALS**
1¼-inch screws, 2×4, 1×4, ¾-inch plywood, Type M mortar, bricks, stones, portland cement

1 To reface existing poured concrete steps, cut forms for the mortar bed from ¾-inch plywood and drive 2×4 stakes next to them. Level the forms with the top edges ½ inch above the top of the steps. To mortar brick to newly poured steps, leave the forms in place and add a ½-inch extension to them. Cut ½-inch strips of plywood to the same length as the tread of each step. Fasten each strip to two 6-inch lengths of 1×4 with the top edges flush. Lay the strips on the top edge of the forms and fasten the 1×4s to the forms. These strips serve as a screeding surface for the mortar bed and don't have to contain the side stresses exerted by concrete.

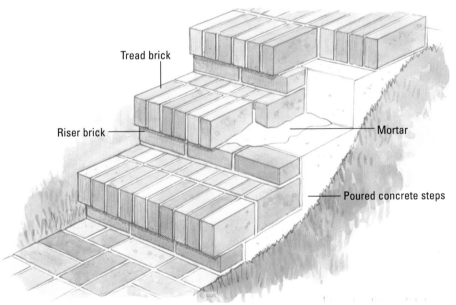

Tread brick

Riser brick

Mortar

Poured concrete steps

Mortaring bricks to steps requires a poured concrete foundation that is solid and whose surface is in good repair. Bricks set in a rowlock (shown) make a strong and durable surface, but you can experiment with other patterns. Bricks set on the treads can overlap risers by 1 to 2 inches, as long as the overlap is equal on each step.

2 Mix a small amount of premix mortar in a mortar box, following the instructions on the bag. Using a mason's trowel, spread about ½ inch of mortar along the bottom and on the face of the first riser.

3 Set the first riser brick in place. The joints on both the landing and the riser are ⅜ inch thick. Make sure the top of the brick is flush with the top of the step. Butter the end of the second and subsequent bricks and set them in place. When you have laid the riser brick, set a level across them to make sure they are level and flush.

Experiment with patterns

Mortared brick lends itself to various patterns. Patterns that use whole brick will save you cutting time. Lay out the bricks in a dry run first to make sure the bricks line up properly and fit the steps.

4 Apply a layer of mortar about ½ inch deep to the surface of the first tread. Spread mortar on the top edges of the riser bricks you have already laid. Cut a 1× or 2× screed to the outside width of the forms and pull the screed across the mortar, working the screed from side to side as you go.

5 Set the bricks on the tread, starting at the rear of the step tread. Keep the bottom joint about ⅜ inch thick, and space the brick on the surface with ½- or ⅜-inch plywood spacers. Bed the brick in the mortar by tapping it with the end of the trowel handle. Remove the spacers as you go, and level the brick with a straightedge.

6 Using the same techniques, continue laying riser brick and tread brick, spacing and leveling each step. Let the mortar set thoroughly. Then mix up mortar for the joints. Squeeze the mortar into the joints with a mortar bag. Fill the joints completely.

7 When the mortar in the joints begins to firm up, tool them with a jointing tool. Smooth the horizontal joints first, then the vertical joints. That way rainwater will have a free path to flow off the front face of the steps. Let the mortar set up, then scrub off the excess with a piece of wet burlap. Allow the mortar to cure for five to seven days before you use the steps.

3 Before you set the stones, mix up a slurry of portland cement and water and brush a very thin coat of the slurry on the stones. The slurry will help the stones adhere to the mortar.

4 Spread a 1-inch mortar bed on the surface of the steps. Starting at the rear of the tread along the riser, set the stones in the mortar and bed them with a rubber mallet. When you have completed the tread, make sure the surface is generally level—check it with a 4-foot level and correct high, low, and tipped stones.

Finishing steps with flagstone

1 For mortared flagstone, choose flat stones at least 1 inch thick and set them on the steps in a dry run. Mark stones so you can cut them to fit the adjacent stones, keeping the joints narrow. When the pattern is right, number the stones and set them aside in the same order. Tread stones can overhang the risers 1 to 2 inches.

2 To cut the stones you have marked, tap a stone chisel with a small sledgehammer to score the cut lines. Then prop the scored section over a scrap of wood or pipe and break it off with a sharp blow from the sledgehammer.

5 Continue setting the stones until the steps are complete. Let the mortar set up solidly. Then fill a mortar bag and squeeze mortar into the joints. Use a trowel to pack the joints if necessary.

6 Allow the mortar in the joints to set up slightly, then tool them with a concave jointer. Scrub off excess mortar with a piece of wet burlap. Let the mortar cure for a week before using the steps.

TILING OUTDOOR STEPS

Tile is an ideal facing for exterior steps, especially if the steps are an integral part of a tiled patio design. Even if they're not, tiled steps are an attractive option that brightens any outdoor entrance. The main provision: The concrete has to be in good condition to provide a solid substrate for the tile.

Inspect the steps, then repair cracks, level the surfaces (especially the treads), and clean off any oily stains that could interfere with the adhesive bond. Install an isolation membrane, if necessary, and roughen the surface.

The edges of concrete stairs are often chipped or otherwise damaged. If left unrepaired, tile you set on them will be unsupported and might break. Repair the edges as shown on these pages, using a sand-mix mortar, not patching compound.

Use nonslip tiles with matching radius caps over the tread nosing. If you can't find radius caps in the style you want, consider V-cap styles as a substitute. If neither is available, use standard field tile and round the edges with a tile stone.

PRESTART CHECKLIST

☐ **TIME**
About 8 to 10 hours for a four-step entry, not counting prep time

☐ **TOOLS**
Tape measure, wet saw, drill, trowels, roller, grout bag, brick set or cold chisel, small sledge

☐ **SKILLS**
Repairing tile, installing tile, cutting tile

☐ **PREP**
Repair existing concrete surface, install backerboard on wood-frame stairs

☐ **MATERIALS**
Mortar, 2×8 form, brick or concrete block, isolation membrane, backerboard, felt paper, mesh tape, tile, tile spacers, joint compound, grout, exterior-grade plywood, caulk

Preparing the steps

1 Repair damaged edges on concrete steps by chipping away loose concrete with a brick set and small sledgehammer. If you don't have a brick set, use a cold chisel, but proceed with caution to avoid removing too much concrete.

2 Sweep away dust and loose material with a hand brush, then wet the area with fine spray from a garden hose. Set a 2×8 against the front of the damaged step, holding it in place with bricks or blocks. Fill the recess with concrete and smooth it along the top of the form.

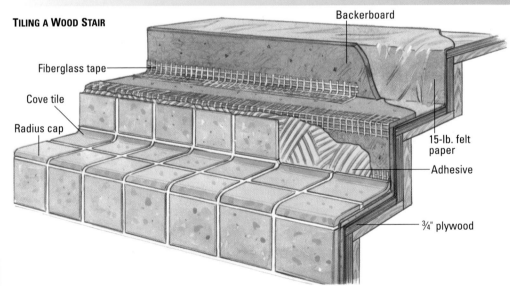

TILING A WOOD STAIR

Backerboard

Fiberglass tape

Cove tile

Radius cap

15-lb. felt paper

Adhesive

¾" plywood

To keep tiles on wood stairs from cracking, make sure the structure is solid and doesn't flex when walked on. Strengthen the stairs by adding a third stringer in the middle if necessary. Cover the treads, risers, and landings with ¾-inch exterior-grade plywood and waterproofing membrane. Then install backerboard over the entire surface of the stairs, taping the joints with backerboard tape and compound. Trowel on mortar and set the tile. Finish the edges with bullnose tile.

3 As an added precaution, apply isolation membrane over patched cracks after the patch dries. Roll on the material with a roller or spread a trowel-applied membrane with the smooth edge of a trowel. Work it to a consistent thickness with the notches, then even it out with the straightedge.

4 Dry-lay the tiles to make sure they fit. To help keep the tiles in place, build forms on the side of the steps that extend about ½ inch above the surface *(page 168)*. Use the same techniques used for tiling a patio *(pages 134–137)*. Spread latex-modified thinset over the bottom riser and comb it with the notched edges of a trowel. Push the tiles into the mortar with a slight twist. Then set the radius cap tiles along the edge. Tile each riser and tread in the same fashion. When the mortar has cured, grout the tiles with a grout bag *(page 170)*.

Use nonslip tiles

Glazed tiles dress up the appearance of any surface, indoors or out, but their slickness makes them unsafe and unsuitable for use on stair treads. Even most unglazed tiles are slick when wet.

Tile used for stair treads must be slip-resistant. For extra safety, install slip-resistant inserts in the tread edges. Typically these metal channels slip under the tread and feature a replaceable plastic or rubber insert that covers the nosing.

As a last resort, or to make an existing tiled surface more slip-resistant, apply self-stick abrasive strips that are manufactured for this purpose. The strips wear, however, and require periodic replacement.

WHAT IF...
You want to tile only the risers?

Tiled risers provide a dramatic complement to hardwood treads. Choose a color that harmonizes with the color of the treads—patterns with earth tones or shades of blue go well with most wood colors. Use wall tiles or stone tiles. Install backerboard on risers that show signs of damage. Otherwise sand the existing finish lightly. Spread and comb thinset, and set the tiles with spacers placed on the bottom and the sides. Seal the top and bottom joints with caulk instead of grout.

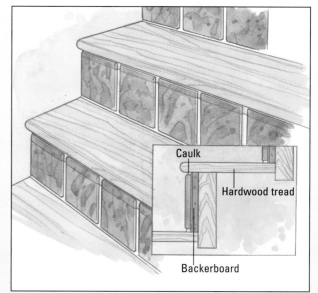

Caulk

Hardwood tread

Backerboard

BUILDING MASONRY WALLS

A masonry wall makes a formidable impression in the landscape, and building one is a formidable task, especially if you've never built one before. But putting up a brick, stone, or concrete block wall is a job well within your reach. You will need determination, skill, practice, and patience. Plan to spend substantial time on the job too; a wall is not a weekend project.

It's tough, but no other project provides quite the satisfaction as a completed masonry wall.

Walls are the dividing lines and corridors of a landscape design. As such they have a number of practical functions: directing traffic, focusing the view,

blocking unsightly objects, guiding travel through your yard. What's more, most of these functions can be adequately carried out with low structures—3 feet often suffices.

Walls are classified in two categories depending on what holds them together. Dry-laid or dry-set walls rely on gravity and friction as the primary bonding agents. Dry-set walls, which are constructed only of stone, do not require a footing. Mortared walls are constructed of brick, stone, or other material held together with mortar, a mixture of cement and other ingredients. You can use any masonry material for a mortared wall, and all mortared walls require a footing.

Walls are also classified according to purpose: freestanding or retaining walls. Freestanding walls have a decorative function and stand by themselves within the landscape. They are built with aesthetic considerations in mind. Retaining walls are aesthetic too but have to be strong because their primary purpose is to hold back earth on a slope or hillside. Retaining walls provide an excellent (and sometimes the only) solution when you want to put a patio at the bottom of a slope and therefore must cut into the slope to make room for it.

No matter what kind of wall you're building, you'll find all the information you need in this chapter.

Masonry walls require practice and patience, but will reward you with a feeling of great accomplishment.

CHAPTER PREVIEW

Running-bond brick wall
page 176

Common-bond brick wall
page 180

Concrete-block wall
page 184

Concrete-block retaining wall
page 190

Interlocking-block retaining wall
page 192

Dry-set stone wall
page 196

Mortared stone wall
page 198

Brick-veneer house wall
page 202

Stone-veneer house wall
page 206

RUNNING-BOND BRICK WALL

Friends, family, and passersby will forever admire your well-laid brick wall. The skills required to lay a wall well come from determination, practice, and patience. If you have not laid brick before, it will pay to practice throwing mortar and setting brick before you start building your wall.

For practice, set a 2×6 or 2×8 between two columns of concrete block, two or three blocks tall, to serve as a practice footing. Review the information about mixing and throwing mortar and setting brick on *pages 92–93*. Then take your trowel and mortar box outside and mix up a small batch.

Practice throwing mortar on two bricks. When you can get it right, try three bricks. You can scrape off the mortar and reuse it for practice until it hardens. Don't use your practice bricks in the actual wall; dried mortar will prevent new mortar from bonding properly.

Brick wall corners (called leads) are built first. Then you work to the center and fill in between. A running bond is the simplest pattern. Each row begins with a half brick, which offsets the joints every other row.

PRESTART CHECKLIST

☐ **TIME**
About 12 to 18 hours to lay a 3×10-foot wall

☐ **TOOLS**
Tape measure, chalk line, level, mason's trowel, brick set, pencil, small sledgehammer, mason's line, line level, mason's blocks, concave jointer, story pole

☐ **SKILLS**
Designing layout, excavating, throwing mortar, setting brick

☐ **MATERIALS**
2×4 lumber, spacers, bricks, mortar

1 Lay out the brick in a dry run and snap chalk lines on the footing. Take up the bricks and spread a mortar bed ¾ inch thick and three bricks long on the footing.

2 Line up the first brick with the chalk lines and push it into the mortar. The joint should be about ⅜ inch thick on the mortar bed. Butter the end of the second brick, then push it into the bed against the first brick, creating a ⅜-inch joint between them. Lay the third brick the same way.

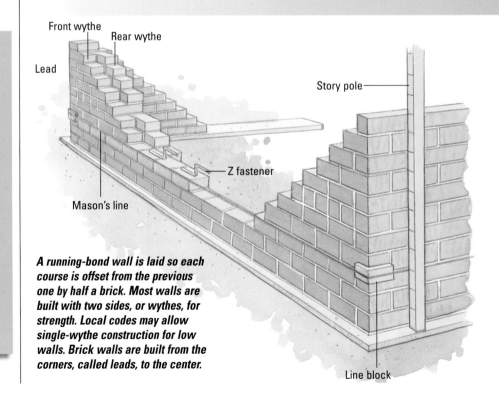

Front wythe
Rear wythe
Lead
Story pole
Z fastener
Mason's line
Line block

A running-bond wall is laid so each course is offset from the previous one by half a brick. Most walls are built with two sides, or wythes, for strength. Local codes may allow single-wythe construction for low walls. Brick walls are built from the corners, called leads, to the center.

3 Check the bricks with a level. Tap them with the end of the trowel handle as necessary to level them and align them on the chalk lines. Lay a second wythe of three bricks parallel to the first along the other chalk line. Check this wythe for level, both along its length and with the first wythe. Scrape off the excess mortar that squeezes from the joints. Using the same techniques, set two three-brick wythes at the other end of the footing, lined up and level.

4 Attach mason's blocks and line at both ends of the first course. Adjust the line until it's about 1/16 inch away from the face of the bricks and even with the top edge of the course. Start the second row with a half brick to offset the joints, and lay two bricks in the second course at both ends, about 1/16 inch from the mason's line. Build up the ends (and any corners) of both wythes to three courses, checking for plumb and level, and moving the mason's blocks up as you go. Check the courses with a story pole (page 96).

TAKING A DRY RUN
Lay out the bricks for guidelines

1 Snap two chalk lines on the footing as far apart as the combined width of both wythes of your wall. The lines should be the same distance from the footing edges.

2 Set out bricks on the line for one wythe without mortar, spacing the bricks with a 3/8-inch plywood spacer. Dry-set the other wythe, starting with a half brick so the joints of the wythes will be offset for strength. Mark the ends of the wythes on the footing.

3 If your wall will turn a corner, snap chalk lines and dry-set the other leg on the footing. Mark the ends of this leg also.

5 At the third course (and every third course thereafter) throw mortar on the bricks and push Z-shape or corrugated metal reinforcements into the mortar to tie the wythes together. Place them every 2 to 3 feet, or as your local codes require. Smooth the mortar over the ties and lay the next course of bricks.

6 Continue laying brick at the ends (building up the leads) until you have laid both wythes to five courses, moving the mason's blocks as you go and starting every other course with a half brick. Then begin to lay brick on the remainder of the footing to fill in between the leads. Butter the end of each brick as you did before and push it into place.

REFRESHER COURSE
Reinforcing brick

You can strengthen brick walls by adding either a corrugated fastener or Z-shape metal ties across the wythes and in the mortar, usually every 2 to 3 feet and every third row.

Modular brick with holes offers another option. You can insert ½-inch rebar into the holes to reinforce the wall. You also can embed ½-inch rebar in the footing to strengthen it. When you pour the footing, space the rebar so it will correspond to the location of the holes when you lay the brick.

Corrugated fastener

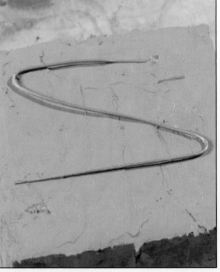

Z-shape metal tie

7 When the bottom row has space for only one more brick (called the closure brick), dry-fit this brick in the space and make sure it will fit with the proper joints. If you've set the brick correctly, it should fit. Trim both ends evenly if it doesn't. Then butter both ends with pyramids of mortar.

8 Holding the closure brick in the center, push it firmly into place. Tap it with the bottom of the trowel handle until it's level and its faces are lined up with the others. Then finish the first course of the other wythe.

9 Working from the ends of each lead toward the middle, lay the courses, moving the mason's blocks and checking your work with a level and a story pole. Scrape off the excess mortar from the joints. When the wythes complete a lead, build the leads higher, then fill in between them.

Checking the leads

Every third course, lay a straightedge on the stepped edges of the brick to check the leads. A properly laid lead forms a straight line at this edge. If a course is too long or too short, don't remove brick to fix the problem. Instead make up the difference a little at a time by laying the rest of the course with joints slightly more or less than ⅜ inch.

10 When the mortar is firm enough that your thumbnail leaves only a slight dent, finish the joints with a concave jointer. Clean excess mortar with wet burlap and after you've laid the last course, cap the wall (page 183).

COMMON-BOND BRICK WALL

A common-bond wall looks very similar to a wall laid with a running bond. However, a common-bond wall is built with a header course (bricks laid perpendicular across the wythes) every second and fifth (or sixth) course.

The headers tie the wythes together, which is why a wall built with this pattern is much stronger than a wall of running bond. Because the headers present their short face and sometimes a slight color difference, they lend visual interest too. You can accentuate this feature by using a different brick color for the header courses.

As always, dry-lay a test run of the layout before using mortar. If the length of the wall is critical and comes out a fraction of a brick short or long in the test run, you can adjust the thickness of the mortar joints as you go to make it fit.

Use grade SW brick in freezing climates and grade MW brick elsewhere.

PRESTART CHECKLIST

☐ **TIME**
18 to 24 hours to lay a 3×10-foot wall

☐ **TOOLS**
Tape measure, chalk line, level, mason's trowel, brick set, pencil, small sledgehammer, mason's line, line level, mason's blocks, concave jointer, story pole

☐ **SKILLS**
Designing layout, excavating, throwing mortar, setting brick

☐ **MATERIALS**
2×4 lumber, spacers, bricks, mortar

1 Lay out the bricks in a dry run with a full brick on the end of each wythe. Mark the edges of the wythes on the footing with chalk lines. Spread mortar on the footing and lay three bricks. Check for alignment and level. Lay three bricks of the second wythe, then lay two identical wythes at the other end of the wall.

2 Cut two bricks to three-fourths their length and throw mortar on the first wythes. Push the cut bricks into place and check their height with a story pole *(see page 96)*. Start the second course at the other end.

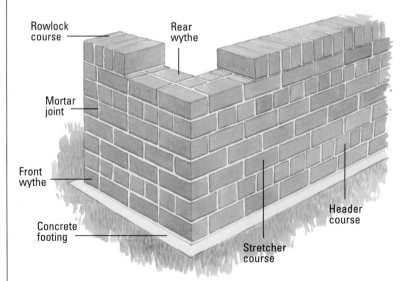

Rowlock course — Rear wythe — Mortar joint — Front wythe — Concrete footing — Stretcher course — Header course

One of the most common ways to lay bricks is aptly called a common bond—essentially a running bond with header bricks laid perpendicular to the others every fifth or sixth row. Start the first course with a full stretcher and the second with three-fourths of a stretcher, then headers. The third row starts with a full stretcher, the fourth row with a header then stretchers, and the fifth course with a full stretcher (just like the first course). Repeat this pattern until the wall is at its finished height.

3 Throw mortar on about two-thirds of the surface of the remaining brick in the first courses. Then butter the long side of a brick (a header brick) and push it into place against the short bricks. Lay two or three more header bricks in this fashion—both on this end and the other end of the wall.

4 Attach mason's blocks and line to the ends of the first course, 1/16 inch away from the bricks and flush with the top edge. Start the third course on both wythes with a full stretcher brick and continue to build the leads with stretchers in this course.

REFRESHER COURSE
Throwing mortar and setting brick

To properly bed mortar, tilt the trowel and sling the mortar onto the brick bed, pulling the trowel toward yourself in the same motion. Compact the outer edges of the mortar with the trowel.

Lightly furrow the center of the mortar bed with the tip of the trowel. Don't make the furrow too deep or it will cause an air gap under the brick.

To place the brick on the mortar bed, push it firmly against the brick already in place. After you've set the brick, tap it gently and check it for level.

5 Working from the leads to the center, finish the first course of stretchers on both wythes, buttering the closure brick on both ends before setting it. Then finish the second course of headers from the leads to the center, moving the mason's block up as you go, leveling and plumbing.

6 Continue filling between the leads on the third course (stretcher course) of the front wythe, moving the line up to guide brick placement. Check the wythe with a level and story pole. Continue building up new leads, starting the fourth course with a header, followed by stretchers, and the fifth course with a full stretcher and stretchers thereafter, exactly like the first course.

7 When the front wythe is even with the leads, build leads on the rear wythe and fill between them the same way. Shift the mason's blocks and line to the rear wythe and move it up for each course. Check every other course for plumb and level. When both wythes are even with the leads, start the sixth course with a three-quarter brick, just like the second course, and build leads in the same order as the first five courses.

WHAT IF...
The wall has corners?

1 Beginning with the front wythe, throw a short length of mortar on both legs of the footing and set a corner brick and one more along each leg of the footing. Then lay three bricks on the rear wythe, inside the front corner. Check for level along and across the wythes, adjusting bricks as needed.

2 To start the second course, cut two bricks into three-quarter and one-quarter lengths (these are called closures). Start the course with a three-quarter brick on both legs. Then set the one-quarter lengths on the rear wythe. Begin laying headers in both directions.

3 Continue laying two or three headers on both legs to complete the second course of the leads. Then build leads on the other end of the footing and lay the rest of the wall as shown on these pages. Check for level and plumb at least every other course.

Building the cap

1 Rowlocks, headers set on edge across the wythes, make an excellent cap for any wall. Because the width of a course set on its edge may equal that of the wall, mark the dimensions of the cap course with a story pole. If you have to trim a brick, set it a few bricks from the end to hide it. You may also be able to adjust the width of the mortar joints to make it come out right.

2 Starting at one end of the wall, throw mortar to a length of about four bricks. Lay this brick and continue throwing mortar and setting brick at the other end. Work from both ends toward the middle. When you reach the last space, dry-lay the closure brick to check its fit. Trim it, if necessary, with a masonry saw. Butter both sides of the closure brick and tap it into place with the trowel handle.

4 To set the cap row on a wall that turns a corner, mark both legs with a story pole to make sure the length of the rowlock course will equal the width of the wall. Set the rowlocks on one leg as shown, then set the other leg.

A margin of error

The last brick in a wythe, the closure brick, is set after you have filled in from the leads to the center of the wall. The closure brick offers you a margin for error if the joints between bricks aren't consistently the same width. If you've set the rest of the brick perfectly, the closure brick will fit easily, but if the space is a little tight, you can trim the closure brick or make the joint a little thinner so the brick fits the opening.

Waterproofing a wall

Although a number of commercial products are manufactured to waterproof masonry structures, a properly laid brick wall should not need a waterproofing application. You may, however, want to seal any bricks below the ground with asphalt.

SAFETY FIRST
Check codes for wall rules

Most local building codes require that walls higher than 48 inches contain reinforcement for strength and stability. Check with your building department before you construct any wall.

CONCRETE-BLOCK WALL

Building a block wall is heavy work, but a few techniques help the job along.

Build the corners (leads) first, then fill in between the leads to form the courses. Build the leads three to five courses high before setting the blocks between them.

When you have to butter the ears of several blocks, set them all on end and butter them at the same time.

To neatly remove excess mortar from the block, let it set up a little before scraping it off; removing soft mortar can produce smears that are hard to clean.

From time to time you'll have to stop setting block so you can strike the joints. You won't be able to complete the wall and strike the joints all at once unless the wall is very small. If you plan to stucco the wall, simply scrape off excess mortar instead of striking the joints.

When the mortar has dried, brush the wall with a stiff brush to remove dirt and fragments of mortar.

PRESTART CHECKLIST

☐ **TIME**
18 to 24 hours for a 3×10-foot wall

☐ **TOOLS**
Tape measure, circular saw, brick set, small sledgehammer, chalk line, pencil, mason's trowel, level, line level, mason's blocks, wheelbarrow, concave jointer, story pole

☐ **SKILLS**
Designing layout, mixing mortar, setting block

☐ **PREP**
Lay out and pour footing

☐ **MATERIALS**
2×4 lumber, concrete blocks, mortar, metal lath

Building end leads

1 Lay out your block in a dry run, spacing it with ⅜-inch plywood spacers. Mark all the edges of the course. Take up the block and spread mortar on the footing. Push the first block into the mortar until it's ⅜ inch above the footing. Mortar the ears of the second block and push it against the first.

2 At this point, you can continue to build up the lead on one corner, then the other, or build both of them at the same time. To start the other lead, push a corner block into mortar at the other end. You can attach mason's blocks and line from one corner to the other to help keep them straight.

CONCRETE-BLOCK WALL

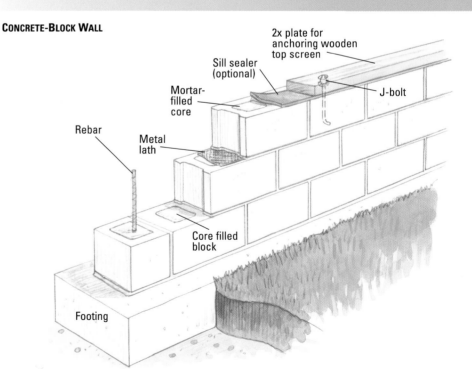

2x plate for anchoring wooden top screen

Sill sealer (optional)

Mortar-filled core

J-bolt

Rebar

Metal lath

Core filled block

Footing

3 Mortar the ears of the next block on either end and push it into place. Adjust the position of the block so it's level along the top of the course and from side to side—tap the blocks into position with the end of the trowel handle. From time to time and after the mortar has set up slightly, trim away any excess with the trowel.

4 Build up the lead on one end of the footing by throwing mortar for the second course and starting this course with a half block. Butter the ears of the second block in this course and continue laying the block three or four courses high. Check often for level, plumb, and square. Periodically check the firmness of the mortar by pressing it with your thumb. When you can just dent it, stop setting block and strike the joints *(page 188)*.

MORTAR THE EARS
Buttering the block ends

1 To butter the ears (the flanges on the ends of a block) first set the block securely on one end. Take up a trowel-length of mortar from your mortarboard and butter the ears with a downward swiping motion of the trowel. Then press down on the mortar on the inside edge of the ear to keep it from falling off when you set the block. If the mortar does fall off, start over with fresh mortar.

2 Slice into the side of the mortar with the edge of the trowel to shape it into an inverted U.

Checking the leads

1 When the lead on one end is three or four courses high, build up the lead on the other end, using the same techniques. Be sure to start alternate courses with a half block. If your wall turns a corner, build the corner with alternating corner blocks. As you go, check that the lead is plumb and level from front to back and side to side.

2 Once a lead is at the correct height, lay a 4-foot level across the edges of the block. If a block extends too far out, tap it in place with the trowel handle. If a block falls short of line, don't adjust it or remove it. Make up the difference across the rest of the course by making some of the joints thicker.

BUILD THE CORNER
Start with a corner block

Full corner block

If your wall is designed with corners, start the first leg with a full corner block. This is a stretcher block with a finished face on one end. After setting the corner block, butter the ears of the adjacent block and set it.

Don't slide the block

Concrete block doesn't require gentle treatment. Grab the block by the sides of the webs and, looking down into the cores, push it into place, lining it up with the others. Don't slide the block into place—you'll displace the mortar and create an uneven joint.

Building between the leads

1 Stretch a line with mason's blocks between the leads. Set the line $\frac{1}{16}$ inch from the face of the block and level with the top of the first course. Lay a mortar bed on the footing between the leads, and set the block, working from both sides to the center.

2 When you reach the center of the wall and have space for only one more block (the closure block), set that block in the space without mortar. It should fit with enough room for $\frac{3}{8}$-inch joints. If there's not enough room, trim the block with a cold chisel or circular saw and a masonry blade. Mortar the ears of the block on both sides and push it into place.

3 Continue building the leads by moving the mason's blocks up to the next course and properly aligning it. Throw mortar for the following course between the leads, butter the ears of each block and set them, working from the leads to the center and keeping the block a consistent distance from the mason's line.

STANLEY PRO TIP: **Butter all the web at corners**

You don't need to throw mortar on the center web. Doing so makes the block more difficult to level and plumb and wastes mortar. The only exception is when you're placing metal reinforcement on the corners of a wall. In this case, butter all the web and embed metal lath into the mortar. You can also cut and bend reinforcement bar into a right angle, and push the reinforcement into the mortar. Then smooth the mortar over the reinforcement.

Core-filling a wall

If you're building a long wall, local building codes may require you to strengthen it by constructing core-filled pilasters at intervals along its length.

The pilasters are made by interrupting the course of the wall with two perpendicular blocks set side by side, alternating with a full block every other course.

In order for the pilasters to receive proper support, you must pour your footing to support them, inserting lengths of rebar into the footing where the cores of the pilaster will be.

Once you have completed the wall to its finished height, fill the pilaster cores with mortar mixed slightly wetter than joint mortar so it pours more easily.

You will also have to install rebar in the footing of a retaining wall and core-fill the wall for added strength.

Finishing touches

1 Remove excess mortar from the block as you go, but let the mortar set up slightly. Then slice off the excess with the edge of the trowel.

2 From time to time, stop laying block and check the mortar by pressing your thumb into a joint. When the mortar will just dent enough to hold a slight thumbprint, it's ready for striking. Run a concave striking tool along the joints, compressing them and smoothing them. Strike the horizontal joints first then the vertical joints to allow water to run freely down the wall. Scrape off excess mortar and strike the joints again.

Control joints

Control joints allow sections of a wall to expand and contract and rise and fall without disturbing other sections. Most backyard block walls won't need control joints; they are necessary for walls more than 60 feet long. A control joint placed every 20 feet on a long wall minimizes the chances it will crack.

Control joints are made in a number of different ways. One way employs a rubber gasket that fits into grooves in the side of the block. Check with your building department for local requirements.

Topping off the wall

Cap blocks are made specifically to hide the top cores and provide a finished look. If you're laying cap blocks, throw mortar on the top edges of the last course and lay the first cap block in the corner. Butter the ends of the remaining block and set them centered on the wall, tapping them level.

Plain mortar makes an acceptable cap for a block wall, but it requires some support. Lay metal lath into the mortar before laying the last course of blocks. Lay the last course, then core-fill it *(page 189),* overfilling by about ½ inch. Level the mortar across the webs, then round its edges to let water drain off more easily.

Core-filling the top course

Embed metal
lath in mortar
(not shown for
clarity)

1 Some wall designs call for filling the cores of the top course with mortar (called core-filling). If you're going to core-fill the top course (for J-bolts, for example) cut a length of metal lath to the width of the block and lay it on top of the next-to-last course. The metal lath will keep the mortar from falling through the blocks to the bottom. Then throw mortar and set the top course.

2 Scoop mortar from your mortar box into a bucket so you can carry it with you as you work across the wall. Scrape mortar from the bucket into the cores, overfilling them slightly. Poke the trowel up and down in the cores a couple of times to make sure the mortar is thoroughly distributed.

3 If you plan to attach a 2× sill or cap to the wall, embed J-bolts into the mortar. Center a bolt in the core and push it down until about 2 inches remains above the cores (about 1½ inches if you will counterbore your 2× cap for the J-bolt nuts). Use a layout square to make sure they're vertical.

4 Smooth the mortar in each core with a small trowel, leveling it to the web of the block and taking care not to disturb the J-bolt. Let the mortar set up before you install the sill or cap.

5 Line up the lumber with the J-bolts and mark the 2× so you can drill holes that correspond to the bolts. Drill the holes and counterbore them, but wait until the concrete has cured before attaching the board.

CONCRETE-BLOCK RETAINING WALL

Concrete block is ideal for building walls to hold back the soil after you dig into a slope for a pathway, patio, or other project. Block retaining walls are generally the same as freestanding block walls *(pages 184–185)*—with a few important differences.

A retaining wall must provide a way to release the water that builds up in the slope behind it. Without a pressure-relief system, the weight of the water in the soil would crack, or even buckle, the wall. Weep holes—lengths of ¾-inch pipe inserted along the top of the first course—escort some of the water out. The other part of the system is a plastic drainpipe covered with gravel. As water accumulates behind the wall, it percolates through the gravel into the drainpipe, which carries it off safely.

Retaining walls must be stronger than freestanding walls. Insert rebar in the footing when you pour it—every three blocks, or at intervals specified by your local codes. As a last step, fill the cores around the rebar with mortar from the bottom to top.

PRESTART CHECKLIST

☐ **TIME**
20 to 36 hours for a 3×10-foot wall

☐ **TOOLS**
Tape measure, brick set, small sledgehammer, chalk line, pencil, mason's trowel, level, mason's blocks, wheelbarrow, striking tool, story pole, shovel, wheelbarrow

☐ **SKILLS**
Designing layout, excavating, mixing mortar, setting block

☐ **PREP**
Lay out and pour footing

☐ **MATERIALS**
Concrete blocks, 2×4 stakes, 2×8 lumber, mortar, gravel, 4-inch perforated drainpipe, landscape fabric, ¾-inch pipe

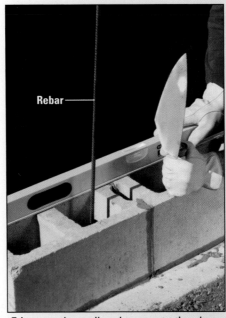

Rebar

Chip a small recess for the pipe

1 Lay out the wall and excavate the slope and the footing trench. Build the footing *(pages 80–81)* and insert rebar into the wet concrete at intervals corresponding to the cores in the blocks. Prepare the footing, spread mortar, and build leads *(pages 184–185),* sliding the block over the rebar as needed.

2 As you lay the second course of block, insert weep holes—¾-inch pipe—into the mortar every third block. Chip off a small recess in the block and trowel a mortar bed for the pipe, sloping it slightly toward the front. Then chip out a recess on the next block, butter the ears, and set the block.

TYPICAL CONCRETE-BLOCK RETAINING WALL

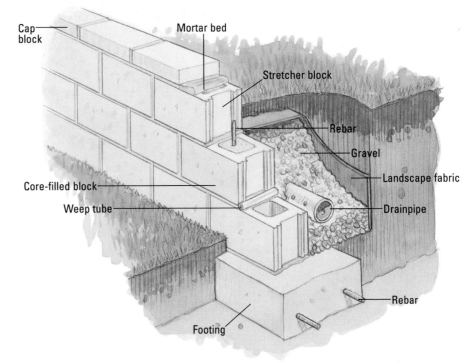

Cap block
Mortar bed
Stretcher block
Rebar
Gravel
Landscape fabric
Core-filled block
Weep tube
Drainpipe
Rebar
Footing

3 Stop occasionally to check the mortar. When it begins to set up slightly, scrape off the excess with an upswing of the edge of the trowel. Do not plug the weep holes with excess mortar as you remove it.

4 After you've laid at least two courses, spread landscape fabric on the soil behind the base of the wall, temporarily laying the excess over the grass on the slope. Lay rocks on the fabric to hold it while you work. Between the rear of the wall and the slope, backfill the wall with gravel, laying perforated drainpipe on the gravel bed level with the top of the first course. Face the holes down.

5 Shovel more gravel on top of the drainpipe. Backfill with additional gravel as you add courses to the wall. Fold the landscape fabric over the top of the gravel fill, and backfill with soil. Replace the sod.

6 When you reach the finished height of the wall, fill those cores containing rebar to the top with mortar. Mix the fill mortar slightly wetter than what you'd use for joints. Smooth the top with a trowel. Spread additional mortar, and lay cap block to finish the wall *(page 188)*.

INTERLOCKING-BLOCK RETAINING WALL

Interlocking concrete block is a way to build a strong wall without mortar. Some such blocks are made with flanges that slip over the rear edge of the preceding course; others rely on a system of pins. With both types, you don't have to practice throwing mortar or setting block, but you will get an attractive addition to your landscape. The flanges slope the wall back into the slope for additional strength.

Interlocking-block walls don't require a footing, but some styles require you to set the first course in a trench to hold the bottom of the wall in place. Cut the slope back 12 to 15 inches from the rear of the trench to leave room for gravel backfill and a drainpipe—a must for retaining walls. Save the topsoil and use any extra as fill elsewhere in your landscape.

PRESTART CHECKLIST

☐ **TIME**
10 to 20 hours to excavate and lay a 3×16-foot wall

☐ **TOOLS**
Tape measure, shovel, tamper, level, circular saw, small sledgehammer, rubber mallet, torpedo level, brick set, caulk gun

☐ **SKILLS**
Digging, designing layout, leveling and laying block

☐ **MATERIALS**
Landscape fabric, gravel, drainpipe, landscape blocks, construction adhesive

1 Lay out the wall and remove the soil from the slope. Following the manufacturer's recommendations, dig and level a trench for the first course. Stake a mason's line to help align the blocks.

2 Starting a foot beyond the top edge of the slope, spread landscape fabric down and over the trench. Put stones on the top to hold the fabric in place. Overlap the fabric edges by 6 inches. Tamp 3 to 4 inches of gravel into the trench and back to the bottom of the excavation.

TYPICAL INTERLOCKING-BLOCK RETAINING WALL

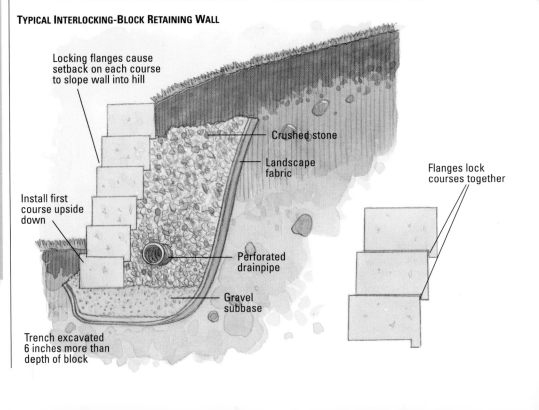

Locking flanges cause setback on each course to slope wall into hill

Crushed stone

Landscape fabric

Install first course upside down

Perforated drainpipe

Gravel subbase

Trench excavated 6 inches more than depth of block

Flanges lock courses together

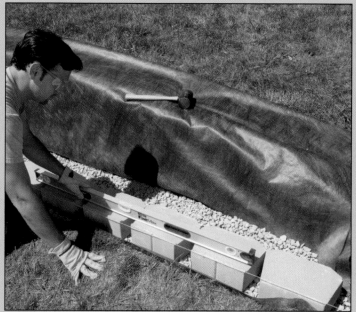

3 Using the line or the edge of the trench to guide you, lay the first course in the trench. The first course blocks are set backwards for many styles. Set each block with a rubber mallet. Make sure each block is level front to back and with the adjoining blocks. Use a 4-foot level to check—shorter levels are not long enough to ensure accuracy. If you need less than a full block at the end of the wall, lay smaller blocks or trim full blocks to fit.

4 Set the remaining courses with the flanges tight against the back of the preceding course. Start every other course with a half or partial block so the joints are offset by at least 3 inches or the amount specified by the manufacturer's instructions. As you work, check the blocks for level. Shim the low end of a block with a small piece of cedar shingle.

WHAT IF...
The blocks have locking pins?

Some blocks have pin-lock systems. One of the most common employs vertical and horizontal pins. Blocks fit over the vertical pins as you lay them. After laying each course, horizontal pins lock the blocks laterally.

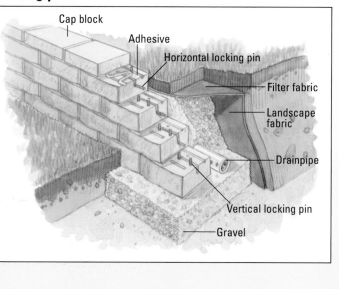

- Cap block
- Adhesive
- Horizontal locking pin
- Filter fabric
- Landscape fabric
- Drainpipe
- Vertical locking pin
- Gravel

TRIM FULL BLOCKS
Making shorter blocks

Precast block is trimmed the same way other masonry materials are trimmed. If you're using solid block, score the line you want to cut with a brick set and small sledgehammer. Repeated blows will split the block. Hollow-core blocks don't break cleanly. Buy half blocks and smaller blocks to fit where you need them, or cut them with a masonry blade.

5 After the third course of block, backfill the area between the wall and the slope with gravel, just about even with the second course. Lay in a perforated plastic drainpipe on the gravel (holes down). Let the pipe daylight beyond the edge of the wall, or run it into a French drain or dry well *(pages 82–83)*.

6 As you build the wall, backfill gravel behind it at least every other course, covering the pipe and bringing the level of gravel up just below the top of the last course you laid.

STANLEY PRO TIP: **Building corners**

If your wall is designed with corners, the corner blocks must overlap at the joints to tie the two legs together. Cut half blocks and alternate them with full blocks as shown, following the manufacturer's instructions. Chisel off the lip of the block if it gets in the way. As you place the block, strengthen the bond with a bead of construction adhesive.

9 The capstones made for block of this or a similar shape cover the V-shaped gaps between blocks in the lower courses. Prepare the next-to-last course by applying a bead of construction adhesive on the surface of each block.

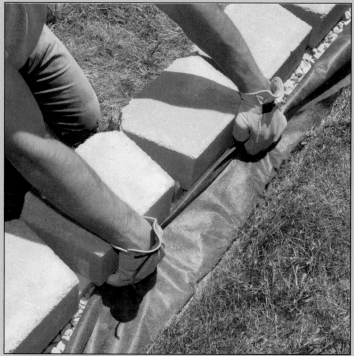

7 Using the same techniques and starting every other row with a partial block, continue building the wall and backfilling it with gravel. When you're one or two courses below finished height, fold the landscape fabric over the gravel and tuck it behind the block.

8 Shovel about 2 inches of the topsoil you removed (not the subsoil at the base of the slope) on top of the landscape fabric. Tamp the soil lightly with a garden rake and replace the sod.

10 Following the manufacturer's instructions place the course of capstones on the wall.

Capstone

11 If you're not building a patio or other structure below the wall, spread and tamp the topsoil you removed from the excavation. Fill in around the base of the wall and level the soil as far forward from the base as the landscape allows. Tamp the soil and replace the sod. Water the sod frequently until it is well established.

DRY-SET STONE WALL

A mortarless, or dry-set, stone wall imparts an old-style character to the landscape. A well-built dry-set wall will last for years. The first settlers in America built walls this way, and many of those walls are still standing today.

Besides not requiring mortar, a dry-set wall doesn't need a footing. It will flex as the earth moves due to freezing and thawing, but it won't fall down. For this kind of durability, however, you must select stones with as much surface contact between them as possible.

Where the contour of the stones form spaces that could cause the stone to move, fill in with small pieces of stone. You'll also need bondstones—long, flat stones that are long enough to span the front and rear wythes of the wall, tying them together.

Taper the sides of the wall inward from bottom to top about 1 inch for every 2 feet of height. You might have to cut the upper course of bondstones to length.

PRESTART CHECKLIST

☐ **TIME**
About 2 days to excavate and set a 3×10-foot wall

☐ **TOOLS**
Round-nose shovel, mason's line, stakes, tamper, circular saw, hammer, mason's hammer, stone chisel, level, cordless drill

☐ **SKILLS**
Designing layout, digging, lifting and setting stone

☐ **PREP**
Prepare site

☐ **MATERIALS**
Gravel, stones, 1×2s (for batter gauge), 1½-inch screws

1 Sort the stones into size groups. Use the largest, flattest stones for the base, smaller stones for the succeeding courses, and smaller chunks for filling in. For the wall footing, lay out and excavate a trench 8 inches deep and 6 inches wider than the wall on each side and at each end *(page 77)*.

2 Shovel about 4 inches of gravel into the trench; level and tamp it. Set bondstones on both ends of the trench. Using stones of different lengths, lay the front wythe (face) of the first course. Place a bondstone every 4 to 6 feet. Set the thinner edge of the stones in the center of the trench.

DRY-SET STONE WALL

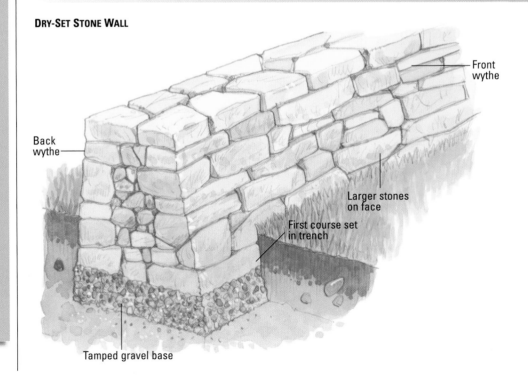

Front wythe

Back wythe

Larger stones on face

First course set in trench

Tamped gravel base

Use staked mason's line as needed to help keep the courses level

3 Lay the back wythe of the wall and fill the space between the two wythes with small stones or rubble. Continue laying the courses, choosing stones with the same thickness but a variety of lengths in each course. Offset the joints of the previous course. Cut stones if needed.

4 Check the batter—the taper from bottom to top—with a batter gauge as you work *(page 101).* Reposition stones if necessary, and vary the width of the stones on alternate courses. Every third course, set bondstones at 3-foot intervals.

5 Choose the flattest, broadest stones for the top course. Mortar the capstones in place if you like. Tip the stones in the top course slightly toward the face of the wall to improve drainage by inserting small flat stones under them.

WHAT IF...
You're building a dry-set retaining wall?

A dry-set stone retaining wall goes up using the same techniques as a freestanding wall but requires thicker stones throughout. Deadmen (long bondstones) are set into the slope to tie in the structure, and a drainage system is required to prevent water from building up behind the wall and exerting pressure on it.

When you cut away the slope for the wall, allow enough room to dig the trench so the wall's rear edge falls 15 to 19 inches from the base of the excavation. Build the wall two courses thick, backfilling it with gravel as you go and setting bondstones every three or four courses. Be sure to batter the wall so the weight of the soil won't push it out.

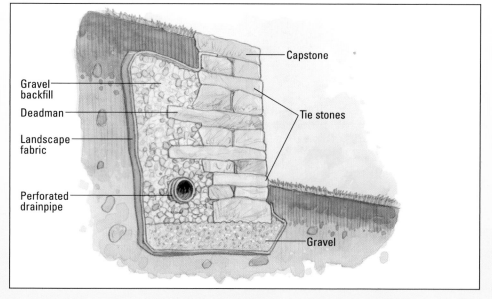

Gravel backfill

Deadman

Landscape fabric

Perforated drainpipe

Capstone

Tie stones

Gravel

MORTARED STONE WALL

An old stoneworker's adage describes how you should lay any stone wall: "One stone over two, two stones over one." Let the old saying guide your selection of stones for a mortared wall. And if you're using fieldstone, take another bit of old advice: "Pick stones that nest." That means choosing stones with contours that mate as closely as possible on their meeting faces.

Mortared stone walls need a concrete footing to keep them from cracking due to frost heave. Because a mortared wall is generally heavier than a dry-set wall of the the same size, local building codes often dictate specifications that affect the footings for mortared walls. Many codes require the use of reinforcing rod *(page 80)*. Check before you build.

PRESTART CHECKLIST

☐ **TIME**
2 to 3 days to lay a 3×10-foot wall

☐ **TOOLS**
Tape measure, chalk line, level, mason's trowel, mason's line, line level, concave jointer, stakes

☐ **SKILLS**
Designing layout, excavating, mortaring, lifting and setting stone

☐ **PREP**
Prepare site and order stones

☐ **MATERIALS**
Lumber for stakes, 1½-inch screws, stones, mortar

1 Lay out the site and pour the footing *(pages 74–81)*. While the footing cures, divide your stones into size groups. Dry-set the first course, starting with bondstones on the ends and every 4 to 6 feet in between. Choose subsequent stones that fit neatly between them.

2 Take up 3 or 4 feet of the stones and set them to the side in order. Then spread a generous layer of mortar—at least 1 inch—on the footing. Set the stones and tap them into place with a rubber mallet.

MORTARED STONE WALL

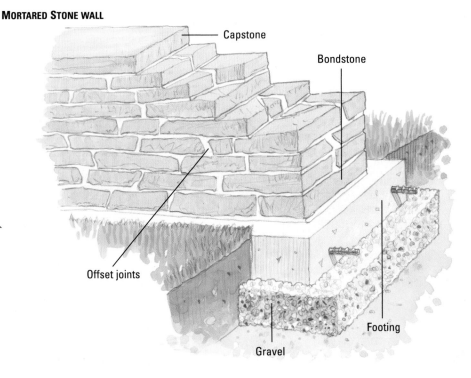

Capstone

Bondstone

Offset joints

Footing

Gravel

3 Continue removing stones, spreading mortar on the footing, and resetting the stones in the first course. Fill the gap between the front and rear wythes with smaller stones and mortar. Set a 4-foot level on the stones to make sure they're approximately level. Since the surface of the stones is rough, you won't get a precise reading from the level, just an average indication.

4 As you work, or after you've completed the first course on a short wall, pack mortar into the joints. For any space in the core that's more than ½ to ¾ inch wide, set in a small piece of stone to fill the gap.

WHAT IF...
You're building a mortared fieldstone wall?

Setting uncut fieldstone takes substantially more time than any other stone wall. That's because the stones in the courses must fit together. You'll find yourself engaged in a lot of trial-and-error fitting.

Like other mortared walls, a fieldstone wall requires a footing. Check your local codes to make sure your plans meet the requirements.

1 Plan the layout so square stones are set at the corners and flat-faced ones line the edges. Use the largest ones you can find but keep the size relatively consistent. Then remove the stones, mortar the footing, and set the stones in the same order.

2 Fill the core with rubble. Depending on the size of the rubble, fill the core in layers, throwing mortar between layers to bind them together. Smaller rubble is best. Then test-fit the stones for the second course.

3 Cover the core with mortar and pack mortar into the joints of the first course. For the next courses, spread mortar one stone at a time. Use enough mortar to form a bed for each stone.

5 When you've completed the first course, drive stakes at each end of the wall beyond the footing and tie mason's line tightly between them. Set the line at the height of the next course and use a line level to level it.

6 Selecting stones from the various piles you set out in Step 1, dry-lay the second course of both wythes. Choose stones that will sit approximately ½ inch below the staked mason's line. Remove these stones and set them aside in the same order. From this point, you can build your wall with leads—build up the corners and fill in between them as you would a brick or block wall *(pages 184–187)*.

CHECKING THE BATTER
Slope the sides

Except for those built as retaining walls, mortared stone walls don't have to be battered, but you can taper their sides if you like the appearance of a battered wall. Make a batter gauge *(page 101)* and use it to check both wythes.

STANLEY PRO TIP: **Using a mortar bag**

As you strike the joints, you'll usually find some places between stones that need extra mortar to make them even with the rest of the joint. Use a mortar bag to fill them. Mix mortar slightly wetter than you would if you were troweling it, fill the bag, then squeeze the mortar into the gaps. The bag is easier to control than a trowel and reduces the amount of mortar spilled on the wall or ground.

7 Continue setting courses, moving the mason's line to help keep them at the same level. Always choose flat, smooth stones for the visible faces of the wall. Fill in the space between the wythes and mortar the stones. Then dry-fit the next row and reset it, checking the batter as you go. Be sure to lay bondstones every third course, at roughly 4-foot intervals. When the mortar begins to set up, stop laying stone and finish the joints. Cap the wall with a course of flat stones large enough to cover both wythes. When you mortar

the capstones, do not finish the joints. Brush them flush with the surface of the capstones to keep water from collecting and freezing there—it could split the mortar or the stone. If you've mixed your mortar slightly wet to make it more workable, don't set any more than three courses a day—the weight of the stones will cause the courses to sag before the mortar sets.

Holding up the stones

Irregular stones are bound to leave gaps that cause the stone to tip before you can get it mortared. Cut a few small wood wedges before you start laying the wall and keep them close. Insert them in the gaps to keep the stone level. Mortar around the wedges and remove them when the mortar is set. Then fill the holes left by the wedges.

FINISH THE JOINTS
Strike joints smooth

1 When the mortar begins to set up, brush off the excess with a whisk broom or stiff brush.

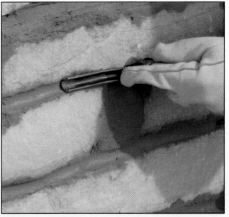

2 If the mortar is firm enough to hold a thumbprint, run a concave jointer over the joints to compact and smooth the mortar. Let the mortar set up a little more and rebrush it if necessary.

BRICK-VENEER HOUSE WALL

Brick cladding, also called brick veneer, will dress up the exterior walls of your home. Brick veneer is essentially a one-wythe wall attached to the house. After a few preparatory steps, you apply it using the same techniques as you would for a running-bond wall *(pages 176–179).*

The first step is to establish a solid bed for the brick to rest on. You can dig a trench, build forms, and set a concrete footing along the wall *(pages 80–81),* or you can fasten 4×4×$\frac{3}{16}$-inch angle iron to the foundation to provide a ledge, as illustrated on these pages. Even a half-high wall is a substantial weight, so fasten the angle iron with lag shields and lag screws.

This layer of brick will trap moisture against the wall; weep holes at the bottom of the wall give trapped moisture a way to escape.

PRESTART CHECKLIST

☐ **TIME**
About a day to lay a 4×10-foot wall

☐ **TOOLS**
Trowel, level, story pole, brick set, small sledgehammer, hammer, concave jointer, brush, open-end wrench, heavy-duty drill and bit, T-bevel

☐ **SKILLS**
Mixing and applying mortar, measuring and leveling, cutting bricks, striking joints

☐ **PREP**
Remove siding on sided surface

☐ **MATERIALS**
Mortar, brick, 4×4-inch angle iron, lag shield, lag screws, 2× lumber, finishing nails, glue

1 Snap a level chalk line on the foundation at the location of the angle-iron ledge. Cut the angle iron to length and drill holes at 1-foot intervals. Hold up (or prop) the angle iron on the line and mark the foundation at the center of the holes. Drill the foundation, insert lag shields, and attach the angle iron with lag screws.

2 Starting at one end of the ledge, throw a 1-inch bed of mortar two or three bricks long. Furrow the mortar with the trowel tip.

BRICK-VENEER WALL

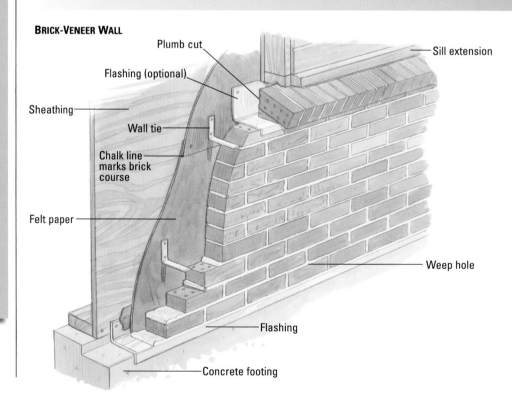

Plumb cut

Flashing (optional)

Sill extension

Sheathing

Wall tie

Chalk line marks brick course

Felt paper

Weep hole

Flashing

Concrete footing

3 Align the first brick with the edge of the foundation ledge and press it into the mortar. Leave a ½-inch airspace between the brick and the foundation. Make the mortar-bed joint ⅜-inch thick. Trim off the excess mortar and throw it back onto your mortarboard or the brick ledge.

4 Butter several bricks and lay them. Every three or four bricks, check them for level, making sure joints are ⅜ inch thick. Use the level to plumb the faces of the brick and make sure they lie on the same plane.

5 About every 2 feet, set a short piece of ¼-inch cord at the bottom of the head joint. Start the cord at the back of the brick. When the mortar starts to set, pull out the cord to create a weep hole.

WHAT IF...
The veneer goes on plywood?

Cover plywood sheathing with felt paper. Staple it to the sheathing and, using a story pole, snap chalk lines every fourth row to help keep the courses straight. Mark vertical lines for the studs so you can attach the corrugated anchors.

STANLEY PRO TIP

Preparing for veneer

Before you brick-veneer an exterior wall, remove the siding. Then staple a layer of house wrap or 15-pound felt paper to the sheathing as a moisture barrier.

Take off the window and door moldings—after you've laid the veneer, the existing moldings won't fit. You'll either have to replace the molding with thicker trim or add extensions to the original moldings (the less-expensive option).

Using a story pole, mark the felt paper just below door and window openings so you can properly position a top rowlock course under them.

Plastic weep tubes

Instead of forming a weep hole with ¼-inch cord, you can insert a plastic tube into the joint. Leave it in place as the mortar cures.

6 Using the same techniques used to build a running-bond wall *(pages 176–179),* build up the leads, starting every other course with a half brick. Check your work frequently for level, plumb, and proper alignment. Continue laying brick to make a five- or six-course lead at each end of the wall.

7 Attach mason's blocks and line at the ends of the first course, aligned with the top of the course and about 1/16 inch out from the front face. Working from both ends to the middle, lay the remainder of the first course.

Building corner leads

If your veneer goes around a corner, install it by building corner leads *(page 186).* The brick goes in two directions, so you won't need to start alternating courses with a half brick—the corner brick acts as a half brick (if the actual width of the brick is exactly half its length).

The number of bricks you lay in the first course in both directions should equal the number of courses you want in your lead. For example, if you want your lead to be nine courses high, lay five bricks in one direction and four bricks in the other. That will make a base for a nine-course lead.

Extending the sill

Blade set to angle of sill

Use finishing nails to fasten extension

The existing trim is cut for the thickness of your siding, so a rowlock course under the window will look out of proportion unless you extend the sill. Fix a T-bevel at the angle of the sill and transfer the angle to a 2× piece of lumber. Cut the extension on a table saw set to the same angle. Sand off or otherwise remove the paint on your old sill. Glue and nail the extension to the old sill.

8 At the middle, dry-set the final brick to make sure it will fit with ⅜-inch mortar joints. If it's too long, trim it slightly. Then butter both ends of the brick and push it in place. Make sure it's level and plumb. Move the line blocks up one course and lay that course. Continue laying courses past the top of the foundation.

9 At this point, and at every fifth course, nail corrugated brick ties into the studs. You can use a story pole to mark the wall at five-course intervals. Find the studs with a stud finder, a tape measure, or by finding the nails in the sheathing. Mortar the ties into the bottom joint as you set the next course of brick. Continue building leads and laying brick until you've reached the finished wall height.

Tooling the joints

From time to time, check the mortar to determine if it's ready for striking. When it has set up just enough that you can leave an impression with your thumb, strike the joints with a concave jointer. After striking the joints, let the mortar set up, then remove the excess with a stiff brush. Clean smears with a damp rag and a brush.

Install rowlock headers

1 To set the rowlock course at the correct angle of the wall and parallel to the window sill, set a T-bevel to the angle of the sill. Then transfer the angle to each of your rowlock bricks and cut them.

2 Install the rowlock course by buttering the sides of the bricks and pushing them into the mortar. If the course doesn't fit exactly, you can adjust the course's length by altering the thickness of the mortar joints.

STONE-VENEER HOUSE WALL

Facing stone, both real rock and synthetic, brings a rustic look to house walls . If you want to use real stone, get split fieldstone. It looks just like a rock wall when installed with attention to the pattern.

Most manufactured stone is more regular in appearance, molded in rough rectangles of different sizes. Installing both materials is much like gluing stones to the wall. Both tend to look better on surfaces that are about 36 inches tall or less, such as a foundation wall or the side of an outdoor barbecue enclosure.

Regardless of the kind of stone you're putting up, the mortar will need a surface with strong tooth to adhere to. Metal lath nailed to the wall is ideal. (Apply felt paper under it on sheathing.) The lath holds the mortar in place. Install the metal lath so the bottoms of the perforations slant down and in toward the wall, not out. Use pressure-treated lumber for the batten and leave it in place. Cover it with soil graded away from the foundation.

1 Fasten metal lath to a masonry foundation wall with masonry nails. Overlap the edges by at least 3 inches and install corner beads. If you're facing a wood-sheathed wall, staple felt paper to the sheathing and nail the metal lath through the felt paper.

2 Dig a narrow trench along the foundation and set a pressure-treated 2×4 rated for ground contact in it. Drive stakes next to the batten. Fasten the batten to them with screws, leveling it as you go. The batten is a ledge for the stones to rest on.

PRESTART CHECKLIST

☐ **TIME**
About 1½ days to veneer a 20-foot foundation wall

☐ **TOOLS**
Small sledgehammer, aviation snips, cordless drill, square trowel, pointing trowel, stone chisel, mortar box, mason's hoe, mason's blocks and line, mortar bag, stiff brush, striking tool

☐ **SKILLS**
Nailing metal lath, spreading mortar, setting stones

☐ **MATERIALS**
Metal lath, concrete nails, pressure-treated 2×4s, stone veneer

STONE VENEER WALL

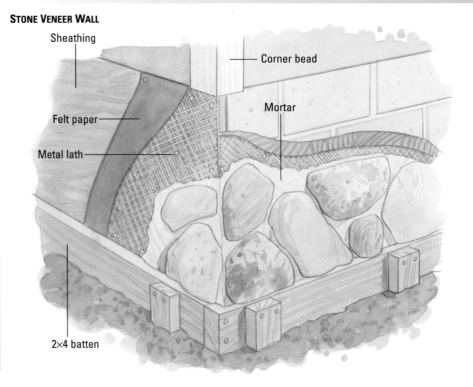

Sheathing

Corner bead

Felt paper

Mortar

Metal lath

2×4 batten

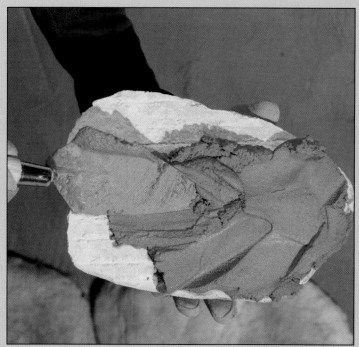

3 Determine the pattern of the stones before mixing the mortar. Then mix the mortar and trowel a coat onto the lath. Embed the mortar fully into the lath, leaving no lath exposed.

4 Back-butter the stones one by one with a generous coat of mortar. Don't worry about applying too much; the excess will squeeze out and become part of the mortared joint.

DETERMINE THE PATTERN
Make a dry run with the stone

Find the best arrangement for your stone veneer before the mortar is on the wall. Dry-lay the stones ahead of time on the lawn or a sheet of plywood. Fit them so the sizes, colors, and shapes are evenly and randomly dispersed throughout the pattern rather than placing most of the large stones on the bottom, as in a fieldstone wall. A stone-veneer house wall would look bottom heavy with such an arrangement.

STANLEY PRO TIP: **Prop up the big pieces**

Lower stones will rest on the batten, but as you work up the wall, stones have to adhere to the mortar to remain in position. Large stones may be too heavy to stick to the mortar on the wall. Prop them up with a 1×4. Cut a notch for the stone in one end and jam the other end into the soil. Stake the prop to increase its stability.

5 Start at the corner. Push the back-buttered stones into the mortar. Arrange stones so the joints are offset. Continuous vertical or horizontal joint lines would not give the effect of an actual stone wall.

6 Starting from the cornerstone, back-butter and set the base stones, letting them rest on the batten. Mist the mortar on the metal lath occasionally so it doesn't set up prematurely. Don't leave the job if there's fresh mortar on the wall and it hasn't yet been covered.

WHAT IF...
You're using manufactured stone?

1 Drive stakes at both ends of the wall and string a level mason's line tightly between them. Check each course for level as you go, nudging the stones into place if necessary.

2 Begin alternate courses with stones of different sizes. Mortar the joints with a grout bag and brush off excess from the face of the stone immediately.

Cutting facing stone

Build a sand bedding box in a 2×4 frame. The sand accommodates the curved face of the stone and keeps the stone steady while you cut it. Cutting stone on a hard surface, such as a driveway, is difficult and could mar the stone face.

7 Starting at either corner, set the next course of stones in the same fashion, placing each stone so it crosses the joint made by the two stones below. Offset the joints across the wall.

8 Set mason's blocks on the edges of the wall and use it to make sure the horizontal alignment of the courses is roughly in line and the faces of the stones are about the same distance out from the wall. When you have finished the wall, let the mortar cure, then finish the joints.

Finishing the joints

1 Grout the joints with a mortar bag. The bag makes clean joints and minimizes the amount of mortar that falls on the face of the stones. Fill the bag with mortar, close the end, and apply pressure to force the grout into the joints.

2 Let the mortar set up slightly, then clean off the excess with a whisk boom or stiff brush. Then let the mortar set up further, until you can just dent it with pressure from your thumb. Strike the joints.

3 You can use a variety of tools for striking facing-stone joints. A standard jointing tool, a pointed dowel, or even an old kitchen spoon will work.

MAINTAINING & REPAIRING MASONRY

Brick, stone, concrete, and tile can take a beating, and a well-made masonry structure promises years of enjoyment and carefree service. However outdoor masonry stands exposed to the ravages of time and weather. Even the best structures need occasional maintenance and care.

Masonry surfaces can crack, chip, spall, or pop out. Mortared stone walls fall victim to water and ice; the cap and top courses are prone to cracks more than anywhere else. After 20 or 30 years, a brick or block wall starts to show its age. If it doesn't crack, mortar simply wears away until it is unsightly and compromises the strength of the wall. Untended cracks in patios or walks allow water to erode the supporting soil or sand and may become homes for annoying weeds. Ice that forms within cracks can lift and damage even the heaviest of surfaces, as can plant roots.

The best maintenance is preventive, and one of the best solutions for avoiding large-scale repairs is to establish and follow a maintenance schedule. Proper maintenance carried out regularly adds years to your enjoyment of the masonry. Inspect the surface every three months or so: Check for damage, stains, loose mortar, and weeds growing where they shouldn't be. The inspection will take five minutes or less, but it will save you time and money if you attend to the problems when you discover them.

Be wary of any damage, even if it first appears superficial. Broken tile, cracked grout or mortar joints, and weeds might indicate a simple surface problem, but they might also be a result of more serious trouble in the structure or its base. Always assess the cause of the damage before making repairs. That way you won't cover up the real cause of the problem—the one that will cost more to repair later.

The best care is preventive— keeping up regular inspections avoids costly repairs.

CHAPTER PREVIEW

Concrete maintenance and repair
page 212

Resurfacing and replacing concrete
page 216

Maintaining patios and walks
page 218

Repairing brick and block walls
page 222

**Repairing a
stone wall**
page 226

**Cleaning and
sealing tile**
page 230

**Repairing
damaged
ceramic tile**
page 232

CONCRETE MAINTENANCE AND REPAIR

Moisture is the chief enemy of concrete. You can minimize moisture damage and improve the appearance of your concrete surface at the same time by painting or sealing it. Either solution entails periodic reapplications. To test whether the concrete needs a new coat of sealer, sprinkle water on the surface. If the water soaks right in, it's time to reapply. On aggregate-concrete surfaces, use an aggregate sealer. It prevents freeze-thaw cycles from popping out the stones.

Other common problems include stubborn stains, rotting expansion joints, and cracks. These are generally small problems that don't call for removing the slab. More serious surface trouble calls for resurfacing. Be sure to consider door height before adding a new surface.

PRESTART CHECKLIST

☐ **TIME**
Varies from an hour or so to several, depending on the repair

☐ **TOOLS**
Stiff brush, paint roller, bucket, cold chisel, small sledgehammer, metal trowel, caulk gun, tamper, pointing trowel, garden hose, paintbrush, hammer, wheelbarrow, mason's hoe, control jointer, edger, broom, bull float, darby, wood or magnesium float (varies with repair), vacuum cleaner, aviation snips, china marker, circular saw and masonry blade, scrap wood, small piece of plywood

☐ **SKILLS**
Cleaning, applying patching concrete

☐ **MATERIALS**
Muriatic acid, acrylic or silicone sealer, expansion strip, bonding agent, patching compound, 2× lumber, wire mesh, concrete, burlap, rubber silicone or polyurethane sealant, latex mortar

Cleaning and sealing

1 A stiff brush and a strong cleaning solution will remove most concrete stains. For stubborn stains, use 1 part muriatic acid added to 9 parts water in a bucket. Scrub the area with a stiff push broom. Muriatic acid is caustic (see "Safety First," *page 222*)—wear rubber gloves and eye protection. Rinse the slab with water.

2 To seal concrete, apply a clear acrylic or nonyellowing silicone sealer with a short-nap roller. Let it dry 48 hours.

Disguising your repairs

Repairs won't blend in well with the old concrete, but you can fix many of those problems with concrete pigments. Experiment with different colors before doing the repair work (to match the old surface as closely as you can).

STANLEY PRO TIP

Keying a crack

Keyed crack is chiseled wider at the bottom than the top

To key a concrete crack, chisel it wider at the bottom. A keyed crack helps keep a patch from popping out. Press patching concrete into the opening, then trowel the surface smooth.

Replacing expansion joints

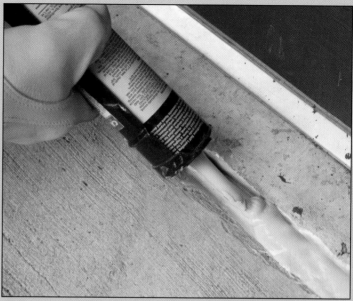

1 Expansion joints allow sections of a concrete slab to shift independently so the slab won't crack. The joints are filled with a fibrous material that acts as a cushion. Over time it may deteriorate. If the expansion strip has rotted, chisel it out with a small sledgehammer and cold chisel. Remove all the loose pieces and vacuum out the joint.

2 Buy a new expansion strip and cut it to size. Slide the new strip into the joint and tap it with a piece of wood scrap until the top is ½ inch below the concrete surface. Caulk the joint with a rubber silicone or a polyurethane sealant.

Repairing pop-outs

1 Enlarge the popped-out area and key it with a cold chisel and small sledgehammer. Clean the hole with a stiff brush.

2 Mist the surface and brush in a latex or acrylic bonding agent. Following the manufacturer's instructions, let the bonding agent dry. Some solutions will get tacky, others will not.

3 Mix up a small amount of patching cement and pack it into the hole. Smooth the surface with a trowel. Keep the area moist until the patch cures.

Repairing chip-outs

Chip out loose material until you reach a solid surface. Brush away the chips and blow out the dust. Trowel in patching or hydraulic cement and smooth the surface, misting it slightly if necessary to help feather it in at the edges. To match a sanded finish, add a light coating of sand to the final troweling. To blend the patch in with a broomed finish, run a brush over it.

Patching large areas

1 Outline the entire damaged area in straight lines with a china marker. Set the bevel gauge of your circular saw at a 15-degree angle, and cut along the lines with a masonry blade. A thin piece of plywood prevents damage to your saw plate.

Repairing damaged stucco

1 Damage to stucco often extends under the visible damage. Tap the edges of the broken area to loosen any weak material. Chip out the stucco, removing loose and crumbled mortar. Be careful not to damage the wall or the metal lath. Brush away any loose residue with a stiff brush.

2 Tap out any remaining bits of mortar still in the metal lath and examine the lath. If it's damaged, cut it out with aviation snips and fit a replacement panel into the hole. In a concrete or brick wall, fasten the lath with concrete nails. Use 10d nails in wood sheathing.

2 Using a cold chisel or stone chisel (it will cut more quickly), remove the damaged concrete within the cut lines until you reach a solid surface. Brush out the loose material, blow off the dust, and mist the exposed surface.

3 Mix up a batch of sand-mix concrete with acrylic additive and trowel it into the damaged area. The patching compound should be slightly thicker at the edges. Feather out the edges and smooth the surface with a wooden float. Broom the surface or otherwise match any existing finishes. Cover the repair with plastic, and don't walk on it for a week.

3 Mix up a batch of latex-modified mortar and trowel it into the lath, forcing it into the recesses. Scratch this coat with a scarifier *(page 109)* and let it dry. Trowel on a brown coat, leaving about ¼ inch for the finish coat. Let the two coats cure.

4 Trowel on a finish coat colored to match the old surface. Then texture the finish coat to match the existing surface.

RESURFACING AND REPLACING CONCRETE

Concrete slabs that are damaged beyond simple repairs must be resurfaced or replaced. Evaluate the condition of your concrete patio or walk before deciding what action to take. If the slab is level and has a solid base with no pronounced settling, you can probably resurface it. This will raise the level of the structure, which may not be a problem for a walk, but a new patio surface higher than the old one might prevent outswinging doors from opening. If you're working with a sliding door exit, the new height of the patio may work.

Removing a slab is hard labor. If you do it yourself, rent an electric jackhammer and have a plan for getting rid of the rubble. Rent a 40- to 50-pound electric demolition hammer, and let the weight of the tool do the work. Removing the wire reinforcing mesh slows the job—cut through it with a hammer and chisel or bolt cutter.

PRESTART CHECKLIST

☐ **TIME**
About 8 hours to form and resurface an 8×8-foot area, 8 to 10 hours to remove it

☐ **TOOLS**
Brush, cordless drill, trowels and tools for finishing concrete, grout float or mortar bag, sticking tool, jackhammer with chipping and cutting bits, wheelbarrow, bucket, shovel

☐ **SKILLS**
Making forms, pouring and finishing concrete, using a jackhammer, mortaring masonry surface materials

☐ **MATERIALS**
Muriatic acid, concrete mix, grout, setting mortar, 2×4s, latex bonding agent

Resurfacing a slab

1 Etch the old surface to prepare it for resurfacing. Use a solution of 1 part muriatic acid added to 5 parts water (see "Safety First," *page 222*). Add the acid to the water in a bucket (never pour water into acid) and brush it onto the slab.

2 Leave the solution on the concrete until it stops bubbling. Then rinse the slab thoroughly with water. Use a strong stream from the hose to make sure you leave no acid on the surface. Acid residue may weaken the bond with the new surface.

WHAT IF...
The slab has to go?

If the surface is beyond repair or exhibits large cracks or broken or tilted sections, you'll have to remove it.

If the slab is small or thin, start in a corner with a 10- or 12-pound sledgehammer and crack small sections. Pry out the pieces with a crowbar. Work your way across the surface, cracking and prying as you go.

For slabs thicker than 4 inches or to remove any slab more easily, rent a jackhammer.

1 Put the chisel end of the jackhammer on the surface near an edge of the slab, push down firmly on the handles, and press the switch to start it. Let the weight of the tool do the work, breaking the concrete and creating new cracks as you go. Follow the cracks with the jackhammer to break up the concrete more quickly.

2 As you finish cracking each section, load the rubble into a wheelbarrow and haul it away. You can use it as fill somewhere in your property (in poured concrete steps, for example) or haul it to an approved dumping place.

3 Prepare the slab for new forms by digging a trench 2½ inches deep and 6 inches wide around the perimeter. Set 2×4s in the trench and stake them against the slab. Place the top edge 1 inch above the surface. Roll a latex bonding agent onto the slab and follow it with the new concrete mix (1 part cement, 2 parts sand, and just enough water to make it workable). Screed with a straight 2×4. Flatten high spots, fill depressions, and screed again.

4 Using the same techniques as you would use for any other concrete slab, float the new surface with a bull float or darby. Edge the new surface, then finish it with a metal trowel, wood float, magnesium float, or broom. Let the concrete cure for three days to a week.

Putting on a new face

All slabs have some cracks. If your concrete walk or patio shows only hairline cracks and no settling, it's a good substrate for a dressier surface of brick, tile, or flagstone. Mortar the new material to the old slab. The new surface will be higher than the old one, so you may need to trim screen doors or make other adjustments.

Place forms around the perimeter of the slab, about 1 inch above the surface. Then trowel on a section of mortar.

Using the techniques appropriate to the material, lay the brick, tile, or stone in the mortar, spacing the pieces with plastic or plywood spacers.

Force mortar or grout into the joints with a grout float or grout bag. Use a concave jointer to strike the joints after the mortar begins to set. Clean the surface, then cover it with plastic to allow the mortar to cure. Don't use the patio or walk for a week.

MAINTAINING PATIOS AND WALKS

Maintaining patios and walks starts with keeping them clean. Sweeping or spraying with a hose may be enough. When removing stains, always start with the least caustic approach and work up to more potent solutions.

If the surface is really dirty, rent a power washer and use a commercial cleaning agent. Be careful with this machine, however. Keep it directed on the patio or walk. A power washer can dig up grass and soil and remove both paint and wood from a wall. It can even mar the face of softer stones like sandstone.

Some stains, such as the chalky residue left after a rainfall, are easily removed with a stiff brush. For oil and grease stains, scrub the stain with mineral spirits, sprinkle it with kitty litter or sand, then sweep it up. Dissolve stains that have penetrated with commercial cleaners. Remove rust stains with bleach and a stiff-bristle scrub brush. If that doesn't work, use oxalic acid.

PRESTART CHECKLIST

☐ **TIME**
From ½ to 2 hours, depending on the nature and size of the repair

☐ **TOOLS**
Stiff-bristle brush, putty knife, rubber mallet, hose, point punch, cold chisel, brick set, plugging chisel, pointing trowel, jointer, small sledgehammer, mixing tub, mortar bag, straightedge, vacuum cleaner, screwdriver, spray bottle, dustpan

☐ **SKILLS**
Basic cleaning and repair

☐ **MATERIALS**
Mortar, mason's sand, grout, thinset, 2×4, bonding agent, concrete, gravel, expansion joint, wire mesh, burlap, muriatic acid or TSP, 2×6, replacement brick or paver

Cleaning pavers

1 Before you clean a walk or patio made of pavers, dig out weeds. Weeds in the joints of sand-set material usually snap off at the top and regrow. To get them at the roots, slide a putty knife along the gaps between bricks. Loosen or cut roots and pull up the plant.

2 Start your stain removal with warm water, a strong soap solution, and a stiff brush. If that doesn't work, use diluted (1:9) muriatic acid or trisodium phosphate (TSP). Don't use acid on stone—it may stain. Sometimes you can clean stained stone or brick by rubbing it with a similar material.

REMOVING STAINS FROM BRICK

Stain	Treatment
Mildew	Mix 1 part bleach, 3 parts water, and some laundry detergent. Scrub this mixture into the stain with a brush, let it soak for 15 minutes, then rinse thoroughly.
Old paint	Pressure-washing may knock off the old paint. If not, scrape off as much paint as possible with a wire brush and putty knife. Then scrub the paint with a mixture of TSP and water. If that doesn't work, use semipaste paint remover. Test first to make sure that the paint remover won't stain the brick.
Graffiti	Spray-paint remover may take off some of the graffiti. Scrape with a wire brush, or try a muriatic-acid solution. Sandblasting is a final option. To paint over graffiti, apply a stain-killing primer first.
Iron/Rust	Mix a solution of 1 pound oxalic acid with 1 gallon water. Scrub this mixture into the stain with a brush. Let it stand for 15 minutes, then rinse thoroughly.
Mortar	Mix 1 part muriatic acid with 10 parts water, and use a wire brush to scrub the stain with this mixture. Let stand for 15 minutes, rinse, and repeat as often as necessary.
Smoke	Mix 1 part laundry detergent, 1 part bleach, and 5 parts water. Scrub this mixture into the stain with a brush. Or use a mixture of 1 part ammonia with 3 parts water.

Repairing sand-bed paving

1 To raise a sunken paver, you must first remove it. Loosen the sand in the joint by running the blade of a putty knife back and forth in the joint. Vacuum the sand from the joint and repeat until you have removed or loosened as much of it as possible. Angle the tip of a wide screwdriver into the joint about ⅛ inch from the surface. Pry the paver loose one side at a time.

2 Add sand in the recess and tamp it to the level of the surrounding bed with a piece of 2× scrap. Mist the sand with a spray bottle, tamp it again, and screed it with a 2×6 cut to fit the width and depth of the recess.

Making new brick look old

If you have to replace a damaged paver (or you damage one when you're removing it), you may have to distress the replacement a little to blend in with the existing brick.

To make a new paver look used, soak it in muddy water. Some of the mud will remain in the pores like a pigment. Rub sand on the surface with another paver to make it look more worn than new. You can also rub the new bricks against one another.

3 Return the paver to its recess and tap it with a rubber mallet. Put your weight on it to make sure it's firmly bedded and not too high or too low. Add or remove sand until the paver is level with the surface.

4 Sprinkle a light layer of mason's sand over the repair area. Then sweep it into the joints with a brush, alternately misting it (to compact it) and sweeping it until the joints are full.

Repairing mortared joints

1 Using a narrow cold chisel (the smaller the better) and a small sledge, chip out the damaged section of mortar plus about an inch more on both ends of the joint.

2 Sweep away the chips into a dustpan with a moderately stiff brush. Vacuum up the remaining dust from the joints. Mist the area with a spray bottle.

3 In a mixing tub, mix up just enough mortar for the repair. Use prebagged mortar and add water a little at a time until it's just workable.

Replacing a brick

1 Using a plugging chisel and a small sledge, break out the mortar in the joint surrounding the damaged brick. Remove as much mortar as you can, but work carefully after the first inch. If you force the body of the chisel into the joint, you'll chip the neighboring brick.

2 Break up the paver with a brick set and small sledge. Even when cracked, the pieces will bind against each other, making them difficult to remove. You may have to use smaller cold chisels to complete the job.

3 Remove the remaining mortar with a brick set, smaller cold chisels, and a small sledge. The sides and bottom of the recess have to be just clean enough for you to replace enough mortar to bed the brick.

4 Make sure the tip on your mortar bag is the correct size for the joints. Fill the mortar bag with mortar and squeeze it into the joints.

5 Let the mortar set up until you can barely dent it with your thumb. Then strike the joints with a striking tool that matches the existing joints. Start the strike on an old joint and follow through into the new mortar so there is no break in the appearance of the joint.

4 Reline the recess with mortar, combining it in ridges with a plastic trowel cut to fit the cavity. Spread it about ½ inch thick.

5 Set the paver into the recess. When it comes into contact with the mortar, rock it slightly until it's just above the surface of the rest of the brick. Tap it a little with a rubber mallet, then check it with a straightedge. Tap again to set it deeper or add mortar to raise it.

6 Mix up mortar and fill a mortar bag. Squeeze the mortar into the joints and let the mortar set up. Strike the joints with a striking tool that matches the existing joints.

REPAIRING BRICK AND BLOCK WALLS

Most repairs to brick and block walls require only basic skills. Catching the damage and repairing it before it spreads wins half the battle for you.

Routinely check a brick or block wall's mortar joints. Soft, crumbling mortar joints let water in to cause serious damage to the wall. Faulty mortar joints call for tuck-pointing—removing the mortar and replacing it. If the brick has lost its glaze, it's vulnerable to water migrating into its body. Seal the brick with a clear sealer. Chipped brick is also a tip-off that water has intruded and frozen. Treat a chipped brick as you would a damaged brick— replace it. If you have ivy growing up the wall, its tendrils won't damage mortar that's in good repair, but the foliage can hide potential problems. Check the wall in the spring before leaves appear. To avoid collapsing a section of wall, replace only a few bricks at a time.

PRESTART CHECKLIST

☐ **TIME**
About 2 hours to replace a brick or a block.

☐ **TOOLS**
Small sledgehammer, masonry chisel, drill with masonry bit, pointing trowel, pointing tool, garden hose, scrub brush, plugging chisel, cold chisels, brick set, mortar box, mason's trowel, burlap, 4-inch grinder, old paintbrush, straightedge, circular saw and masonry blade

☐ **SKILLS**
Chiseling, mixing mortar, pointing mortar

☐ **MATERIALS**
Muriatic acid, mortar, brick, stone, concrete block, wooden wedges

Tuck-pointing brick

1 Adjust the blade of a 4-inch grinder to cut the mortar to about one-half its depth. With the rear of the grinder guard on the face of the brick, turn the grinder on, and ease the blade into the joint.

2 Brush the loose mortar from the joint with an old paintbrush. You can also blow out the dust on a small area with an air hose. In all cases, wear eye protection. After cleaning, mist the joint with a sprayer.

WHAT IF...
Only a small amount of mortar is damaged?

You won't have to grind out mortar for small tuck-pointing jobs. Cut out the mortar with a raking tool or narrow cold chisel. Then replace the mortar as shown above.

SAFETY FIRST
Using muriatic acid

Muriatic acid is a diluted form of hydrochloric acid. Handle it with care.

Wear old clothes, safety glasses, and rubber gloves. Always pour acid into water to dilute it, don't pour water into the acid.

When water is poured into the acid, it causes a reaction that produces heat. This reaction can make the solution expand rapidly, creating a large acid bubble that can burst up and out from the container and splash onto you, possibly causing burns.

Rinse acid-washed surfaces thoroughly to dilute the acid and flush it away. Store the acid in its original, marked container.

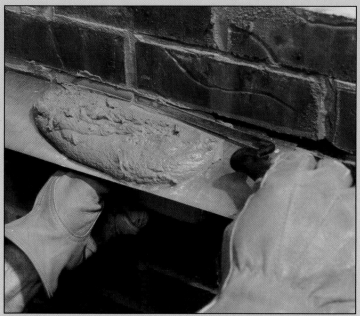

3 Replace the mortar in the joint by sliding it off the face of a flat trowel and into the recess. Use a narrow trowel or a thin piece of scrap wood to put mortar into the joint and not on the brick. Press the mortar into the joint until it's solidly filled—mortar will start oozing at the edge of the tool when the joint is full.

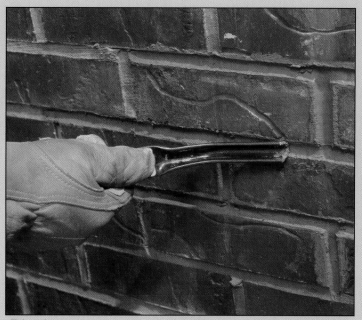

4 Let the mortar set until it's fairly stiff and you can just dent it with pressure from your thumb. Then tool the joints with a striker that matches the profile of the original joints. Tool the horizontal joints first, then the vertical joints.

Removing efflorescence

One of the most common brick problems is efflorescence, a powdery white residue that forms on the surface. The culprit: salts in the brick or mortar that rise to the surface.

Recently placed mortar is particularly prone to developing efflorescence, especially if it rained while the wall was under construction. This type of efflorescence usually goes away on its own within a year.

Poorly finished (or maintained) mortar joints and poor seals that allow water in around moldings and flashings cause the efflorescence on older structures.

If efflorescence is found near the ground, the problem may be due to poor drainage in the soil around the foundation of the structure. Before treating the efflorescence, deal with its cause. Make sure the wall dries completely between rains.

1 To remove efflorescence, start by wetting down the entire surface with a garden hose. Then loosen the deposits with a stiff-bristle brush. Don't use a wire brush—it will leave metal marks on your masonry. Follow with a strong rinse from a power washer.

2 If the efflorescence continues to reappear, scrub the surface with a solution of 1 part muriatic acid and 12 parts water. Work carefully: Muriatic acid is extremely corrosive. Rinse with a power washer. On concrete blocks, use only water; acid can damage them.

Replacing a damaged brick

1 To remove a damaged brick, drill several ¼-inch holes in its center. Next chip out the old mortar with a plugging chisel and small sledge. Using a brick set, break the brick into pieces and remove them. Brush away debris, blow out the dust, and dampen all surfaces of the cavity.

2 Mix latex-fortified mortar, tinting it with pigments if necessary to match the existing color. Using a pointing trowel, apply a 1-inch-thick layer of mortar to the bottom side of the recess.

Replacing a damaged block

1 Use a masonry drill to drill holes into the cores of the block. Then chip out the mortar around the block with a plugging chisel and small sledge, being careful not to damage the surrounding blocks. Set a cold chisel in the holes and break out the front face of the cores.

2 Using a cold chisel, chip out the block face just enough to leave all but the front 2 inches of the webs. This provides a bonding surface for the replacement face. Chip out the mortar on the sides of the recess also.

3 Butter the top and ends of the replacement brick with mortar and set the brick on a pointing trowel. Slide the new brick off the trowel and into the recess, holding the trowel on the mortar in the cavity to keep it as undisturbed as possible. Pry the brick as necessary to make the joints evenly thick. Set a straightedge on the brick and push it level with the wall.

4 When the mortar has stiffened slightly, scrape away any excess with a masonry trowel and brush the area with a stiff brush. Let the mortar set up until it's fairly stiff and you can just dent it with pressure from your thumb. Then tool the joints with a striker that matches the profile of the original joints. When the mortar dries to a crumbly surface, brush it again.

3 Using a circular saw with a masonry blade, cut through the side webs at the thickness of the face and score the top and bottom of the center web. Then cut away the face from the center web with a cold chisel. Apply an inch of mortar to the perimeter of the new block face, as well as to the center and edges of the rear surface. Set the new face in place, slipping it in with a pointed trowel.

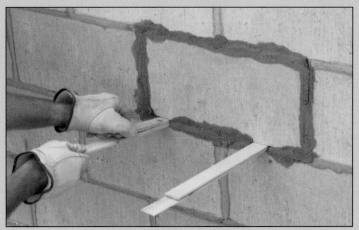

4 Center the block face in the opening by driving wood wedges in the mortar. Let the mortar set up and remove the wedges. Then mortar the holes left by the wedges, and strike the joints.

REPAIRING A STONE WALL

Frost heave often causes structural damage to a stone wall. Erosion and the gradual deterioration of stones by freezing and shifting are other common problems.

Mortared walls are less subject to erosion because of their footing, but their mortar joints—and the surface of the stones themselves—can crack and take in water, then freeze and split. A damaged wall that doesn't receive timely attention poses a safety hazard.

You may be tempted to replace damaged stone with synthetic stone made from epoxy or cement-based materials. Such imitation stone is less expensive. Though the patches may look good at first, they will become conspicuous with further exposure to the elements and ultimately mar the appearance of the wall.

PRESTART CHECKLIST

☐ **TIME**
From 6 to 16 hours, depending on the nature of the wall, the extent of damage, and the kind of stone

☐ **TOOLS**
Small sledgehammer, wooden wedges, tamper, 2×4 beater block, crowbar, marking chalk, cold chisel, spray bottle, pointing trowel, stiff-bristle brush, circular saw and masonry blade

☐ **SKILLS**
Cutting and handling stone

☐ **MATERIALS**
Mortar, replacement stone (if required), gravel (for erosion repairs), carpet-covered 2×4 lumber

Replacing a popped stone

1 To return a popped stone to its original position, drive wedges between stable stones to take the weight off the popped stone. Work the popped stone out of the wall carefully, without dislodging the other stones. Drive the wedges into the wall slightly further.

2 Reinsert the popped stone in its cavity and tap it home with a carpet-covered 2×4 and a small sledgehammer. Use a crowbar to take the weight off the wedges and remove them. You may have to work the wedges and the crowbar back out of the wall at the same time.

Maintaining stonework

Maintenance of stonework requires attention to details. These tips that can help you keep your wall, walk, and patio in good repair.

■ Climbing plants pose no danger to hardened mortar, but roots disturb footings and tendrils take hold in cracks. Plant life in the wrong places displaces stones or bricks, blocks rainwater runoff, and hides other damage. To remove plants, cut the main stem above ground level and treat it with a product recommended by your local extension service.

■ Residues of some weed killers can cause spalling on some stone surfaces.

■ If stone-faced steps are worn, you may be able to reuse them by turning them over.

■ Choose the most gentle cleaning method that can handle the job. Start with water cleaning, the most gentle method, then turn to chemical-base cleaners or mechanical methods such as sandblasting only if you need to.

■ Water increases damage to badly deteriorated mortar. Repair the mortar before cleaning with water.

■ A pressure washer can be an effective cleaning method, but also may erode softer stones like sandstone.

■ Steam cleaning is an effective method for removing embedded soil and poses less risk than sandblasting. Sandblasting is a method of last resort.

■ A poultice of absorbent material mixed with a solvent can remove many chemical stains without damaging the stone. Keep the poultice on the stain as long as necessary to remove the stain.

■ Always test your cleaning agent in an inconspicuous spot before using it on the entire surface.

Rebuilding a damaged wall

1 A collapsed section of wall can often be repaired without total replacement. Inspect the wall and visualize a V-shape section that you'll need to remove. Mark the area on the wall with marking chalk. Don't use spray paint. Then number the stones with chalk so you can replace them to their original positions. Take a photo of the wall to further help you replace the stones in the right order.

2 Working above the marked section, chisel away any mortar that anchors the capstones and take them off the wall. Dismantle the damaged section.

WHAT IF…
Erosion has caused the damage?

Soil erosion is often the cause of a toppled wall section. This is a problem that does not usually show up for many years. To repair the damage, remove stones from the damaged area and at least two stones wider. Dig a 6- to 8-inch trench where you have removed the stones. Fill the trench with gravel a little at a time and tamp it as you go. Rebuild the section of wall. The gravel will allow water to drain under the wall without washing out its support.

3 Using the snapshot as a guide, rebuild the wall, working from the leads toward the center. Set the stones using the same techniques used to build it. Be sure to replace any small stones used to keep larger ones in place. Fill in the center recess between the wythes with cracked rubble. Replace the capstones.

Repairing stone mortar joints

1 Carefully chip out the damaged mortar with a thin cold chisel and a small sledgehammer. Clean the joint until you reach solid mortar.

2 Mix mortar to a consistency for use with a mortar bag and fill the bag. Mist the joint with water from a spray bottle and squeeze mortar into the joints.

3 Pack each joint tightly with a pointing trowel, adding more mortar if necessary. Tool the joints to match the original and remove excess mortar with a stiff brush.

Repointing mortared fieldstone

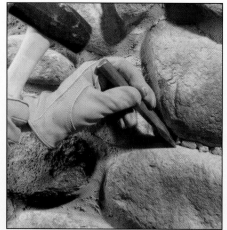

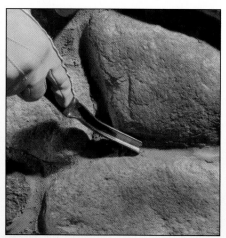

1 Chip out cracked mortar with a 1-inch cold chisel and small sledgehammer. Brush away the loose material. Chip out the joint until you reach solid mortar.

2 Mist the joint lightly and push mortar into it with a small pointing trowel. Compress the mortar as much as possible. When the mortar has set up slightly, tool the joints to match the original.

Replacing a mortared stone

1 Remove the damaged stone by chiseling out the mortar around the stone. Angle the chisel in the direction of the damaged stone to avoid damaging others. Then pry out the stone. Using a wider cold chisel, remove as much mortar as possible from the cavity. Brush or blow out the cavity to remove loose mortar and dust (wear eye protection).

2 Hold a new stone slightly larger than the recess against the wall and mark cut lines so you can cut it to fit properly.

3 If the stone is thin enough, cut it with a circular saw and masonry blade. Cut thick stones as shown on *page 103.* Then using a mason's hammer, carefully chip the replacement stone until it fits the recess with enough space for the mortar joints. Be careful not to cut too much off the stone; doing so makes the joints wider than those on the rest of the surface and calls attention to the repair.

4 Mist the cavity and spread mortar on the bottom of the cavity and the top and sides of the replacement stone. Insert the stone and push it into place using the pointing trowel. Pack mortar against all sides of the stone. When the mortar has set, tool it to match the original.

CLEANING AND SEALING TILE

Regular cleaning will keep ceramic tile in good condition, but surfaces around an outdoor kitchen, barbecue, or dining space may become stained.

To remove a stain, start with the steps outlined in the chart, below right. If these solutions don't work, ask a tile supplier to recommend a cleaning agent that's compatible with your tile.

A cleaning agent mixed with baking soda, plaster of Paris, or refined clay often is enough to remove stubborn stains. Deodorant-free cat litter also works well. Mix the ingredients into a wet paste and apply it to the stain. Tape a plastic bag over the paste and let it sit for a couple of days. Then brush off the paste.

Unglazed tile usually requires a sealer. Penetrating sealers soak into the tile and preserve its natural color. Topical sealers lie on the surface of the tile and may change the tile color or surface sheen. Topical sealers wear off and require reapplication. If tiles look dull, it's probably time to strip and reseal them. Even presealed tile needs to be stripped and resealed periodically.

PRESTART CHECKLIST

☐ **TIME**
About 45 minutes to vacuum and damp mop a 15×20-foot kitchen, 90 minutes to strip it, about the same time to seal it

☐ **TOOLS**
Stripping: scrub brush and mop or floor machine, vacuum cleaner
Sealing: vacuum cleaner, applicator, buffer

☐ **PREP**
Vacuum and clean surface

☐ **MATERIALS**
Stripper, sponge, sealer, bucket, rags

Stripping tiles

1 To remove old sealer, use a sponge or mop to spread stripper in an area that you can clean before the liquid dries (about 25 square feet). Scrub the area with a brush or with a floor machine. Don't let the stripper dry on the surface.

2 Remove residue with a sponge mop or rags. Some water-base strippers allow removal with a wet-or-dry vacuum. Rinse with clean water and wipe dry.

REMOVING STAINS FROM TILE

Stain	Treatment
Ink, coffee, blood	Start with a 3 percent hydrogen peroxide solution; if that doesn't work try a nonbleach cleaner.
Oil-base products	Use a mild solvent, such as charcoal lighter fluid or mineral spirits, then a poultice of household cleaner. For dried paint, scrape with a plastic (not metal) scraper.
Grease, fats	Clean with a commercial spot lifter.
Rust	Use commercial rust removers, or try household cleaner.
Nail polish	Remove with nail polish remover.

Always rinse the stained area with clear water to remove residue.

Applying sealers

1 On newly tiled surfaces, wait 48 hours before sealing. On existing tile, vacuum the surface thoroughly so dirt and dust won't become embedded in the new sealer.

2 Clean the tile with a commercial tile-cleaning product, following the manufacturer's directions. Rinse with clear water.

3 Apply sealer with a sponge, paint pad, brush, or mop, as recommended by the manufacturer. Prevent the sealer from puddling or contacting walls. Some sealers can't be overlapped. Allow time to dry between coats. Reapply one or two additional coats.

SAFETY FIRST
Tile-care products can be toxic

Many strippers and sealers are solvent-base and highly caustic. Even water-base products contain harmful chemicals. All tile-care products are potentially dangerous so be sure to observe the manufacturer's safety precautions.

Wear rubber gloves, long-sleeve clothing, pants, and eye protection. Wear a respirator to avoid breathing toxic fumes and put a fan in the window to provide adequate ventilation. Keep children and pets out of the area during maintenance.

Working with waxes

Wax is a good finish for many unglazed tile surfaces. Some waxes contain pigments that enhance the color of the tile.

To renew a waxed surface, strip the old wax and wash the surface thoroughly with a mild detergent. Rinse with clear water and let it dry completely. Wax the surface in successive thin coats with the applicator recommended by the manufacturer. Allow each coat to dry, and buff between coats. Several thin coats produce a brighter shine than one thick coat; they also reduce wax buildup.

A dull shine doesn't necessarily call for rewaxing. Clean the tile with a soap-free cleaner and buff with a cloth or rented floor machine. When using a buffer, start in the middle of the area with the brush level. Tilt the handle up or down slightly to move the machine from side to side. Don't push the machine. Buff across the surface.

REPAIRING DAMAGED CERAMIC TILE

Tile is durable, but it can be damaged. Improper installation, poor adhesive bonds, and falling objects can cause it to crack or chip.

Repairs start with removing the grout and tile. Before replacing them, diagnose the problem to see if you need to make structural repairs to prevent subsequent damage.

If the grout is soft and powdery, remove it and regrout. If the cracked grout is hard, remove it and fill the joint with a matching colored caulk.

Cracked tiles on a long length of floor are caused by either a faulty adhesive bond or an underlying crack. Before you remove the tiles, tap them lightly with a metal object, such as a wrench. If you hear a hollow sound, the bond is probably at fault. A thorough cleaning and new mortar will fix the problem. If the wrench "rings," the bond is probably solid; you may need to isolate the crack with a membrane.

PRESTART CHECKLIST

☐ **TIME**
About 1½ hours to remove and replace grout and tile, at least a day to regrout a large area

☐ **TOOLS**
Grout saw or utility knife, small sledgehammer and cold chisel, putty knife or margin trowel

☐ **SKILLS**
Breaking tile with a hammer and cold chisel, driving fasteners, troweling

☐ **MATERIALS**
Replacement tiles, thinset, grout, tape

Removing and replacing damaged tile

1 To repair damaged tile, remove the grout with a grout knife. Using a small sledgehammer and cold chisel, break the tile, working from the center to the edges. Wear eye protection.

2 Pull out the chips of broken tile. Scrape up the fine pieces with a margin trowel or putty knife. Using the same tool, scrape off any adhesive remaining in the recess. Dust out or vacuum the area so the adhesive bonds securely.

Removing ceramic tile

1 Crack one tile with a cold chisel and small sledgehammer and to create a starting point in a central area. Grip the chisel firmly and strike it with a sharp blow of the hammer. Wear eye protection.

2 Break out the remaining area of the tile with the sledgehammer and brush the loose pieces out of the recess. Chip out the grout along the edge of the adjacent tiles.

3 Using a margin trowel or wide putty knife, apply adhesive in the recess. Use the same general type of adhesive (mastic or thinset) as the original.

4 Back-butter the replacement tile with a margin trowel or putty knife and push the tile into the recess until the adhesive oozes from the grout joints. Check the tile for level with the rest of the surface, wipe off the excess adhesive, and let it cure.

3 Tap a wide chisel at an angle under the edge of the adjoining tile, and pop off the tile. Repeat the process for each tile until you have removed the entire surface. Dispose of the broken tile and scrape off any remaining adhesive.

Repairing a cracked slab

Remove tiles and grout along the length of the crack, going at least one tile beyond the damage. Following the manufacturer's instructions, apply an isolation membrane. Trowel thinset into the recess and back-butter each tile. Replace the tiles and level them. Grout when the mortar is dry.

GLOSSARY

Actual dimensions: The actual size of a masonry unit as measured with a tape or ruler. *See nominal dimensions.*

Additive: Any of several chemicals or compounds added to a concrete mix to modify the concrete's properties.

Aggregate: Gravel or crushed rock; it's mixed with portland cement and water to make concrete.

Ashlar: Rectangular blocks of stone of uniform thickness used mainly to build dry-laid walls.

Back-butter: To apply mortar or adhesive to the rear face of a masonry unit before setting it.

Backfill: To replace or add soil to an excavation or along the edge of a structure.

Bat: A half-brick. Bats are used to start offset courses and to fill in when whole bricks won't fit.

Batter: Tapering the sides of a stone wall toward the top to give it additional stability.

Beater block: Manufactured or homemade tool with a soft face, often carpet. Used to level a surface composed of masonry units.

Bed joint: The horizontal layer of mortar between two courses of masonry units.

Bisque: Ceramic material that has been fired but not glazed. Bisque tile can be decorated with glazes or other materials.

Bond: (noun) Any one of several patterns in which masonry units can be arranged. (verb) To join two or more masonry units with mortar.

Bond strength: The measure of an adhesive's ability to resist separating from a masonry unit and setting bed when cured.

Brick set: A wide-blade chisel used for cutting bricks and concrete blocks.

Brick veneer: Any of several products in various thicknesses made of clay or other materials and additives, whose appearance resembles brick.

Building codes: Ordinances established by local communities to govern construction methods and quality for structures.

Bullnose tiles: Flat tile with at least one rounded edge. Used to trim the edges of a tiled installation. Also called caps.

Butt joint: A joint that forms when two surfaces meet exactly on their edges, ends, or faces.

Caulk: A compound used to seal surface gaps or joints. Applied in semiliquid form from tubes or a caulking gun, it dries to a flexible bead that keeps out liquids. Caulk is available in a wide range of colors and in sanded or unsanded mixtures.

Cement-Bodied tile: Tile made of cement instead of clay.

Ceramic tile: Tile composed of refined clay usually mixed with additives and water, and hardened by firing in a kiln to a minimum of 1800°F. Can be glazed or unglazed.

Chink: A narrow piece of stone driven into cracks or voids in a stone wall to achieve added stability.

Cleft stone: Stone paving pieces that have been formed by splitting smaller pieces from larger rock.

Closure brick (or block): The final unit laid in a course of bricks or blocks.

Coefficient of friction: The force required to move an object across a horizontal surface—used as a measure of slip resistance.

Control joint: An intentional gap cut or formed in a concrete surface to control surface cracks.

Corner lead: The first few courses of masonry laid in stair-step fashion at a corner to establish levels for the remaining units in those courses.

Darby: A long-bladed wood float used to smooth the surface of fresh concrete.

Dry-Laid wall: A wall of masonry units laid without mortar.

Efflorescence: A powdery white substance that forms on the surface of masonry walls, caused by the evaporation of water from dissolved salts.

Expansion joint: An intended space or gap built into materials subject to cracking. Allows materials to expand and contract with temperature changes without damage to the remainder of the surface.

Exposed-aggregate: A concrete surface finish with embedded aggregate.

Extruded: Tile shaped by pressing the clay through a die.

Field tiles: Flat tiles with unrounded edges used within the edges of a tiled installation.

Flashing: A layer of material, usually metal, inserted in masonry joints and attached to adjoining surfaces to seal out moisture.

Float: A flat, rectangular wood or metal hand tool with a smooth face used for smoothing mortared surfaces.

Flush: Having the same surface or plane as an adjoining surface.

Footing: A thick concrete support for walls and other heavy structures built on firm soil and extending below the frost line.

Frost line: The maximum depth frost normally penetrates the soil during the winter. The depth varies from place to place.

Frost resistance: Rating applied to a masonry unit indicating its suitability for exterior applications subject to freezing.

Gauged stone: Stone cut into tiles of uniform shape and dimensions.

Glaze: A hard, usually colored, layer of lead silicates and other materials fired to the surface of a tile. Used to protect and decorate the tile surface.

Grade: One of six ratings applied to ceramic tile, indicating its suitability for use in certain applications.

Granite: A naturally occurring stone composed of quartz and other minerals. Colors are generally reds or browns.

Green bisque: Clay that has not been fired; not a reference to its color.

Grout: A mortar mix used to fill the joints between masonry units attached to a base material. Available in many colors and in sanded or unsanded mixtures.

Grout float: A float with a soft rubber surface used to press grout into tile joints.

Head joint: The mortar joint between the ends of adjoining masonry units.

Impervious tile: Tiles whose density completely resists the absorption of liquids. Generally used in wet areas as well as hospitals, restaurants, and similar locations.

Inside corner: The plane on which walls or other surfaces form an internal angle.

Isolation membrane: A flexible sheet or liquid product applied to a substrate to allow cracks to expand without telegraphing into the tile surface.

Latex-modified thinset: Thinset mortar mixed with latex additive to increase its flexibility, resistance to water, and adhesion.

Layout lines: Chalk lines snapped to guide the placement of tile.

Level: (adjective) Having all surfaces exactly on the same plane. (noun) A hand tool used to determine level.

Marble: A naturally occurring hard variation of limestone marked with varied color and vein patterns.

Margin trowel: A narrow rectangular trowel used for mixing mortar and applying it in narrow spaces.

Masonry cement: A powdered mixture of portland cement and hydrated lime used for preparing mortar. Used to bind sand or other aggregate materials together.

Mexican paver: A handmade tile, generally low-fired or sun-dried and unglazed, characterized by blemishes, imperfections and irregular edges.

Mortar: (noun) Any mixture of masonry cement, sand, water, and other additives. (verb) The action of applying mortar to surfaces or joints.

Mud: Trade jargon for cement-base mortars, usually used for installations where it is applied in a thick layer, as in shower stalls or in the brown and scratch coats of stucco.

Nippers: *See tile nippers.*

Nominal dimensions: The stated size of a masonry unit, representing the ratio of one side to the other including the width of its standard grout joint. Not necessarily the actual dimensions of the material. *See actual dimensions.*

Nonvitreous tile: A low-density tile whose pores absorb liquids readily. Generally used indoors in dry locations.

Open time: The amount of time a mixed mortar can be used before it starts to set up.

Organic mastic: One of several petroleum or latex-base adhesives for setting tiles. Exhibits less strength, flexibility, and resistance to water than thinset adhesives.

Outside corner: The plane on which walls or other surfaces form an angle.

Pavers: Any of several unglazed vitreous clay, shale, porcelain, or cement-bodied floor tiles, from 1/2 to 2 inches thick.

Penetrating sealer: A sealer that penetrates the pores of tile and grout to form a water- and stain-repellent layer.

Perimeter joint: An expansion joint around the edge of a surface, used to allow the material space in which to expand.

Permeability: A measure of the ability of a substance to absorb moisture.

Plumb: A surface that lies on a true vertical plane.

Plumb bob: A weight, typically pointed, suspended on a line or string, used to determine if a surface is truly vertical.

Polymer-modified: A grout or mortar mixed with an acrylic or latex ingredient to increase its strength and workability.

Porcelain: Any of several hard-bodied vitreous tiles formed from purified clay that's fired at very high temperatures.

Premix: Any of several packaged mixtures of dry ingredients used for preparing concrete or mortar.

Quarry tile: Unglazed, vitreous or semivitreous tiles, usually 1/4 to 1/2 inch thick, most often used on floors.

Ready-mix: Concrete that is mixed in a truck as it is being transported to the job site.

GLOSSARY *(continued)*

Rebar: A textured steel bar or rod used to reinforce concrete and masonry.

Reinforcing wire mesh: Steel mesh used to reinforce concrete projects such as walkways, drives, and patios.

Retardant: A chemical added to grout or mortar to slow its curing process.

Rod saw: A cylindrical blade coated with tungsten-carbide and installed in a hacksaw frame to cut curves in tile.

Rowlock course: Bricks laid side by side on their faces and pitched slightly (when used outdoors) to shed moisture. Used below windows and as wall caps.

Saltillo tile: A soft handmade tile dried in the sun instead of fired in a kiln.

Sanded grout: Grout containing sand, which increases the strength and decreases the contraction of the joint.

Screed: (verb) To level poured concrete and other materials by pulling a long board, often a 2×4 or 2×6, across the surface. (noun) The board used to screed.

Sealer: Any of several topical or penetrating products used as a protective coating on grout and unglazed tile surfaces.

Semivitreous tile: Tile of moderate density that is partially porous.

Setting bed: Any mortared surface on which tile is set.

Setup time: The amount of time an adhesive can be used before it hardens.

Slake: To allow a masonry mixture to stand for a time after initial mixing so the solids can thoroughly absorb the liquid.

Slate: A naturally occurring stone composed of compressed shale deposits, generally rough-surfaced and gray or black.

Slump: A measure of the wetness of a concrete or mortar mix; the wetter the mix, the more it spreads out, or slumps.

Snap cutter: A bench-mounted tool with a carbide scribing wheel and a pressure plate that makes straight cuts in tile by snapping it along a scribed line.

Spacers: Small plastic pieces, usually X-shape, used to ensure consistent grout-joint width between tiles.

Spalling: Cracking or flaking that develops on a concrete surface or brick faces.

Square: (adjective) Two lines or surfaces exactly perpendicular or at 90 degrees to each other. (noun) A hand tool used to determine square.

Stone tile: Naturally occurring materials cut from quarries and sliced or split into thin sections for use as tile. Marble, granite, flagstone, and slate are the usual materials.

Story pole: A measuring device, often a straight 2×4, with a series of marks used to verify that a course of masonry units is at the proper height.

Straightedge: A length of metal or wood with a perfectly straight edge used to mark a straight line on material or to determine if edges or surfaces are straight.

Strike: To finish a mortar joint.

Terra-cotta: A low-density tile made of unrefined natural clay and fired at low temperatures.

Terrazzo: Small pieces of granite or marble set in mortar often in a pictorial pattern, then polished.

Thinset mortar: Term that describes a wide range of mortar-base tile adhesives.

Tile nippers: A hand tool similar to a pliers but with sharp jaws of hardened steel. Used for cutting notches and curves in tile.

Trim tile: Tiles with at least one rounded or otherwise configured edge, used at corners or to define the edges of an installation. Common examples are cove trim, bullnose, V-cap, quarter-round, inside corners, and outside corners.

Trowel: Any of several flat and rectangular or pointed metal hand tools used for applying and smoothing adhesives and mortars.

Tuck-pointing: The process of repairing old masonry joints with new mortar.

Veneer: A layer of bricks or stones that serves as a facing.

Vitreous tile: An extremely dense ceramic tile with a high resistance to water absorption. Used indoors or outdoors, in wet or dry locations.

Waler: A horizontal brace on the outside of a concrete form to strengthen it against the pressure of the concrete as it is poured.

Weep holes: Openings made in mortar joints to facilitate drainage of built-up water.

Wet saw: A high-speed power saw equipped with a water-cooled carbide blade used for making straight cuts in tile.

Yard: A unit of volume equal to 1 cubic yard (27 cubic feet).

INDEX

METRIC CONVERSIONS

U.S. Units to Metric Equivalents			Metric Units to U.S. Equivalents		
To convert from	Multiply by	To get	To convert from	Multiply by	To get
Inches	25.4	Millimeters	Millimeters	0.0394	Inches
Inches	2.54	Centimeters	Centimeters	0.3937	Inches
Feet	30.48	Centimeters	Centimeters	0.0328	Feet
Feet	0.3048	Meters	Meters	3.2808	Feet
Yards	0.9144	Meters	Meters	1.0936	Yards
Square inches	6.4516	Square centimeters	Square centimeters	0.1550	Square inches
Square feet	0.0929	Square meters	Square meters	10.764	Square feet
Square yards	0.8361	Square meters	Square meters	1.1960	Square yards
Acres	0.4047	Hectares	Hectares	2.4711	Acres
Cubic inches	16.387	Cubic centimeters	Cubic centimeters	0.0610	Cubic inches
Cubic feet	0.0283	Cubic meters	Cubic meters	35.315	Cubic feet
Cubic feet	28.316	Liters	Liters	0.0353	Cubic feet
Cubic yards	0.7646	Cubic meters	Cubic meters	1.308	Cubic yards
Cubic yards	764.55	Liters	Liters	0.0013	Cubic yards

To convert from degrees Fahrenheit to degrees Celsius, first subtract 32, then multiply by $\frac{5}{9}$.

To convert from degrees Celsius to degrees Fahrenheit, multiply by $\frac{9}{5}$, then add 32.

KNOWLEDGE IS THE BEST TOOL

STANLEY COMPLETE **Decks**
STEP-BY-STEP INSTRUCTIONS • DECKS AND ACCESSORIES • PLANNING AND CONSTRUCTION

STANLEY COMPLETE **Trimwork & Carpentry**
STEP-BY-STEP INSTRUCTIONS • REMODELING TIPS & IDEAS • FROM FRAMING TO TRIMMING

STANLEY COMPLETE **Built-Ins, Shelves & Bookcases**
STEP-BY-STEP INSTRUCTIONS • CUSTOMIZING TIPS AND IDEAS • PROJECTS FOR EVERY HOME

STANLEY COMPLETE **Tiling**
STEP-BY-STEP INSTRUCTIONS • FLOORS, WALLS, & COUNTERTOPS • DECORATIVE PROJECTS

STANLEY COMPLETE **WIRING**
STEP-BY-STEP INSTRUCTIONS • REPAIRS & UPGRADES • NEW CIRCUITS & FIXTURES

CONSTRUCT · REJUVENATE · PLAN & REPAIR · ENHANCE · MAINTAIN

LOOK FOR THESE EXCITING HOME IMPROVEMENT TITLES WHEREVER BOOKS ARE SOLD

STANLEY®
MAKE SOMETHING GREAT™